LEAVING CERTIFICATE

LATER MODERN HISTORY OF EUROPE AND THE WIDER WORLD   TOPIC 4

division and realignment in europe
1945–1992

PAT CALLAN
MÁIRE DE BUITLÉIR
FRANK CLEARY

THE EDUCATIONAL COMPANY

First published 2004
The Educational Company of Ireland
Ballymount Road
Walkinstown
Dublin 12

A trading unit of Smurfit Ireland Ltd.

The
paper used in
this book comes
from Managed
Forests in
Northern
Europe
For
every
tree
felled, at
least one new
tree is planted

0123456789

Editor: Aengus Carroll
Design and Layout: Design Image
Cover Design: Design Image
Printed by: Future Print

Acknowledgements

AKG London, Bettmann Archive, Bridgeman Art Library, Centre for the Study of Cartoons and Caricature (University of Kent), Collection Kipa, Corbis Photo Agency, Getty Images, Hulton-Deutsch Collection, Novosti, Punch Magazine, Time Life Pictures, TopFoto Picture Agency.

FOREWORD

Division and Realignment in Europe 1945–1992 covers Topic 4 in the Later Modern Europe section of the Leaving Certificate History Syllabus.

The story of Europe in the second half of the 20th century is full of exciting and radical events. Europe in the West tried to rebuild after the war, while Eastern Europe came to terms with Socialism and sovietisation.

The study of history is stimulating. Examining original sources, studying contemporary images, reading an engaging story, all increase the ability of the student to understand the world in which they live at the start of the 21st century.

History gives students the opportunity to establish links between events. History provides an understanding of change over time, and helps students to see events from the point of view of participants. Students develop the ability to reach conclusions, and place events in a proper historical context.

Three Perspectives are set out in the syllabus – Politics and Administration, Society and Economy, Culture, Religion and Science. The syllabus fosters the inclusion of the experience of women as an important aspect of study. This book covers the listed Elements for each Perspective.

This book emphasises the role of evidence in the study and writing of history. It sets out to promote a spirit of enquiry and critical thinking. Where appropriate, the student is presented with important evidence of the past. The original sources should be read as an important part of the text, and students should practise the analysis of images and other documents, by interrogating those documents.

The material is taught to both Ordinary and Higher levels. Students study the same content, but Higher Level students aim to have a broader and deeper understanding of the syllabus. For Ordinary Level students, the Key Personalities and the Case Studies are particularly important. Also, Ordinary Level students are expected to give a 'narrative' account of the Case Studies, while Higher Level students have to give a 'discursive' account.

Division and Realignment in Europe 1945–1992, has three listed Case Studies – the 1956 Hungarian Uprising, the 1973 Oil Crisis and the Vatican Council. These Case Studies are dealt with in detail, and the principal events and trends are identified for each Case Study.

Division and Realignment in Europe 1945–1992, is a contemporary topic, and many teachers will have vivid memories of events that they have lived through. Study of events of the recent past will allow students to appreciate the complexities of the world in which they live.

The authors hope that students and teachers will benefit from a study of the theme of 'division and realignment', and that they will find the learning journey along the way to be stimulating and enjoyable.

Pat Callan
Máire de Buitléir
Frank Cleary

August 2004

WEBPAGE

WEBSITES OF INTEREST

Imperial War Museum London
http://www.iwm.org.uk

The History Channel
http://www.historychannel.com
http://www.spartacus.schoolnet.co.uk

BBC Online
http://www.bbc.co.uk/history

The Biography Channel
http://www.biography.com

Channel 4 Interactive History
www.channel4.com/historyquest

Spartacus Educational
http://www.historyinternational.com

The Quotations Page
http://www.quotationspage.com

The Internet Movie Database
http://www.imdb.com

Has documents on Western Europe, Eastern Europe, religion after 1982 (including Vatican Council), the growth of science and the Internet, popular culture and feminism:
http://www.fordham.edu/halsall/mod/modsbook.html

Political, economic, social and cultural aspects relating to individual European countries are found in this collection of primary documents:
http://library.byu.edu/~rdh/eurodocs/

Excellent site with plenty of material (including activities for students) on Europe after 1945:
http://www.bbc.co.uk/history/

One of the great encyclopaedias:
http://www.britannica.com

A history collection specifically for secondary school students:
http://www.spartacus.schoolnet.co.uk/history.htm

Two substantial sites on the EU:
http://www.eu-history.leidenuniv.nl/
http://vlib.iue.it/hist-eur-integration/Index.html

Deals with the collapse of the Soviet Union:
http://www.cnn.com/SPECIALS/cold.war/

US history of Germany after 1945:
http://motherearthtravel.com/history/germany/

History of the computer:
http://www.hitmill.com/computers/computerhistory.asp

Very detailed history of the events of the Cold War, using many primary documents:
http://www.cnn.com/SPECIALS/cold.war/

History of the Berlin Wall:
http://userpage.chemie.fu-berlin.de/BIW/wall.html

History of the Hungarian uprising 1956:
http://historicaltextarchive.com/books.php?op=viewbook&bookid=13

Marshall Plan site:
http://www.lcsys.com/fayette/history/plan.htm

Pope John Paul II:
http://www.catholic-forum.com/saints/pope0264.htm
http://en.wikipedia.org/wiki/Pope_John_Paul_II

Migration after 1945:
http://www.let.leidenuniv.nl/history/migration/1945.html

Michael Gorbachev:
http://www.time.com/time/time100/leaders/profile/gorbachev.html

CONTENTS

SOURCES
AND HOW TO USE THEM

Historians use sources to find out about the past. These sources can be **primary** (i.e. from the time being studied) or **secondary** (i.e. a book in which a historian sets out the result of her/his researches). In this book (which is a secondary source) you will find many references to both kinds of sources. As part of your course you will examine some primary sources and do a research project. These tasks will help you to learn and practice some of the skills of the historian. In order to do this well, it is useful to know what those skills are and how a historian finds out about the past.

How does a historian begin?

Historians usually begin their research with a question: What happened at that time? Who killed those people? Who was responsible for this event? Why did that person act that way?

When they have decided what question they want to answer, historians read all the secondary sources they can find about their topic. From that they learn what other historians already know and where they got their information.

Examples of written primary sources

Government records like census returns, statistics or reports of enquiries.

Bills and acts of parliament.

Official documents like birth or death certificates.

Newspaper reports.

Letters.

Diaries.

Pamphlets.

Speeches.

Business records.

Minutes of meetings.

Memoirs and autobiographies.

Looking for primary sources

After that they go looking for relevant primary sources. Almost anything can serve as a primary source. Many are written documents, like those mentioned in the box on the right. Most documentary sources are stored in **libraries** and **archives** where they can be looked after properly.

Apart from written sources, historians can also get information from paintings, drawings, photographs or cartoons. Oral interviews with people who were involved in an event the historian wants to examine are important for the study of more recent history, while buildings or artefacts are important for people who lived before writing became common. Many artefacts are kept in **museums**.

How do historians approach primary sources?

Whatever primary source they use, historians never take it at face-value. They always want to ask questions about it. The first of these questions could be called the 5 Ws – what, who, when, where and why. These are explained more fully below. As the historian answers these and other questions she/he **makes notes of the answers** and enters them on a **record card**.

Keeping careful notes about one's sources is one of the historian's most important skills. These should be at least one record card for each primary source consulted.

Questions to ask of written and oral sources	Answers	What you do
What kind of a source is this?	Is it a private letter, a newspaper article, an official document like a birth certificate or a census return, a published memoir? If it's a tape recording, is it an interview with a historian (i.e. a secondary source), or with a person involved in the event (i.e. a primary source)? It is important to fit a document into a category as this helps to understand what it was for.	Make a note of the kind of source you are dealing with.
Who wrote/ produced it and what do we know about him/ her?	Look for the name of the author. It may be on the title page or in the description that goes with the document. Sometimes there is additional information, e.g. about the author's job or involvement in the topic being studied. If that is not there, ask yourself if you know anything about the author. That may help you to decide how reliable he or she is as a witness. Sometimes no author's name is given. Then we should try to guess who wrote it. If it is an official document, perhaps the author was a civil servant: what would such a person's point of view be? If it is a newspaper article, do we know what the newspaper's attitude was on the topic we are studying? A journalist would probably be influenced by the point of view of the owner of the newspaper.	Note the name of the author and any additional information you have about him/her. If there is no name, given suggest who might be responsible for the source.
When was it produced?	Sometimes this is easy to answer. A letter may be dated; a book or an official document has the date it was published. Knowing the date allows us to decide how near to the events the writer was. A report written the day after something happened will tell us different things from a memoir written by the same person 20 years later.	Add the date to your other notes about the source.
Where was it produced?	Often harder to find than the date. Letters usually have addresses but writers whose books were published in London did not always live there. Sometimes we can guess the answer from something the author says.	Note the place of publication, if it is available.
Why was it produced? Who was the author aiming it at?	This important question is often overlooked. Who was the source aimed at? What effect did its author want to produce? If he was making a speech, who was he trying to win over? If he was writing his memoirs, did he want to make himself look more important than he really was? If it is a letter, would the author be likely to lie to the person he is writing to?	Write a sentence explaining what you think the aim of the source was.

It is important to remember that historians may not be able to answer all of these questions. That does not matter. What does matters is that we always ask them when we first approach a source.

After answering these questions, the historian reads the document to find out what is in it.

QUESTIONS TO ASK OF WRITTEN AND ORAL SOURCES	ANSWERS	WHAT YOU DO
What does the document mean?	Read it through once. Note any words you do not understand. Remember words change their meaning over the centuries. Most dictionaries show the older meanings as well as modern ones. Look for one that fits.	Use dictionary to look up words and note the meanings.
Who is mentioned?	Note any people whose names you know. Can you find out about people you have not heard of before?	Identify the people mentioned.
What are the author's points?	Identify the main point(s) the author makes.	Make a short summary of these in your own words.

Next the historian interprets the document.

Is the author a reliable witness?	What is the relationship between the author and the events dealt with in the document? Did the author write at the time or much later? How did the author get his/her information?	Note your conclusions, giving reasons for them.
Does the author have a point of view?	Does the author give an opinion about events? What is it? Is the author prejudiced or biased? Which side did he/she favour? How much faith should we put in it? Was the author present or only reporting what she/he heard?	Give the author's point of view and your reasons for saying so.
What audience was the author addressing?	Who did the author write for? Is he/she trying to persuade someone? To please someone? To justify his/her actions?	Note your conclusions and the reason for them.

Once the historian understands what the document says, he/she tries to fit the information into the bigger picture gathered from other sources. This is called 'putting the source in context'.

Do the versions match?	Does the evidence here support or contradict what I already know from other sources? Should I trust this source more than them? If so, why?	Pick out words/ passages which support or contradict.
How do I check out contradictions?	What other sources could I use to decide which is the more accurate story, or to fill in missing parts of the evidence?	List other sources to be consulted.
Does this make me change my mind?	Is the evidence in this source reliable enough to make me re-think my ideas about my topic?	Give your conclusion.

By this time you should have one or more record cards containing information you have gleaned from the document. File it away so that you can use it with information from other sources that you will read later.

HOW TO USE PICTURE SOURCES

Up to the 1860s the only picture sources we had were paintings, drawings, cartoons and maps. Since then we have had photographs and from the 1890s, moving pictures.

Pictures look simpler to handle than documents, but, even so, historians want to ask questions about them. Here are the main ones.

QUESTIONS TO ASK ABOUT PICTURE SOURCES	ANSWERS	WHAT YOU DO
What is it?	Is it a painting or drawing, a portrait of someone, a photograph or a cartoon?	Note the answer.
Who does it show?	Who are the people in it? If it is a cartoon, the 'people' may represent something, e.g. 'John Bull' is England and 'Erin' is Ireland.	Name the people or what they represent.
What's going on in it?	Work out what is shown happening.	Write down what you see.
In a drawing or painting, what was the artist's aim?	Why did the artist draw this event/person? Was he paid to show a king/politician in a good light? Does the way a scene is presented tell us anything about the artist's point of view? Does this affect his/her reliability as a witness?	Note your conclusions with the reasons for them.
In a photograph what was the photographer's aim?	Did the photographer take these images to make us feel sorry for the people shown? Or because they were 'quaint'? Does that make any difference to the reliability of the image?	Note your conclusions with the reasons for them.
In a movie scene, was it real or was it staged?	Are these real pictures from the time or were they part of a movie made later? Were the scenes staged for the camera or did they really happen like this?	Note your conclusions with the reasons for them.
What is the context of this picture?	What do I know about the events/people recorded in this picture source? How do the images fit with what I knew from other sources?	Note your conclusions with the reasons for them.
How can I check out the reliability of an image?	Are there any other sources I could use to check how reliable these images are?	List other sources.

PRACTISING THE SKILLS OF THE HISTORIAN

When the historian has consulted all possible sources, both secondary and primary, it is time to try to answer the question with which he/she began the research.

The answer takes the form of a report which tells what happened. As the historian writes, he/she mentions the source from which each piece of information came and gives the evidence upon which every conclusion is based.

The skills we learn from history

In producing this work, the history student has begun to develop **the skills of the historian**. They include:

Research:	Finding out where to get information.
Note taking:	Keeping a careful record of each source consulted and the conclusions drawn about it.
Reading for meaning:	Extracting information from sources, both primary and secondary, written and pictorial.
Critical analysis:	Asking questions about the authorship and purpose of every source – never taking any information at its face value.
Contextualisation:	Understanding that any one source only makes sense in the context of a wider picture.
Writing a report:	When the research is done, putting together a final report of the results.

Even if you never do historical research again, these are skills you will find useful in any way of life you chose to follow later.

1

INTRODUCTION: POST-WAR EUROPE

Words you need to understand

Superpower: A country with great economic wealth, political influence and military power after the second World War.

Communism: A political and economic doctrine that believes that all the means of production and distribution should be owned by the people.

Capitalism: An economic doctrine that believes in individual ownership of wealth and profit.

Democracy: A system of government where authority rests with the people.

Cold War: A state of tension and suspicion between countries.

Reparations: Compensation for war damage.

Buffer zone: An area used to protect another area.

Spheres of influence: An area considered important to a country's interest over which it can exercise a degree of political and economic control.

Sovietisation: Extension of control by the Soviet Union (USSR) in Eastern Europe.

De-Nazification: Removing Nazi influences in Germany after the second World War.

Satellite state: A state that depends on another, more powerful state.

INTRODUCTION: POST-WAR EUROPE

The second World War began in September 1939 when Hitler invaded Poland. By May 1945 the war in Europe was over. Hitler and Nazism had been defeated by the Allies (Britain, the USA and the USSR). However, the war in the Pacific continued until August 1945, when the USA dropped two atomic bombs on the Japanese cities of Hiroshima and Nagasaki, forcing Japan to surrender. The most destructive war in history was over.

The war had brought devastation to Europe. Twenty million soldiers died, while the civilian death toll from bombings, starvation and Nazi extermination policies is estimated at another 24 million. Roads were clogged with refugees trying to return to their own countries or escaping to find new

Courtesy: Bettmann/Corbis

● Although much of central Berlin was devastated by Allied bombing, citizens there tried to bring their lives back to normal. Here we see Berliners in 1945 waiting for buses amongst the ruins.

places to settle in. Entire cities had been destroyed: Cologne, Berlin, Dresden, Warsaw, Rotterdam and many other cities and towns were reduced to rubble, while factories, businesses and places of production were in ruins.

The task of reconstruction seemed daunting. None of the leading powers in Europe before the war were in a position to take on this challenge. Britain, France and Germany were left demoralised and economically broken by the war. Only two countries were capable of commanding and organising the huge investment of financial, political and psychological support Europe needed to get back on its feet. Those two countries were the wartime allies of the USA and USSR.

1.1   AN UNEASY ALLIANCE

The alliance between Britain, the USA and the USSR during the second World War was a marriage of convenience. They joined together to fight a common enemy: Nazi Germany.

At the beginning of the war the USA was neutral, but sympathetic to the British cause against Germany. In August 1941, American president, Franklin Roosevelt, and the British Prime Minister, Winston Churchill, met at sea off the coast of Newfoundland. They issued a joint declaration, the **Atlantic Charter** (see the Source Document on page 3). In it they stated their war aims and their plans for a new world order once Germany was defeated.

Franklin Delano Roosevelt (1882–1945): Born into a wealthy New York family; educated at Harvard and in Europe. He became president of the USA in 1932, during the Great Depression. He introduced the 'New Deal', a programme of social and economic reform. After the outbreak of the second World War he favoured an Atlantic alliance and sent war supplies to Britain. Following the Japanese attack on Pearl Harbor the USA joined with Britain and the USSR against Germany and its allies. He attended wartime conferences with Churchill and Stalin and often acted as mediator between them. He died in April 1945, before the war ended.

Courtesy: Bettmann/Corbis

Though still technically neutral in August 1941, the USA supported Britain in the fight against Nazism in Europe. By the end of 1941, however, events were to change American neutrality and turn the war into a global conflict. In December 1941 Germany's ally, Japan, attacked the American naval base at Pearl Harbor. The USA declared war on Japan, and three days later Germany declared war on the United States.

Churchill, Roosevelt and their advisors met in Washington over Christmas 1941. Their alliance was now put on a military footing. They agreed to focus their combined efforts on fighting Germany in Europe.

Winston Churchill (1874–1965): Son of Lord Randolf Churchill, Winston Churchill served in Lloyd George's government during the first World War. He was Chancellor of the Exchequer 1924–1929. During the 1930s he was a firm critic of the policy of appeasement. When Neville Chamberlain resigned as Prime Minister in 1940, Churchill succeeded him, leading a wartime coalition government until July 1945. He met with Roosevelt and Stalin at a series of wartime conferences. He was suspicious of USSR policy in Eastern Europe after the war. In 1947 he made his famous 'Iron Curtain' speech. In 1951 he was again elected Prime Minister. At the age of 80, he retired from politics in 1955 and died ten years later.

Courtesy: Corbis

Meanwhile, the situation in Eastern Europe had also changed, bringing the USSR into the alliance with Britain and the USA. At the beginning of the war the USSR was actually an ally of Germany. In August 1939, the two countries had signed a ten-year non-aggression pact, the **Nazi-Soviet Pact**. Hitler, however, broke this pact when he invaded the USSR in June 1941. The common threat from German aggression now formed the basis for a coalition between the USSR, the USA and Britain. Immediately after Germany's attack on the USSR, Prime Minister Churchill offered the Soviet Union economic and technical help to fight Hitler.

The alliance between the USA and Britain was formally extended and given a clear direction in the Atlantic Charter in January 1942. Following a series of conferences in Washington DC, 26 anti-aggressor nations led by the USSR, the USA, Britain and China signed an agreement promising to combine their efforts to work together to defeat Germany and its allies. These nations supported the principles of the Atlantic Charter.

Source Document

Eighth Clause of the Atlantic Charter, 14 August 1941

They believe that all the nations of the world for realistic as well as spiritual reasons must come to the abandonment of force. Since no future peace can be maintained if land, sea, or air armaments continue to be employed by nations which threaten, or may threaten aggression outside their frontiers, they believe, pending the establishment of a wider and permanent system of general security, that disarmament of such nations is essential. They will likewise aid and lighten for peace-loving peoples the crushing burden of armaments.

Signed   Franklin D. Roosevelt
          Winston S. Churchill

QUESTIONS ON THE DOCUMENT

1. Why do you think the leaders of the USA and Britain met in August 1941?
2. In the document, what do the leaders think is the most serious threat to world peace?
3. What do the leaders plan to do to protect future world peace?

CASABLANCA AND CAIRO, 1943

In 1943, Churchill and Roosevelt met at Casablanca (Morocco) and at Cairo (Egypt). Stalin was invited to attend both conferences. However, Stalin was busy with the defence of the USSR in the early months of 1943 and did not wish to leave Moscow at this time. Roosevelt and Churchill brought their military advisors with them to Casablanca.

Two decisions made at Casablanca were of vital importance to Stalin and the USSR:
- Germany would have to make an 'unconditional surrender' to the allies. This decision was designed to remove fears in the USSR that the Western powers might do a deal with Hitler at the expense of the USSR.
- The allies would move from North Africa to launch an invasion of Germany through Italy.

Stalin had called for the opening of a 'second front' in Western Europe. The Soviet Red Army faced a three-pronged attack by over three million German troops and 100,000 tanks, along a huge 2,000-mile battle front. Opening a second front in Western Europe would relieve pressure on the Red Army. At the Casablanca Conference, however, the Allied leaders decided to postpone opening a second front in Western Europe. Instead the combined British and American forces would focus the attack on Southern Europe. The decision angered Stalin and confirmed his suspicions that the Western Allies cared little for the plight of the USSR. It also convinced him that his British and American allies welcomed the showdown between Nazism and Communism and that they secretly hoped they would destroy each other. The signs of future tensions between the Western Allies and the USSR were already evident.

TEHERAN, 1943

In November–December 1943, an Allied conference was held at Teheran, in Iran. This was the first time all three leaders attended. By this stage the Red Army was in a strong position, advancing against the retreating Germans into central and Eastern Europe. At Teheran, Churchill voiced concerns about the post-war situation in Eastern Europe. He did not trust Stalin and feared victory over the Nazis would leave the USSR in control of Eastern Europe. He proposed a combined Anglo-American invasion of the Balkans. Stalin rejected this suggestion. Roosevelt was reluctant to alienate Stalin. Furthermore, the most important issue for Roosevelt was to defeat Germany before making any decisions on post-victory territorial claims. Churchill's proposed second front in the Balkans was rejected in favour of an Anglo-American invasion of France, i.e. Stalin's second front in Western Europe, which he had called for over nine months earlier.

Stalin (1879–1953): Son of a former serf, Stalin joined the Bolsheviks and was exiled to Siberia for revolutionary activities. Released after the February Revolution, he played a minor role in the October Bolshevik Revolution. Lenin appointed him General Secretary of the Communist Party in 1922. When Lenin died in 1924, Stalin sought to discredit Trotsky, Lenin's natural successor. By 1927 he had become the sole ruler of the USSR. He introduced a series of five-year plans in industry and agriculture, which transformed the USSR, making it into a leading economy by the 1930s. A ruthless dictator, he eliminated all opposition through imprisonment and execution of his opponents.

Courtesy: Bettmann/Corbis

During the second World War Stalin joined the Western Allies (Britain and the USA) in the fight against Nazism. After the war he imposed Communist governments in Eastern Europe. Feared rather than loved by his own people, he died in 1953.

The Allied leaders held three conferences in 1945. They met at Yalta, a Soviet resort on the Black Sea, in February 1945, at San Francisco in April and at Potsdam (Berlin) in July.

YALTA, SAN FRANCISCO AND POTSDAM, 1945

The Yalta Conference took place when the Allies were close to a final victory over Germany. Roosevelt assumed the role of mediator between Churchill and Stalin at this conference. He tried to avoid giving Stalin the impression that he and Churchill stood together against USSR interests. Roosevelt in fact did have differences with Churchill. The American president found the British Prime Minister's devotion to colonial and empire interests outdated.

● The 'Big Three' at Yalta, February 1945.

Courtesy: Hulton-Deutsch Collection

By February 1945 Stalin was in a very strong position. The Red Army had reached Poland. Stalin had already taken steps to set up a 'friendly' government there. Churchill supported the Polish government in exile in London and wanted it returned to power in post-war Poland. At Yalta a compromise was worked out. Poland would have a coalition government. No decision was made on where Poland's borders would be drawn after the war.

There was general agreement between the three leaders on how to deal with Germany: it was to be disarmed, demilitarised and divided into four zones, occupied by Britain, France, the USA and the USSR. Berlin would also be divided into four zones. Germany would pay reparations. Roosevelt got the backing of the other two leaders for his plans to set up an international organisation to replace the League of Nations. It was decided to hold another conference in San Francisco to draw up a charter for the **United Nations**.

As in Teheran in 1943, areas of potential conflict between the wartime Allies were glossed over. However, tensions and suspicions between the Western leaders and Stalin were plain to see. Stalin did get Churchill and Roosevelt to agree to the idea of Eastern Europe becoming a sphere of influence for the USSR. In exchange for greater control in Eastern Europe, the USSR agreed to declare war on Japan and join forces with the USA to defeat Japan when the war in Europe ended.

Courtesy: Swim Ink/Corbis

● A typical image of the 1940s, portraying a united front of protection for the world. Such posters did not point to the emerging divisions following the second World War.

The San Francisco Conference met on 25 April. Roosevelt had died two weeks earlier on 12 April. Hitler committed suicide on 30 April. The Red Army had arrived in Berlin. The Conference sat for two months. It drafted a charter for a new international organisation, the United Nations.

The USA was represented by its new president, Harry S. Truman. A general election took place in Britain after the conference opened. Churchill was replaced as Prime Minister by Clement Attlee. Stalin, alone among the original leaders of the Alliance, remained in power. At Potsdam Stalin had moral and diplomatic advantages over the two newcomers, Truman and Attlee. Furthermore, he was in a strong bargaining position, since the Red Army had gained control in Eastern Europe. Stalin was determined to hold on to gains the USSR had won in Eastern Europe.

Harry S. Truman (1884–1972): In January 1945 Truman became vice-president to Roosevelt, succeeding him as president that April. He took the decision to use the atomic bomb to end the war with Japan. A committed anti-Communist, Truman was determined to halt USSR advances after the second World War. He launched the Marshall Plan for economic recovery in Europe and issued the *Truman Doctrine*. He was president when the Cold War began. He refused to recognise the Communist government in China after 1949 and he supported the policy of containment.

Courtesy: Bettmann/Corbis

The Potsdam Conference was mainly concerned with the future of Germany. It confirmed the decision made at Yalta to divide Germany into four zones, as a temporary arrangement, until Germany was demilitarised and democratised:

■ War criminals would be brought before an international court.

■ Germany would pay reparations to the occupying powers.

■ A council of foreign ministers was set up to handle the peace treaties with the defeated powers.

The question of Poland was raised again at Potsdam, but no final agreement was made on the future of its borders. Stalin succeeded in getting the other two leaders to accept the USSR-supported Lublin government in Poland. He gave an undertaking to allow free elections in Poland after the war. The USSR would retain the Polish lands they had taken in 1939, and the new state of Poland would be compensated with lands in the West, taken from Germany.

Relations between the Allied leaders were cool at Potsdam. Truman and Stalin dominated the proceedings. Truman had both a personal dislike for Stalin and a strong aversion to Communism. He felt that Roosevelt had given in too much to Stalin's demands. While attending the Potsdam Conference, Truman received news that the atomic bomb had been successfully tested. He informed Stalin of a 'new secret weapon' but did not offer to share the technology with the USA's wartime ally, the USSR. Stalin took this as proof that the USA intended using the weapon against the USSR if the post-war settlement did not work out to American advantage.

Truman, for his part, adopted an uncompromising approach with Stalin. As sole possessor of the atomic bomb America no longer needed the support of the USSR. The Potsdam Agreement was intended to be temporary. More permanent decisions were expected to come when the Allies met later. However, by July 1945, the 'uneasy alliance' had fallen apart. The common enemy was defeated, but the coalition between the Western powers and the Soviet Union was unable to sustain itself beyond victory over Hitler and Nazism. A new crisis now faced Europe and the world, known as the **Cold War**. The main players in the Cold War would be the USSR and the USA – the post-second World War superpowers.

Source Document

Lend-Lease Agreement of the United States and Great Britain, 23 February 1942

Article 1   The government of the United States of America will continue to supply the government of the United Kingdom with such defence articles, defence services and defence information as the president shall authorize to be transferred or provided.

QUESTIONS ON THE DOCUMENT

1. According to the document, what would the USA continue to supply to Britain?
2. The USA had been supplying the British with aid since 1941. What event happened in late 1941 that brought the USA-British alliance closer?
3. Why do you think the USA helped Britain before December 1941?

QUESTIONS

1. Explain why the USSR joined the Western powers in an alliance during the second World War.
2. List some of the issues that caused tension between the Western Allies and the USSR at Teheran in 1943.
3. Explain why the USSR and the USA dominated the Potsdam Conference in July 1945.

1.2   EMERGENCE OF THE SUPERPOWERS

THE UNITED NATIONS

In April 1945 the United Nations was set up to replace the League of Nations. The UN Charter was signed in San Francisco in June 1945 by 51 countries. Each of the original 51 member states had been involved in the war against the Axis powers.

The two central agencies of the UN were the **General Assembly** and the **Security Council**. The Assembly was intended to be a world parliament, where each member state was represented and had equal status. The Security Council was intended to be the executive power of the UN. It was made up of five permanent members and ten elected for a two-year term. The primary function of the Security Council was to maintain world peace. Britain, the USA, the USSR, France and China held permanent seats, each with the right to veto. The Security Council could act only when decisions were unanimous.

● San Francisco, 1945. The conference where the UN Charter was signed by 51 countries.

Courtesy: National Archives (US)/Corbis

Although the Security Council provided for five permanent seats, in reality there were only two powers in a position to influence the United Nations. Britain and France were in a weak economic and military position after the war. China, a newcomer on the international scene in 1945, had many internal political problems. During the war the Allies had supported the nationalist government of Chiang Kai-Shek against Japanese advances into China. After 1945 a bitter civil war developed between the nationalists and the Chinese Communists under Mao Tse-tung. Lasting until 1949, the civil war eventually brought the Communists to power in China. In the immediate post-war years China was in no position to act as a leading world power.

Source Document

Use of the veto in the United Nations

List of instances in which proposals before the Security Council obtained the required seven affirmative votes out of 11 (five permanent and six non-permanent members) but were not carried as a result of the negative vote of one or more *permanent* members of the Security Council.

Question before the Security Council	Date	Permanent member voting in negative
1. Syrian and Lebanese question: withdrawal of foreign troops	16 Feb. 1946	USSR
2. Spanish question: investigation of Franco regime	18 June 1946	USSR
3. Spanish question: resolution for observation of	26 June 1946	USSR
4. Spanish question: vote on president's ruling	26 June 1946	USSR, France
5. Spanish question: resolution	26 June 1946	USSR
6. Admission: Transjordan	29 Aug. 1946	USSR
7. Admission: Ireland	29 Aug. 1946	USSR
8. Admission: Portugal	29 Aug. 1946	USSR
9. Greek question: border incidents	29 Aug. 1946	USSR
10. Corfu Channel question	25 Mar. 1947	USSR
11. Greek question: US recommendation	29 July 1947	USSR

QUESTIONS ON THE DOCUMENT

1. Why do you think the USSR used its veto so frequently during 1946–1947?
2. List the number of countries the USSR stopped from joining the UN during 1946–1947.
3. What other permanent member of the Security Council used the veto during this time?

Courtesy: Corbis

● These are 'Little Boy' and 'Fat Man', which were the atomic bombs dropped on Hiroshima and Nagasaki by the US in 1945.

THE SUPERPOWERS

Of the five permanent members of the UN Security Council, only the USSR and the USA were strong enough to make a difference in international affairs. Both of these powers emerged from the second World War stronger than they had been before the war.

Despite suffering enormous losses during the war, the USSR still had a strong economy. When Hitler invaded in June 1941, Stalin moved industries eastwards beyond the Urals, out of German reach. In addition, the USSR had the largest army in the world in 1945. At the end of the war the USSR occupied most of Eastern Europe, giving them immense military advantage.

The USA suffered no wartime damage on American soil. Its economy provided Britain and the USSR with war supplies and as a result boomed during the war years. In 1945 the USA had the strongest economy in the world. After Hiroshima in August 1945, they also had sole control of the most powerful weapon the world had ever known, the atomic bomb. Possession of this military technology gave the USA undisputed dominance in international affairs. Furthermore, American armies were in control of Western Europe.

THE COLD WAR

The USA and the USSR, with their vast resources of land, large population and industrial, technological, economic and military strength, overshadowed all the other powers in 1945: they were superpowers.

From 1945 on, rivalry between the superpowers developed into frequent clashes of interests and ideas. The hostile relations between them became known as the 'Cold War'. This was a war of words, using weapons of propaganda, espionage and fear.

The superpowers dominated rival 'blocs': the USA the **Western bloc** and the USSR the **Eastern bloc**. No actual fighting occurred between the superpowers during the Cold War. Instead, each of them manipulated the international situation to suit their own national interests. They each supported opposing sides in local conflicts in Europe and in different parts of the world.

Source Document

Courtesy; Corbis

● American and Soviet troops meet at Targau, Germany, April 1945. Here they congratulate each other on the defeat of Germany.

QUESTIONS ON THE DOCUMENT

1. Why do you think the American and Soviet troops are smiling and shaking hands?
2. Do you think the photograph accurately represents the relations between the USA and Soviet Union at this time? Give reasons for your answer.

QUESTIONS

1. What countries signed the UN Charter at San Francisco in April 1945?
2. How many countries had seats on the UN Security Council? How many were permanent?
3. Explain the term 'superpower'. Why were there only two superpowers in 1945?

1.3   ORIGINS OF THE COLD WAR

The hostility between the USA and the USSR caused deep suspicion between the superpowers after 1945. Neither side trusted the other. In order to fully understand the origins of the Cold War we must examine the reasons for this distrust. These reasons can be looked at under two broad headings: ideological and historical.

1.   *Ideological* **refers to ideas. Each of the superpowers held very different ideas about how countries should be governed.**

The USA was a capitalist and democratic state. Under capitalism, individuals or companies are free to make their own choices about spending and investing their wealth as well as free to own private property. Government regulation of the economy is kept to a minimum. Under a democratic system citizens vote freely in elections, where they have choices between a variety of parties. Individual liberty is protected by law and citizens are free to express their opinions.

The USSR had a Communist system of government, in which only one party was allowed to exist, i.e. the Communist Party. Only members of the Communist Party were allowed hold positions in government. At elections voters chose candidates who all belonged to the Communist Party.

The government controlled all aspects of life in the USSR, including the economy. There was no private ownership of property. All shops, farms, factories, businesses, etc. were owned by the state. There was no freedom of speech and the state controlled newspapers, radio and the media in general.

The two ideologies had a fundamentally different understanding of the idea of freedom. For the USA, freedom meant civil liberties, freedom of speech, association, beliefs, etc. and the right to own and accumulate personal wealth.

For the USSR, on the other hand, freedom meant economic freedom from material want, the right to employment, housing, education, health, etc. The right to accumulate wealth was restricted by the state, as were the rights to civil liberties.

Both sides accused the other of denying freedom to their respective citizens. Each believed that their particular system offered the best model of government for all the countries in the world to follow. The USA, confident in its tradition of the modern world's first democratic model of government, felt a sense of mission, even duty, to uphold the ideas of individual liberty, capitalist free enterprise and the American way of life. After 1945, this sense of mission extended to imposing their model of capitalist democracy on Europe and the rest of the world.

The USSR, the world's only Communist country before 1949, saw themselves as defenders of the working classes around the world. They too had a sense of mission, believing that their model of government, offering economic equality to all citizens, would give the rest of the world a better future.

2.   *Historical* **refers to events and experiences in the past. What follows are some of the major events from 1917–1939, which led to the distrust between the USSR and the West.**

In the October Revolution in 1917, the Bolsheviks seized power in Russia. Led by Lenin, they set up the world's first Communist state. Events in Russia in 1917 had two main effects on Western Europe and the USA at that time:

- The Bolsheviks, later called the Communists, promised to support any country attempting to overthrow its government and to replace it with a Communist one.
- In 1917 the USA, Britain, France and Russia were fighting Germany and its allies in the first World War. Germany faced a two-front war in Europe: Britain, France and the USA in the west and Russia in the east. Once in power the Bolsheviks signed the Treaty of Brest-Litovsk, withdrawing Russia from the war and betraying the Western powers. The new Communist government in Russia announced that it would not honour any debts owed to the West before 1917.

Following the Treaty of Brest-Litovsk, civil war broke out in Russia. The enemies of the Communists became known as the 'Whites'. Britain, France and the USA supported and helped to finance the White campaign. The Communists would not forget this Allied intervention in the civil war. It showed them that the West could not be trusted in the future.

By 1920 the Red Army had won the civil war. In 1922 the Union of Soviet Socialist Republics (USSR) was set up. In 1924 the USSR adopted a constitution, claiming that by setting up the USSR 'a decisive step by way of uniting the workers of all countries into one World Soviet Socialist Republic' had been taken. Western countries, including the USA, blamed the USSR for the growing threat of Communism inside their own countries.

Source Document

From *Punch*, 1947

Courtesy: *Punch* magazine

QUESTIONS ON THE DOCUMENT

1. Name the two coach drivers in this cartoon.
2. What are the two destinations the buses refer to?
3. What impression does the cartoonist give you about the two destinations? Give reasons for your answer.

The USSR was excluded from the peace settlements at Versailles after the first World War and was not permitted to join the League of Nations until 1934. The USA did not formally recognise the USSR until 1933.

By 1929 Stalin had become leader in the USSR. With the rise of Fascism in Germany and Italy, Stalin tried to convince Britain and France that international action was needed to stop Hitler and Mussolini. The failure of Britain and France to stand up to the Fascist leaders convinced Stalin that the West favoured Fascism as a bulwark against Communism. Hitler had declared his intention of destroying Communism and invading the USSR. Stalin urgently needed allies to defend the USSR against German aggression. In 1934, Russia joined the League of Nations.

Between 1933 and 1938 Britain and France, anxious to avoid war with Germany, followed a policy of appeasement. They gave in to Hitler's demands for German expansion. Stalin grew increasingly suspicious of the West and did not trust either their ability or desire to deal with the Fascist threat.

MUNICH AGREEMENT

During the summer of 1938, Hitler claimed Germany's right to the Sudetenland, in Czechoslovakia. On 29 September Hitler, Mussolini and the British and French Prime Ministers met in Munich to discuss Hitler's demand. The USSR was not invited to Munich. Hitler insisted that the Sudetenland would be his 'last territorial demand in Europe'. In the final act of appeasement the other powers gave in to Hitler. Germany took over the Sudetenland on 1 October 1938.

Stalin denounced the Munich Agreement, believing that Britain and France were now concerned only with directing German expansion eastwards, away from themselves and towards the USSR. In order to safeguard the security and interests of the USSR Stalin would have to look beyond the Western powers and the League of Nations.

Source Document

Courtesy: The Centre for the Study of Cartoons and Caricature

● Peep under the Iron Curtain. This cartoon was first published in 1946.

QUESTIONS ON THE DOCUMENT

1. Who is Joe, referred to in this cartoon?
2. Who stated that Europe was divided by an Iron Curtain in 1946?
3. What impression does the cartoonist give of life on the Russian side of the Iron Curtain?

In August 1939 Germany and the USSR signed the Nazi-Soviet Pact. In the West the Nazi-Soviet Pact was regarded as betrayal by the USSR. On 1 September, Germany invaded Poland. Two days later Britain and France declared war on Germany. On 17 September the USSR invaded Poland from the east. By the end of September 1939, the Polish state no longer existed. Poland was partitioned between Germany and the USSR. It was only when Hitler broke the terms of the Nazi-Soviet Pact by invading Russia in 1941 that the USSR joined the Western alliance to fight Germany.

ALLIED VICTORY, 1945

In June 1944 the combined American and British invasion of Europe began. They landed in Normandy, France. By August, Paris was liberated from Nazi control and in September the Western Allies crossed the borders into Germany itself. Meanwhile, in 1944 the USSR army drove the German army across Eastern Europe into Poland. By February 1945 they were only 64 km (40 miles) from Berlin.

In March 1945 the Allies crossed the Rhine into Germany, and by April they were at the Elbe, 90 km from Berlin. Stalin saw Berlin as the USSR's prize and compensation for the sacrifices his country had made in winning the war against Germany. On 7 May, the Allies accepted Germany's 'unconditional surrender'. The war in Europe was over.

DROPPING THE ATOM BOMB

On 6 August 1945, the war in the Pacific came to an end when the USA dropped an atomic bomb on Hiroshima. The following day another atomic bomb was dropped on Nagasaki. Japan surrendered unconditionally.

American use of the atomic bomb alarmed the USSR and contributed to the distrust that was already building up between the former allies.

GROWING RIFT BETWEEN THE SUPERPOWERS

Since it entered the war the USA had been sending supplies and financial aid to the USSR. When the war ended this aid was stopped. Stalin viewed it as yet another example of Western coolness towards the Soviet Union and as an act of abandonment by its former allies.

Courtesy: Fotoware/TopFoto

● D-Day landings at Normandy.

THE QUESTION OF GERMANY

The two superpowers again came into conflict over the issue of German reparations. The USA wanted to see full German economic recovery after the war. Stalin, however, wished to use Germany to rebuild the USSR, as compensation for the war damages caused by the German invasion.

At Potsdam the Allies had agreed on the division of Germany into four occupied zones. They also agreed that Germany should pay reparations. In the spring of 1947, the foreign ministers of the four occupying powers in Germany (Britain, France, the USA and USSR) met in Moscow. The USSR insisted on a $10 billion reparation settlement from Germany. The Western powers saw this as a threat to German and Western European economic recovery and an attempt by Stalin to build up the economy of the USSR, thereby strengthening Communist control in Europe. The Western powers refused Stalin's demand and took steps to rebuild the German economy in their zones of occupation.

The American, British and French united their zones in 1948. In their zones they increased German industrial production. In June that year the Western Allies introduced currency reform to stop inflation and to encourage economic recovery. A new currency, the Deutschmark, was introduced. The Western Allies united their zones in Berlin as well, and introduced the Deutschmark there.

THE TRUMAN DOCTRINE

In 1947 the USA had put forward the **Truman Doctrine** (see p. 22), offering military aid to any country fighting a Communist takeover. At the same time, Secretary of State George Marshall announced a programme of economic aid to all European countries to help them with post-war recovery. This became known as the Marshall Plan (p. 22). The USSR denounced these moves as capitalist imperialism. Stalin turned down the offer and refused to allow countries under USSR control in Eastern Europe to participate in the programme. The USSR, feeling encircled and mindful of previous betrayals by the West, was determined to protect its own interests in Eastern Europe.

On 24 June 1948, the USSR blocked all road, rail and canal access to Berlin, thus cutting off West Berlin from the rest of Germany. Stalin hoped that the **Blockade of Berlin** would drive the USA, Britain and France out of West Berlin, leaving the city under USSR control. The Western powers responded with a massive airlift of food and supplies to the people of West Berlin. By May 1949, Stalin realised that the West would not give up West Berlin and called off the blockade.

German Democratic Republic
The term 'democratic' here reflects the Soviet understanding that freedom from material want and the right to employment, housing, education and health facilities constitute genuine democracy.

The Berlin Blockade led to the division of Germany into two separate states. In May 1949 the three Western powers established the Federal Republic of Germany (West Germany). In October 1949 the USSR set up the German Democratic Republic (East Germany). Berlin remained divided – the western side of the city was part of the new Federal Republic, the eastern section part of the new Democratic Republic.

In the Federal Republic elections were held and the leader of the conservative Christian Democratic Party, Konrad Adenaeur, became the first chancellor of the new state. The city of Bonn was chosen as the new capital. In 1949 a provisional constitution was introduced, setting up a federal system of parliamentary government, with a president as head of state and a chancellor as head of government. After the Berlin crisis, the Cold War tensions reached new heights. Each superpower formed military alliances against each other. Europe was now divided into two hostile camps.

Konrad Adenauer (1876–1967): As mayor of Cologne, Adenauer served two prison terms under Nazi rule. He became chancellor of West Germany in 1949 and worked to achieve the post-war reconciliation of France and Germany. He was a strong supporter of the Western democratic bloc during the Cold War. He remained in power for 14 years, during which time he presided over the economic recovery of West Germany. He retired in 1963.

Courtesy: Corbis

1.4   SATELLITE STATES

After the second World War the USSR secured control of an unbroken belt of countries along its western borders. These included Poland, Hungary, Romania, Bulgaria and Czechoslovakia and were known as 'satellite states'. After 1948, when the division of Germany became permanent, East Germany came firmly under Soviet control. Stalin wanted to establish 'friendly' governments in all of these countries to ensure protection for the USSR. He wanted a 'buffer zone' here of satellite states between the USSR and Western Europe. In his own lifetime, Stalin had witnessed two German invasions of his country, in 1914 and 1941. He was determined that the USSR would never again face the threat of invasion from the West. The establishment of satellite states in Eastern Europe was thus part of a defensive policy and vital to the future security of the USSR, according to Stalin.

Following the announcement of the **Truman Doctrine** and the Marshall Plan, Stalin became alarmed. He feared that a USA-backed conspiracy was being directed against the USSR. In offering aid to countries fighting Communism, the **Truman Doctrine** was seen in the USSR as a direct threat to the very existence of the Soviet Communist state. He believed that the economic aid package proposed under the Marshall Plan was an attempt to lure countries away from Communism. Stalin prohibited countries under USSR control from availing of the Marshall Plan. To tighten control in the satellite states and to defend the Communist system against capitalist encirclement, Stalin set up the 'Communist Information Bureau', or **Cominform**. Cominform's main function was propagandist, to counteract 'American imperialism' and bind all the European

Communist parties closer together. In 1949 **Comecon** was set up, providing aid to countries in Eastern Europe to develop their economies and to integrate them with the Soviet economy. This was a kind of Marshall Plan for Eastern Europe.

Source Document

Courtesy: The Centre for the Study of Cartoons and Caricature

• This cartoon first appeared in the *Evening Standard* (British) on 18 November, 1947. It is titled 'Toeing the new line'.

QUESTIONS ON THE DOCUMENT

1. What is the message in this cartoon?
2. Who does the figure in uniform holding the tin of paint represent?

There was another reason why Stalin felt control of Eastern Europe was necessary for the USSR. This reason had more to do with economic expediency than with security or defence. The USSR suffered huge damages in the war. They expected to be compensated for their losses by German reparations after the war. The Western Allies, as we have seen, did not want to cripple Germany economically and resisted Soviet demands for compensation. Stalin began removing raw materials and equipment from East Germany, using them for the reconstruction of the economy in the USSR. Control of satellite states in Eastern Europe would supply the USSR with both the means to rebuild its economy and provide markets for its products. Exploitation of the countries in the 'buffer zone' ensured the economic recovery of the USSR.

The consolidation of the USSR's control of the satellite states in Eastern Europe happened in stages. Military occupation by the Red Army allowed the Russians a free hand in ensuring that key people sympathetic to Moscow were put in positions of power in Eastern Europe. Native Communist leaders, many of them trained in the USSR, were given dominant ministries in post-war coalitions, gaining control of the police and the courts. In the immediate post-war months the USSR wanted to make its control of Eastern Europe seem legitimate to the West. It allowed broad-based coalition governments to rule.

Courtesy: Corbis

However, by 1948 the Communists had succeeded in outmanoeuvring all other parties in these coalition governments. Across Soviet-controlled Eastern Europe, single one-Party states were set up, firmly under Communist control. Leaders of opposition parties were silenced. Native

• Russian Army troops, in February 1945, marching through Budapest, Hungary.

Communist leaders were replaced by Soviet ones. In Poland the Secretary of the Communist Party, Gomulka, was removed from office. In Bulgaria, Hungary and Albania native Communist ministers were dismissed and executed. Coalition governments were replaced by 'Peoples' Democracies' under tight control from Moscow.

CZECHOSLOVAKIA, 1948

The coalition government in Czechoslovakia lasted longer than in other Eastern bloc countries. The liberal leaders, Eduard Benes and Jan Masaryk, had hoped that Czechoslovakia might become a bridge between East and West. Many in Czechoslovakia hoped to participate in the Marshall Plan. Hopes were dashed, however, when the Communists, backed by the Red Army, staged a *coup* in February 1948. Stalin imposed a Communist government on Czechoslovakia.

Courtesy: Corbis

• As part of the Five-Year Plans, this giant tractor factory was constructed in Soviet Belarussia in 1947.

The sovietisation of Eastern Europe extended beyond politics into control of social and economic life as well. Churches were repressed and their lands confiscated. Media was strictly controlled under rigid censorship laws.

Five-year plans, based on the Soviet model, were introduced in industry. Consumer goods were in short supply. Industrial output did improve, but as the emphasis was on supplying the economic needs of the Soviet Union, the countries of Eastern Europe saw little improvement in their standards of living. Economic reorganisation in these countries after 1945 was directed towards making them serve the needs of the economy of the USSR. By 1951, 92 per cent of Bulgaria's trade was with the USSR, while Poland's trade with the USSR increased from 7 per cent before the war to 48 per cent by 1951. Collectivisation of agriculture, modelled on the Soviet practice, was also introduced to the satellite states.

As in the USSR, life in the Soviet-controlled Eastern bloc was tightly controlled by a secret police. Between 1949 and 1953 a new series of purges began in the USSR. Stalin became suspicious of leading Communists and military leaders, seeing them as rivals to power. His commissar for state security, Beria, was given wide-ranging powers to seek out real and imagined enemies of Communism, and of Stalin. Moscow-inspired terror, arrests, imprisonments and executions were extended to the satellite states. By the time of Stalin's death on 5 March 1953, the sovietisation of Eastern Europe was complete.

QUESTIONS

1. Give two reasons why Stalin wanted to control Eastern Europe after 1945.
2. Why was the USSR able to build up a buffer zone between itself and the West after 1945?
3. How did the USSR succeed in getting control in the satellite states?
4. How were the economies of the satellite states run?

GENERAL ESSAY QUESTIONS ON CHAPTER 1

1. "The alliance between the USA, Britain and the USSR during the second World War was a marriage of convenience." Discuss.
2. Account for the emergence of the USA and the USSR as superpowers after the second World War.
3. Assess the importance of the ideological differences between the USA and the USSR in contributing to Cold War tensions.
4. With reference to two or more countries, how successful was the 'sovietisation' of Eastern Europe between 1945 and 1990?

2

MILITARY ALLIANCES AND THE MAIN EVENTS OF THE COLD WAR

Words you need to understand

Containment: US policy to limit the spread of Communism after the second World War.

Crisis: A time of serious danger or difficulty.

Doctrine: A statement of policy or belief.

Free elections: Vote in secret for a party or individuals of choice.

Guerrilla war: Hit-and-run surprise tactics to fight a war.

Inflation: Sharp rise in prices.

Nuclear deterrent: Possession of nuclear weapons to stop another nuclear power from attacking.

Rationing: Restriction of supplies, e.g. food, fuel, etc.

Ratify: Accept and act on an agreement.

Treaty: An agreement signed between two or more states.

INTRODUCTION

On 7 May 1945 the Allies accepted the 'unconditional surrender of all German forces'. The next day, 8 May, was declared **V-E Day** (**Victory in Europe Day**). All fighting in Europe stopped. The war was over.

Once Germany was defeated, the wartime unity between the USSR, the USA and Britain quickly disappeared. In this chapter we will see how different aims in the post-war world led to setting up new military alliances that divided both Europe and the world into two hostile, armed camps.

The superpowers, the USSR and the USA, independently formed alliances with friendly countries. These became satellite states to each of the superpowers. After the second World War the world was split into two opposing blocs:
■ The Eastern bloc – the USSR and its satellites.
■ The Western bloc – the USA and its satellites.

In 1945 the USA alone had nuclear weapons. By 1949 the USSR had developed a nuclear bomb. Rivalry between the superpowers for military and political supremacy resulted in an **arms race**. Each side became capable of destroying not only each other, but also the entire world. Both the USSR and the USA spent vast amounts of money on defence budgets between 1945 and 1990. The threat of nuclear attack strengthened the alliances between each superpower and its own satellite states. One American historian, John Gaddis, referred to the atomic bomb as 'the impotence of omnipotence'. He explains that neither of the superpowers wished to use the atomic bomb, but in times of conflict between them it could act as a powerful deterrent and an effective tool for defence.

At various times during this period the Cold War threatened to become 'hot' and develop into open conflict between the superpowers. These were times of acute danger for world peace. The main crises of the period are examined in this chapter.

2.1   SELF-DETERMINATION VS. SECURITY

When the war ended it was clear that the former allies had very different plans for the future government and administration of Germany and Eastern Europe.

The Western allies, the USA and Britain, based their plans for post-war Europe on the Atlantic Charter. This called for government by consent, or self-determination: 'the right of all peoples to choose the form of government under which they will live'.

TWO WORLD VIEWS

Courtesy: *Punch* magazine

• This 1946 cartoon contrasts the perspectives of the two superpowers – the one on the left is the Soviet view and that on the right is the USA's. Explain why only the Soviet Union and the USA are in control of the world in these cartoons.

Stalin, however, had other interests, which the Atlantic Charter ignored. Soviet national security interests were his primary concern. Any post-war settlement that did not fulfil these interests would be unacceptable to the USSR. For Stalin, Soviet security meant control of Eastern Europe. Unfriendly states on its western borders would present a threat. Self-determination and free elections in Poland, Hungary, Romania, Albania, Bulgaria and Czechoslovakia would not produce pro-Soviet states. Western attachment to the idea of self-determination was in direct conflict with the Soviet demand for its own security.

By April 1945 the Red Army controlled Eastern Europe as far as the river Elbe. That month Stalin announced, "Whoever occupies territory also imposes his own social system as far as his army can reach. It cannot be otherwise." Short of going to war with the USSR, the USA and Britain had no choice but to accept Soviet control of these countries.

The wartime allies had agreed to the division of Germany into four zones after 1945. The four zones of occupation would be administered by Britain, France, the USA and the USSR. The issue of German reparations caused friction between the USSR and the Western allies and it did not augur well for future joint policy between them in dealing with Germany. The USSR also differed with their former allies on the question of Eastern Europe. Stalin had no intention of allowing democratic, Western-style governments to be set up within his sphere of influence.

● How Western and Eastern Europe divided, after 1948.

The growing tension between the USSR and its former allies was not confined to Germany and Eastern Europe. Stalin's determination to safeguard Soviet security and trade interests led him to push for oil rights in Azerbaijan, Iran. During the war the British occupied the south of Iran while the USSR occupied the north of the country. It was agreed that both powers would withdraw completely from Iran after the war. The region had been a target for Russian expansion since the 19th century. Stalin took the opportunity to set up a Communist government in northern Iran in December 1945. However, Britain and the USA were not prepared to allow Soviet expansion in this area. They could not stop Stalin in Eastern Europe, but they did force the USSR to withdraw its forces from Iran.

The Balkans was another region that Russia (USSR) had always wanted to control. Control of the Dardanelles, the straits leading from the Black Sea to the Mediterranean, would strengthen Soviet defence of the Ukraine. It would also give access to the Mediterranean for trade purposes. Stalin put pressure on Turkey to allow joint Soviet-Turkish control of the Dardanelles. The Western powers resisted this and insisted that the Black Sea be left as an open waterway for all countries. Stalin was forced to back down, but saw the decision to grant access to the Black Sea to foreign powers as a security risk to the Soviet Union's southern ports.

Whether Stalin acted defensively to protect the USSR or aggressively to spread Communism, the West became convinced that tough action was needed to stop further USSR expansion.

QUESTIONS

1. How did the USSR and the West differ in their plans for post-war Europe?
2. How did the USSR try to strengthen its security arrangements after 1945?

2.2 DISARMAMENT

After the USA dropped atomic bombs on Japan in August 1945, the Western leaders felt more secure in following an uncompromising policy with the USSR.

In 1945 the USSR had the largest army in the world. During the war the Red Army had nearly 12 million men, but by 1948 it was reduced to under three million. It also had 50,000 tanks and 6,000 aircraft. Even with demobilisation after the war, the USSR remained a strong military power.

In the USA public opinion wanted 'the boys brought home'. Military leaders reluctantly gave in to public pressure. In 1945 the USA's armed forces numbered 12 million soldiers. By mid-1946 it had been reduced to three million and by 1947 stood at 1.6 million.

Courtesy: Corbis

In January 1946 the USA proposed a plan to control the manufacture of atomic weapons. The UN, acting on the American initiative, set up an **International Atomic Energy Commission**. The US representative, Bernard M. Baruch, put forward a proposal for international control whereby an international agency, answerable to the UN, would take charge of atomic energy. This agency would prevent the manufacture of atomic bombs by national governments. It would also have the power to send international inspectors into all countries to ensure that atomic weapons were not being developed. However, Baruch warned that the US would not reveal its atomic secrets until the UN provided for 'immediate, swift and sure punishment for those who violate the agreements that are reached by the nations'. He also insisted that the five permanent members on the UN Security Council should give up their veto rights on all matters relating to atomic energy.

● Much testing of nuclear bombs was carried out by the USA in the Pacific Ocean throughout the 1940s and 1950s, feeding into the fears of a third World War, and adding to the tensions of the Cold War.

The USSR vetoed the proposal when it came to a vote on the Security Council. Instead they proposed that the USA destroy its atomic bombs and called on the UN to declare atomic warfare illegal. They also called for a commitment from all nations not to manufacture atomic bombs. The USSR firmly rejected inspections by any international agency, saying this would pose a threat to their national security. By the end of 1946 any chance for international control of atomic weapons had been lost. The USSR and the USA proceeded with their separate atomic research and development programmes. In September 1949 the Soviets successfully tested their own atomic bomb. This alarmed the USA and Britain and increased the tensions and distrust between East and West.

QUESTIONS

1. What plans did the USA and the USSR have to control nuclear weapons in 1946?
2. How did the failure of attempts to disarm after the second World War increase tensions between the superpowers?

2.3   CONTAINMENT

In January 1946 Harry S. Truman, president of the USA, wrote to his Secretary of State (foreign minister), "Unless Russia is faced with an iron fist and strong language another war is in the making ... I'm tired of babying the Soviets." Truman was losing patience with the USSR and was preparing to take tough action against America's former ally.

In February Stalin announced that capitalism and Communism were incompatible. The West saw this statement as a declaration of Soviet intention to continue the conflict between the superpowers. Two weeks later, George Keenan, a senior US diplomat in Moscow, sent a telegram to the government in Washington. He said:

> "The Kremlin's [USSR government] neurotic view of world affairs is the traditional and instinctive Russian sense of insecurity ... Russian rulers have learned to seek security only in patient but deadly struggle for the total destruction of rival power, never in compacts with it." Stalin was "only the last of that long succession of cruel and wasteful Russian rulers who have relentlessly forced their country on to ever new heights of military power."

Keenan later warned Washington that the Kremlin would never accept compromise with the USA until it had control of Western Europe. He called on the USA to follow a policy of "long-term patient but firm and vigilant containment of Russian expansive tendencies". Keenan's idea of containment became the basis for the USA's policy towards the USSR during the Cold War.

IRON CURTAIN

In March 1946 former British Prime Minister Winston Churchill made his famous speech at Fulton, Missouri. He said "... an Iron Curtain has descended across the continent" [Europe]. He declared that the USSR wanted "infinite expansion of their power and doctrines" and condemned "the police governments" in Eastern Europe. He urged vigilance and military action to stop Soviet imperialism. This, he said, called for a "fraternal association of English-speaking peoples" and "intimate relationships between our military advisors" as well as "joint use of all naval and air force bases in the possession of either country all over the world."

Courtesy: Hulton-Deutsch/Corbis

● Churchill with Truman at a rally in Missouri where Churchill delivered his famous 'Iron Curtain' speech, March 1946.

Churchill was calling on the USA to join with Britain to defend the principles they had fought for in the second World War: "This is certainly not the liberated Europe we fought to build up, nor is it one that contains the essentials of permanent peace."

President Truman sat on the platform with Churchill while he delivered his speech. Within days he took firm action with the USSR by sending a US battleship to the eastern Mediterranean and warned the USSR against putting any further pressure on Turkey or Iran.

A week after Churchill's speech Stalin responded with this statement: "There can be no doubt that Mr Churchill's position is a call for war on the USSR."

The issue of German occupation led to a further rift between the superpowers.

In September 1946 US Secretary of State, James Byrnes, announced that his country would no longer seek Soviet co-operation in the occupation of Germany. Instead America would strengthen its own zone and work to rebuild Germany.

Courtesy: Bettmann/Corbis

Events in Greece caused further conflict between the former wartime allies. In 1946 a pro-Western democratic Greek government, backed by Britain, was set up. The Greek Communists staged a revolt against the new government and a bitter civil war followed. Greece was geographically cut off from Western Europe. After the war it found itself surrounded by new Communist states in Albania, Yugoslavia and Bulgaria. By early 1947 the British Labour government, faced with enormous post-war economic strain at home, was under pressure to deal with urgent domestic problems. In February 1947

• American-equipped Greek commandos firing on Communist 'guerrillas', 1948.

British Foreign Secretary, Ernest Bevin, informed the USA that "economic necessity dictates the relinquishment of British burdens in Greece."

THE TRUMAN DOCTRINE

The USA wrongly believed that Stalin was sending aid and arms to the Greek Communists. President Truman decided to act promptly. In March 1947 he asked the US Congress [parliament] to vote for a military and economic aid package for Greece. In his speech requesting the aid Truman said, "I believe that it must be the policy of the United States to support free peoples who are resisting attempted subjugation by armed minorities." He also wanted to commit the USA to a worldwide crusade against Communist expansion. This policy became known as the **Truman Doctrine** and represented a turning point in post-war East-West relations. The USA was now committed to a policy of actively preventing the spread of Communism around the world.

Courtesy: Corbis

The US Congress endorsed the **Truman Doctrine** and voted in favour of a $400 million aid package to Greece. This massive aid soon ended the Communist threat in Greece and Turkey. The Greek government defeated the Communists in the civil war. The success of the policy in Greece inspired the USA to set up a general policy offering financial aid to other countries faced with Communist takeovers.

In June 1947 the Truman Doctrine was given a more global and permanent edge when the new Secretary of State, George Marshall, announced an American programme of economic aid to all European countries, including the USSR and its satellites in Eastern Europe.

Marshall's aid package, the **Economic Recovery Program** (ERP), aimed at setting up "political and social conditions in which free institutions can exist". He made European co-operation a condition of getting the aid. These conditions discouraged the USSR from participating. Stalin saw the ERP as a Western attempt to extend capitalism in Europe. Western European countries responded with enthusiasm to Marshall's plan, but Stalin refused to participate and also forbade the Soviet satellites in Eastern Europe to have anything to do with it.

• The Fruit of Co-operation was the title of this Unity poster from 1947.

Source Document

A

Courtesy: TopFoto

B

Courtesy: *Punch magazine*

- The left-hand image is the West German view, while the right-hand cartoon shows the Soviet view of the Marshall Plan.

QUESTIONS ON THE DOCUMENT

1. Study the two cartoons. What is the West German view of the Marshall Plan? What is the Soviet view?
2. Explain what the flags represent in Source A.
3. Explain what the dollar sign represents in Source B.

Instead of uniting Europe the Marshall Plan caused a further rift between East and West. Like the Truman Doctrine, it represented Keenan's idea of containment.

In response to the Truman Doctrine and the Marshall Plan, in September 1947 Stalin set up the **Communist Information Bureau**, or **Cominform**.

In January 1949 Stalin introduced a plan to help the economies of Eastern Europe. The **Council for Mutual Economic Assistance**, or **Comecon**, was the USSR's version of the Marshall Plan. It drew the economies in the Eastern bloc closer to the USSR and also brought benefits to the Soviet economy in much the same way as the Marshall Plan did to the economy of the USA.

QUESTIONS

1. Why did George Keenan suggest a policy of 'firm and vigilant containment' in 1947?
2. Churchill suggested ways of limiting further Soviet expansion in his Fulton, Missouri speech in 1946. List some of them.

2.4   MILITARY ALLIANCES

On 4 March 1947 Britain and France signed a military defence agreement, called the **Treaty of Dunkirk**. The two countries promised to co-operate on military and economic matters and to work together to fight any military threat from Germany. Both Britain and France feared a revival of German military strength. A British diplomat, Frank Roberts, wrote in 1946: "Any comparison between the German menace before the war and a Soviet menace today, must allow for … fundamental differences … There is, therefore, infinitely less danger of a sudden catastrophe with the Russians than with the Germans."

During the summer of 1947 there were heated exchanges between the Eastern powers and the USSR over the Marshall Plan. The British and French governments proposed to the USSR that their three foreign ministers meet to consider the Plan.

Many of the Eastern European satellite states were keen to participate in the Marshall Plan. In July the British and French governments invited 22 European countries to attend a conference in Paris to discuss Marshall's offer. Czechoslovakia accepted the invitation. Molotov, the Soviet Foreign Minister, attended the Paris Conference. He and the other Soviet delegates walked out in protest before it ended. Stalin issued an ultimatum to the Czech government, forcing them to withdraw from the conference. Moscow radio announced that the USSR and the Eastern European countries would not participate in the Marshall Plan.

PRAGUE COUP, 1948

Czechoslovakia was geographically situated in Central Europe. The Communist Party had been popular in Czechoslovakia before the war and Stalin had no reason to fear a hostile outcome from free elections. In May 1946 elections took place. The Communists won 114 of the 300 seats in parliament, giving them the dominant position in the coalition government formed after the election.

The new Czech government tried to follow an independent line, keeping good relations with both Stalin and the West. It worked hard to ensure that democracy survived in Czechoslovakia and followed the USSR in foreign policy. Good relations were maintained with Moscow between 1945 and 1947.

Courtesy: Hulton-Deutsch/Corbis

● This is an early Communist rally in Prague, Czechoslovakia, 1948. Rallies such as these prompted the coup d'etat by the Communists later that year.

In the summer of 1947, however, popular support for the Communists declined in Czechoslovakia. The reasons for this were:

■ Stalin's pressure on the Czech government to withdraw from the Paris Conference, ending Czech hopes of participating in the Marshall Plan.

■ The policies of the Czech Minister of the Interior, who began removing non-Communists from the police force. Freedoms enjoyed by Czech citizens since 1945 were now being eroded by the activities of the secret police.

New elections were due in May 1948. The Communists reorganised the government, removing all non-

Communists. On Soviet instructions, dissidents were arrested. With control of the police and backed by the Red Army, the Communists succeeded in taking over. This is known as the **Prague Coup** and it brought an end to democracy in Czechoslovakia. It turned the only Eastern European country with a democratic government into another Soviet satellite state.

In the May elections only Communists were allowed to stand. A new constitution was introduced which put Czechoslovakia firmly under Communist control.

Events in Czechoslovakia convinced the USA and the Western powers that the policy of containment was the only way to deal with the Soviet threat. Within a year of the Treaty of Dunkirk, Britain and France came to the conclusion that their alliance was directed against the wrong enemy. It was the USSR, not Germany, that presented a military threat to Europe.

NATO

On 17 March 1948 Britain, France, Belgium, Luxembourg and the Netherlands signed the **Treaty of Brussels**. Under the terms of this treaty, if any one of the five countries was attacked the other members of the alliance would help them with "all military and other aid and assistance".

The five countries that signed the Treaty of Brussels knew they could not meet the threat of a Soviet military attack on their own. Western Europe needed the support of the USA.

On 4 April 1949, 12 countries signed the **North Atlantic Treaty Organisation** (**NATO**) in Washington, DC. This military agreement was signed by representatives from Britain, France, Belgium, Luxembourg, the Netherlands, Italy, Portugal, Norway, Denmark, Iceland, Canada and the USA. Under the terms of the agreement, any attack on a NATO member state would be taken as an attack against all the members (see Source Document on pp. 26–7). The military forces of all the NATO partners were put under joint military control and were to be kept prepared to "resist armed attack".

Courtesy: Bettmann/Corbis

● The ceremony in Washington for the NATO signing, April 1949. Twelve countries signed up initially.

The setting up of NATO gave Western Europe a strong military defence. It guaranteed security against Soviet advances and had the backing of US air and atomic strength. General Eisenhower, a respected second World War American military leader, was appointed first commander of NATO forces. As well as being a military alliance, NATO was also a political alliance. Its members promised to defend each other against attacks on "freedom, common heritage and civilisation of their people".

EXPANSION OF NATO

West Germany was not included in the NATO alliance when it was first set up. Some of Germany's neighbouring countries feared a revival of its military strength. Lord Ismay, NATO's first Secretary General, expressed this fear when he said that they would "keep Americans in, the Germans down and the Russians out".

In May 1949 the Western zones merged and set up the German Federal Republic. In October that year the USSR established the German Democratic Republic in East Germany.

When war broke out in Korea in 1950 (see page 35), the USA became concerned about the weakening of the defence of Western Europe, as US troops were withdrawn to serve in Korea. They tried to persuade their NATO allies to permit Germany to rearm. The French in particular were unhappy with this. Instead, France suggested an integrated European army. Germany could be involved, but France hoped to keep that involvement to a minimum. In Paris on 27 March 1952 France, West Germany, Italy, Belgium, the Netherlands and Luxembourg signed a treaty to establish the **European Defence Community** (EDC). The plan for a common European military union set out in the EDC never got off the ground. France and Italy were reluctant to give up control of their military forces. In August 1954 the French parliament refused to ratify the EDC agreement.

Under pressure from the USA, France agreed to expand the 1948 Treaty of Brussels to include Germany and Italy in October 1954. The following May, West Germany joined NATO. French fears of German military recovery were eased when Britain promised to keep some of its forces in Europe. For Germany, membership of NATO meant that foreign troops stationed in the country were now allies and not forces of occupation. Greece and Turkey joined NATO in February 1952.

Courtesy: The Centre for the Study of Cartoons and Caricature

• Reviewing the Paper Troops. This is a cartoon portraying Eisenhower and the 'NATO big 4' in front of row after row of paper cut-out soldiers. Why are they shown as paper troops?

During the 1950s and 1960s tension often developed between the USA and some of the European members of NATO. As the Soviet threat to Western Europe declined some member states rejected American domination of NATO. The growth of the European movement for integration often led to conflict of interests in which the USA found itself at odds with its European NATO allies. France in particular frequently clashed with the USA. In 1966 President de Gaulle withdrew French forces from NATO and consequently NATO headquarters were moved to Brussels. There were also tensions between Greece and Turkey over Cyprus. In 1964 the Greeks withdrew their forces from NATO, but rejoined again in October 1980. In May 1982 Spain's application for membership of NATO was accepted.

QUESTIONS

1. Explain why Britain and France signed the Treaty of Dunkirk in 1947.
2. List the countries that signed the North Atlantic Treaty Organisation in 1949.
3. Why was West Germany allowed to join NATO in 1955?

Source Document

The North Atlantic Treaty
Washington DC, 4 April 1949

The Parties to this Treaty reaffirm their faith in the purposes and principles of the *Charter of the United Nations* and their desire to live in peace with all peoples and all governments.

They are determined to safeguard the freedom, common heritage and civilisation of their peoples, founded on the principles of democracy, individual liberty and the rule of law. They seek to promote stability and well-being in the North Atlantic area.

They are resolved to unite their efforts for collective defence and for the preservation of peace and security. They therefore agree to this North Atlantic Treaty:

Article 3

In order more effectively to achieve the objectives of this Treaty, the Parties, separately and jointly, by means of continuous and effective self-help and mutual aid, will maintain and develop their individual and collective capacity to resist armed attack.

Article 5

The Parties agreed that an armed attack against one or more of them in Europe or North America shall be considered an attack against them all and consequently they agreed that, if such an armed attack occurs, each of them, in exercise of the right of individual or collective self-defence recognised by *Article 51 of the Charter of the United Nations*, will assist the Party or Parties so attacked by taking forthwith, individually and in concert with the other Parties, such action as it deems necessary, including the use of armed force, to restore and maintain the security of the North Atlantic area.

Any such armed attack and all measures taken as a result thereof shall immediately be reported to the Security Council. Such measures shall be terminated when the Security Council has taken the measures necessary to restore and maintain international peace and security.

Article 10

The Parties may, by unanimous agreement, invite any other European State in a position to further the principles of this Treaty and to contribute to the security of the North Atlantic area to accede to this Treaty. Any State so invited may become a Party to the Treaty by depositing its instrument of accession with the Government of the United States of America. The Government of the United States of America will inform each of the Parties of the deposit of each such instrument of accession.

QUESTIONS ON THE DOCUMENT

1. According to Article 3, how will NATO members keep prepared 'to resist armed attack'?
2. According to Article 5, what will happen if any member is attacked in Europe?
3. How does Article 10 show that the USA dominated NATO?

WARSAW PACT

The expansion of NATO to include West Germany alarmed the USSR. The rearming of West Germany was seen as a military threat not only to the Eastern bloc, but the USSR itself. The Soviets were also concerned about a NATO presence in Germany.

Cominform (1947) and Comecon (1949) had already formalised ties between the USSR and Eastern Europe. Following West Germany's entry into NATO, the Soviets felt encircled by the West. Within days of West Germany joining NATO, the Soviets moved to consolidate their military hold on their satellite states.

On 14 May 1955 the **Eastern European Mutual Assistance Treaty**, known as the **Warsaw Pact**, was signed. It was an agreement between Albania, Bulgaria, Czechoslovakia, Hungary, Poland,

Romania, the German Democratic Republic (East Germany) and the USSR. The Warsaw Pact was a military alliance that set up a unified military command and created an Eastern bloc army. This joint command force had its headquarters in Moscow and had a Soviet general in charge. Each country promised to help each other if any one or more of them were faced with an armed attack in Europe. They all agreed to allow Soviet troops to be stationed in their countries. Annual joint military manoeuvres were held as a show of military force to both the satellite states and the West. Europe was now divided into two armed camps, each controlled by a nuclear superpower.

In 1956 Hungary unsuccessfully tried to leave the Warsaw Pact. In 1968 an uprising took place in Czechoslovakia. The USSR led a Warsaw Pact invasion to crush these revolts. The ending of the Cold War made the Pact redundant. It was dissolved by its members in 1991.

QUESTIONS

1. What prompted the USSR to set up the Warsaw Pact agreement in May 1955?
2. List some of the terms of the agreement.
3. Give examples to show how the USSR controlled the Warsaw Pact alliance.

2.5   THE MAIN CRISES OF THE COLD WAR

THE BERLIN BLOCKADE

The first serious confrontation of the Cold War happened in Berlin in June 1948. The city had been divided into four zones. Britain, France, the USA and USSR each took over the administration and military occupation of a zone. Situated 150 km inside the Soviet zone, West Berlin was isolated from the other Western occupied zones of Germany. Access to the Allied sectors of Berlin was through the Soviet-controlled part of Germany.

To improve economic administration and to allow Germany to benefit from Marshall Aid, the three Western powers decided to merge their zones. In June 1948 the British, French and American zones were merged to form one administrative zone where, later that month, they introduced a new currency, the Deutschmark, which was intended to reduce inflation and promote economic growth.

The presence of the Allies in Berlin annoyed the USSR. They wanted them to leave West Berlin and thus secure Soviet control of all of East Germany. In June 1948 the USSR closed all road, rail and canal links between Berlin and the Western zones of Germany. Gas and electricity supplied to West Berlin from the Soviet zone were also cut.

The USSR believed the Western Allies would not risk a confrontation that might lead to war. They hoped that the Western powers would either leave Berlin or start new negotiations that would give the USSR control in the city.

Courtesy: Hulton-Deutsch/Corbis

● A police raid on a Berlin 'Black Market' in 1948, trying to curb the illegal currency exchange, following the introduction of a new currency in the East.

War was actually a greater possibility than the Soviets realised. The US commander in Germany, General Lucius Clay, suggested that a train full of American troops should be sent to Berlin and open fire if the Soviets tried to stop them. This proposal was not acted upon. The USA did not wish to run the risk of war with the USSR. However, they were determined to defy the blockade. They decided to organise an airlift to keep access to West Berlin open.

OPERATION VITTLES

The four powers had never made a formal agreement about access to Berlin by land or water. They did, however, have an agreement that allowed air access. Stalin was technically within his rights when he blockaded the city in 1948. However, he did not block air routes. This allowed the Western powers to maintain and support their presence in West Berlin. Stalin did not try to stop them using air routes, knowing that if he did war would have been inevitable.

The Western powers launched Operation Vittles, a massive airlift lasting for 324 days. Supplies of food, fuel, machinery, medicines and other goods were flown in every day. Even sweets for the children were dropped in tiny parachutes made from handkerchiefs. Tensions ran high as Soviet planes flew close to Allied planes heading for Berlin. Any provocation by either side could have led to another war. By May 1949 Stalin realised that the Western powers would not leave Berlin. On 12 May he reopened land and water routes through East Germany, calling off the blockade of West Berlin.

• West Berlin 1948. Children wave to a US plane bringing supplies during the Soviet Blockade.

BERLIN, 1949–1981

West Berlin remained a Western hostage surrounded by Soviet-controlled East Germany. The Western powers were determined to improve economic life in West Berlin. They used funding from Marshall Aid to develop industries and provide services. West Berlin prospered and standards of living improved greatly. East Berlin, in contrast, remained poor. Low wages, food and housing shortages, lack of consumer goods and poor living standards in general led to widespread discontent. East Germans could travel freely into West Berlin. Many were attracted by the better living standards there and did not return to the East.

Stalin died in March 1953. In June, strikes and riots broke out. Workers in East Berlin marched in protest, demanding reforms. When the government failed to meet the workers' demands, violence erupted. The East German government called in Soviet tanks and troops to restore order. The new leader of the USSR, Khrushchev, agreed to give financial assistance to the GDR.

The prosperity of West Berlin was a cause of concern for the USSR. The flight of refugees was a constant reminder that living conditions in the West were superior. This undermined East German support for the USSR and the GDR.

• Lifting of the Berlin Blockade – one of the first cars to pass through, 14 May, 1949.

Nikita Khrushchev (1894–1971): Nikita Sergeyevich Khrushev was born in the Ukraine in 1894. During the Russian civil war, 1919–1922, he served in the Red Army. He rose in the ranks of the Communist Party during the 1930s. In 1949 Stalin put him in charge of Soviet agricultural production. After Stalin's death in 1953, he became Party secretary. In 1956 he denounced Stalin. He called for 'peaceful co-existence' with the West. However, when Poland and Hungary rebelled against Soviet rule later that year he sent the Soviet army to suppress the uprisings. Between 1958 and 1964 he was Prime Minister of the USSR and head of the Communist Party. Despite his peaceful gestures to the West, the Cuban Missile Crisis of 1962 brought the USSR close to war with the USA. Khrushchev's poor relationship with the Chinese leader Mao Tse-tung led to a serious rift between the USSR and China. Khrushchev was forced to resign in 1964 and died in 1971.

The Western powers refused to recognise the German Democratic Republic (GDR) as an independent state. Unlike other Eastern European states under USSR control, the GDR had been an artificial creation. Poland, Hungary and all the other Eastern bloc countries had existed before 1945. The GDR, however, was a new state, established by the USSR. It had no legitimate status, according to the West. They insisted on dealing with the USSR and not the East German authorities in all matters relating to Berlin.

The Soviets, on the other hand, regarded East Berlin as part of the GDR. The Western presence in Berlin denied the USSR complete control of the eastern part of Germany. They wanted the West to recognise the GDR as an independent state and to withdraw from West Berlin. In November 1958 Khrushchev demanded Western withdrawal from Berlin within six months. He called for the setting up of a neutralised, "free Berlin". He threatened to hand over control of all the routes into the city to the GDR if the West did not comply. The West did not want another crisis situation like the Berlin Blockade. Neither did they want to give in to the Soviet demand. They decided to put the choice to the people of West Berlin. In a referendum 98 per cent of West Berliners voted against Western withdrawal. Khrushchev backed down, at least for the moment.

On 1 May 1960 a CIA (American secret service) agent, Gary Powers, flew a spy plane over the USSR. Similar spying missions had been happening for several years, but the Soviets shot down Powers' plane. Khrushchev decided to use this incident for propaganda purposes. Two weeks later, at a meeting in Paris between the USA, Britain, France and the USSR, Khrushchev demanded an apology from the USA. The American president, Eisenhower, refused, but did promise that there would be no more spying missions. The meeting ended abruptly. The USSR withdrew from the talks and cancelled their invitation to Eisenhower to visit Moscow the following year.

Courtesy: Bettmann/Corbis

● 1961 – Communist People's Police officers string barbed wire along a fence – the first stages of the construction of the Berlin Wall. Each work party has guards who keep their guns raised at all times. The wall stretched for almost 160 km.

THE BERLIN WALL

Khrushchev left Paris for East Berlin. The Western leaders feared that the city would again become the scene for another East-West confrontation. However, nothing happened this time.

In June 1961 Khrushchev again put pressure on the West to leave Berlin. He met the new American president, John F. Kennedy, in Vienna. He told Kennedy that if the Western powers did not sign an agreement recognising the GDR he would hand over administration of Berlin to the East German authorities, which would end access to the city from West Germany. Following this meeting both leaders increased military spending. Khrushchev made war-like speeches. Kennedy announced a call-up of army reserves and advised Americans to build bomb shelters.

On 13 August the East German authorities blocked all traffic between East and West Berlin. The next day they began erecting a high wall with observation towers and stationed armed guards along the border between East and West Berlin. The guards were given orders to shoot any East Germans attempting to escape to the West.

John F. Kennedy (1917–1963): John Fitzgerald Kennedy was born in Boston in 1917. During the second World War he served in the US navy in the Pacific. He entered politics in 1946 and in 1960 he was elected president. As president he followed a policy of containment, which frequently brought him into conflict with Khrushchev. In 1961 the USA carried out the unsuccessful Bay of Pigs invasion of Cuba. Two years later Kennedy took firm action with the USSR in the Cuban Missile Crisis, forcing the withdrawal of Soviet missiles from Cuba. He sent military advisors to Vietnam. In June 1963 he visited the divided city of Berlin, only weeks before the Berlin wall was built. In November 1963 he was assassinated in Dallas, Texas.

Courtesy: Corbis

The building of the **Berlin Wall** caused outrage in the West. Use of American tanks to breach the wall was considered, but no action was taken. By not acting, the West appeared to concede that East Berlin was within the Soviet sphere of influence. In June 1963 President Kennedy visited West Berlin. He made an emotional speech at the wall and warned the Soviets that any interference by them outside East Germany would be treated as an attack on the Western powers.

The Berlin Wall became a symbol of the Cold War, a physical expression of the reality of the Iron Curtain. For the next 28 years it stood as a grim reminder of the divisions between East and West. In 1989 popular movements in Eastern Europe finally brought about the collapse of Communism. On 9 November 1989 the wall was taken down by the people of Berlin. The city that had been at the centre of so many crises since 1945 was at last united. On 3 October 1990 East and West Germany were reunited as one state. The Cold War was over.

Courtesy: Peter Turnley/Corbis

● East German soldiers stand guard over celebrants at Potsdamer Platz (East) in November 1989.

QUESTIONS

1. Why did the USSR blockade Berlin in June 1948?
2. Why did the USSR want the Western powers to leave Berlin?
3. Why was the Berlin Wall built in August 1961?

Source Document

From *Punch*, 1947
The Berlin Blockade

Courtesy: *Punch* magazine

QUESTIONS ON THE DOCUMENT

1. In this cartoon, what do the storks represent?
2. Who is the man with the gun?
3. Why doesn't he shoot at the storks?

PEACEFUL CO-EXISTENCE

When Stalin died in March 1953, relations between the superpowers improved in the short term (see pages 43–45, Poland and pages 73–87 for Hungary). The Western powers had blamed Stalin for the Cold War tensions. In July 1955 Khrushchev, Stalin's successor, met the American president, Eisenhower, in Geneva. This was the first meeting of US and Soviet leaders since Potsdam (June–July 1945). No major decisions were made, but the atmosphere was friendly.

In February 1956 Khrushchev made a speech in which he criticised Stalin. He also talked about "peaceful co-existence" with the West. However, events in Poland and Hungary later that year would damage the new spirit of reconciliation between the USSR and the West.

The people of the Eastern bloc countries were encouraged by Khrushchev's speech. They hoped the new leader would bring reform.

POLAND, 1956

Poland was the first Eastern European country to demand reforms.

Courtesy: Hulton-Deutsch/Corbis

● Wladyslaw Gomulka in 1956.

In June high food prices and low wages led to riots and strikes. Khrushchev sent Soviet troops to restore order. He flew to Warsaw and began negotiations with the Polish Communists. Their leader, Gomulka, reassured him that Poland would continue to support Soviet foreign policy and remain committed to the Warsaw Pact alliance. Khrushchev accepted Gomulka's leadership in Poland and agreed to allow the Polish Communist government some control over internal affairs.

HUNGARY

In October 1956 riots occurred in Hungary, influenced by events in Poland. Students and workers took to the streets demanding reforms. Nagy (see page 74), the popular Communist leader, was brought to power. On 1 November he announced that free elections would be held and that Hungary would leave the Warsaw Pact. This alarmed Khrushchev. He decided to send the Red Army to deal with the revolt. On 4 November the invasion began and 6,000 Soviet tanks rolled into Hungary. The uprising was crushed.

The Soviet invasion of Hungary was condemned in the West. Eisenhower was criticised for not sending help to the Hungarian rebels. However, the Western powers realised that sending any assistance to the Hungarians would have provoked a dangerous confrontation with the USSR. This decision showed that the Western powers accepted that Eastern Europe was within the Soviet sphere of influence. They would not go to war over Eastern Europe.

SUEZ CRISIS

The Suez Canal connects the Mediterranean to the Red Sea. It runs through Egypt and is an important trade route. In 1888 the Suez Canal Company was set up to run the canal. The British government and private French investors were the main shareholders. When the Company was set up it granted 'free and open' navigation of the canal. British troops guarded the canal.

In 1952 a nationalist revolution in Egypt brought Colonel Nasser to power. He wanted to develop closer ties with other Arab states and to remove European influences from the region. He also wanted to industrialise Egypt. To help achieve this he planned to build a dam on the river Nile, at Aswan. The USA agreed to help finance the building.

When Britain made a defence pact with Turkey and Iraq (the **Baghdad Pact**) in 1955, Nasser saw his hopes for a united Arab defence union destroyed. He began to establish links with the Eastern bloc. He ordered arms from Czechoslovakia and gave recognition to Communist China. The USA was alarmed at these developments and in July 1956 decided to withdraw its offer of assistance to build the dam. One week later Nasser nationalised the Suez Canal Company. He planned to collect fees from ships using the canal. With this revenue he would build the dam.

• The Suez Canal, from an Israeli bridge, towards Egypt in 1957.

Arab countries had refused to recognise the state of Israel when it was set up in 1948. Resentment between Israel and its Arab neighbours continued to grow. In 1955 Nasser closed the Suez Canal to Israeli shipping. When he nationalised the canal in July 1956, Israel, Britain and France found they had a common enemy, Nasser.

In October, Israel invaded Egypt. Expecting American backing, the British and French attacked Egyptian bases in November. The United Nations condemned the actions of Israel, Britain and France. The USSR stood behind Egypt and threatened to launch rocket attacks on London and Paris. It seemed as if war was on the horizon. The USA, however, decided not to assist their Western allies this time. They had no wish to alienate the Arab world or to risk an open conflict with the USSR. A UN resolution, sponsored by the Americans, proposed sending a peace-keeping force to Suez. British and French troops withdrew and the crisis ended.

British and French collusion with Israel in the Suez affair drove Nasser closer to the USSR. The Soviets provided the finance to build the Aswan dam, giving them a foothold in the region. The crisis had another advantage for the USSR: it took attention away from Soviet military action in Hungary (see Chapter 5).

The failed Suez invasion was a humiliating experience for Britain and France. It showed them that without the support of the USA their power to influence international affairs was limited.

QUESTIONS

1. What effect did Khrushchev's speech in February 1956 have on Poland and Hungary?
2. The USSR reacted differently to the events in Poland and Hungary. Explain.
3. Explain how the Suez Crisis became a Cold War conflict.

CZECHOSLOVAKIA, 1968

Since 1948 Czechoslovakia had remained loyal to the Soviet Union (see pages 50–52). However, like in other Eastern European countries, people were discontented with economic conditions. Wages were low and food prices were high. Consumer goods were in short supply. Students demonstrated and demanded reforms in 1967.

In January 1968 a new leader, Alexander Dubcek, came to power. Dubcek promised reforms and assured the USSR that Czechoslovakia would remain in the Warsaw Pact.

In April 1968 Dubcek introduced a number of domestic reforms, which became known as the **Prague Spring**.

• Stalinist propaganda was an everyday sight for Czechoslovak citizens in the late 1940s.

Source Document

• The Prague Spring. Political slogans, flowers and poems were the protests made against the Warsaw Pact invasion.

Courtesy: Miroslav Zajíc/Corbis

QUESTIONS ON THE DOCUMENT

1. Why did people paint street slogans like these in Prague in 1968?
2. What are the messages in these slogans?

The USSR was concerned that the unity of the Eastern bloc would be threatened and that Czechoslovakia was moving towards a Western style of government.

In August the USSR sent tanks and 400,000 Warsaw Pact troops to Czechoslovakia. Fearing widespread revolution and bloodshed, Dubcek called on people not to fight. Instead a policy of **passive resistance** was followed.

Courtesy: Bettmann/Corbis

• This girl shouts her protest "Ivan go home" to soldiers sitting on tanks in the streets of Prague.

Czech protesters painted anti-Soviet slogans on walls and jeered at the invading troops. Dubcek was removed from power and replaced by the pro-Soviet Husak. Soviet troops remained in Czechoslovakia and reform was abandoned.

The West condemned Soviet action in Czechoslovakia, but did not interfere. Tensions increased between the superpowers. The French Communist intellectual, Jean-Paul Sartre, said that "the Soviet action was 'pure aggression, such as is defined in terms of international law as a war crime'."

However, as in Poland and Hungary in 1956, by following a policy of non-intervention in Czechoslovakia, the USA and its Western allies accepted Soviet control in Eastern Europe.

QUESTIONS

1. How did the West react to the uprising in Czechoslovakia in 1968?
2. Why was there an uprising in Czechoslovakia in 1968?

Source Document

Dubeck's demands

- By law, everyone was guaranteed equal rights.
- More trade to be allowed with non-Communist countries.
- No more censorship of newspapers.
- Elections to be more democratic.
- The secret police to have their powers reduced.
- Less state control of the economy.
- People to be allowed to travel freely outside the country.
- The Czech parliament to be allowed to criticise the government.

QUESTIONS ON THE DOCUMENT

1. List the reforms mentioned in this document.
2. Which of these reforms presented the greatest threat to the USSR's control of Czechoslovakia?

CHINA

In October 1949, following a bitter civil war, the Chinese Communists, under Mao Tse-tung, came to power. The USA saw Communism as a global conspiracy and was alarmed by events in China. It refused to recognise the legitimacy of Mao's government. The USSR initially welcomed the new regime in China and gave the new Communist government financial support.

KOREA

After the second World War Korea was divided in two. North of the 38th parallel was occupied by Soviet troops, while the USA occupied south of this line. As was the case in Germany, the superpowers failed to agree on a common policy for Korea. The occupying forces withdrew and two separate states were set up there. In June 1950 North Korean troops invaded South Korea in an attempt to unite the country.

Courtesy: Bettmann/Corbis

● More than 10,000 Seoul citizens gather to demonstrate against the Chinese Communist intervention in the Korean War, 1950.

Believing that the USSR was behind the invasion, the Americans sent troops to assist the government of South Korea. At the UN a resolution condemning the invasion was passed. Since the USSR was boycotting the UN Security Council at the time, the US managed to get approval to send a UN military force to South Korea. This force was mainly made up of American troops.

The North Koreans were driven out of South Korea, but when UN troops advanced as far as the Chinese border a crisis developed. Mao sent a large force of Chinese troops into North Korea.

The war dragged on for three years. The North Koreans received Soviet and Chinese support, while the USA sent aid to the Southern government. Eventually in July 1953 a ceasefire was called. Korea remained divided at the 38th parallel.

The Korean conflict confirmed the Western European powers' dependence on the USA for military defence. The threat to security in Western Europe led to closer co-operation between them. It also helped bring about a change in attitude towards Germany. In May 1955 West Germany became a full member of NATO. The real enemy in Western Europe was now the USSR, and West Germany became the front line of Western defence against Soviet attack (see pp. 25–6).

VIETNAM

Since 1883, Indochina (which included Laos, Cambodia and Vietnam) formed part of the French empire. During the second World War Japan occupied Vietnam. After the war, the French tried to regain control in Vietnam, but the Vietnamese now wanted independence.

Between 1946 and 1954 the Vietnamese nationalists, the Viet Minh, led by Ho Chi Minh, fought the French. In May 1954 the French were eventually defeated. Vietnam was divided along the 17th parallel. Ho Chi Minh set up a Communist state in the north. A right-wing dictator, Ngo Dinh Diem, set up the state of South Vietnam. Diem was supported by the Western powers. Ho Chi Minh wanted to unite Vietnam and to end Western influence.

Civil war broke out in 1957. South Vietnamese guerrillas, **Viet Cong**, backed by Ho Chi Minh, tried to overthrow Diem's regime. The USA believed that the USSR and China were supporting the Viet Cong.

Fearing the spread of Communism, they decided to help South Vietnam. Eisenhower, and later Kennedy, sent military advisors, but were reluctant to involve American ground troops in a war in Vietnam. By 1960 there were 16,000 American 'advisors' in South Vietnam.

Courtesy: Bettmann/Corbis

• Burnt houses in Saigon, 1968. A typical scene of devastation in South Vietnam.

In March 1965 President L.B. Johnson sent US troops to help the South Vietnamese. He expected to fight a limited war and secure an easy victory over the Vietnamese Communists.

During the Vietnam War the USSR and China sent arms and supplies to the North Vietnamese. By 1968 there were 500,000 American troops in Vietnam. American casualties were high and public opinion at home turned against the war. A ceasefire was agreed in January 1973. The USA left Vietnam and the country was reunited under a Communist government in 1975.

The Vietnam War was the first televised war in history. It proved to be a propaganda disaster for the Americans. Reports and images of US brutality against the Vietnamese shocked the world. The use of chemical warfare – napalm and Agent Orange – turned world opinion against the Americans. In Europe, TV coverage of the war was a catalyst for student discontent. Students in Italy, West Germany, France, Britain and Northern Ireland as well as in Eastern Europe demonstrated against the war. One recent historian claims "Young European radicals felt a sense of guilt by association with American-led intervention in South-east Asia".

The French president, de Gaulle, denounced American imperialism in South-east Asia. In June 1966 he visited Moscow and urged European co-operation from the Atlantic to the Urals.

QUESTIONS

1. Why did the USA become involved in Korea and Vietnam?
2. What effect did the Vietnam War have on Europe?

THE CUBAN MISSILE CRISIS

The most dangerous crisis of the Cold War happened in 1962, in Cuba. In 1956 revolutionaries, led by Fidel Castro, began a guerrilla war in Cuba. They wanted to overthrow the corrupt dictatorship of General Batista.

Cuba is situated less than 150 km from the Florida coast of the USA. Many American companies and private investors owned land and businesses there. The Cuban economy mainly depended on sugar exports to the USA.

In January 1959 Batista was driven from power by Castro, who then introduced a number of social and economic reforms. The state took over factories and large sugar plantations.

The USA was annoyed with Castro's reform programme, afraid he would turn Cuba into a Communist state. Furthermore, Americans had owned many of the factories and lands taken over by the new Cuban government. They were angry that they were now forced to abandon their lucrative investments and leave Cuba without compensation.

When Castro visited the USA in 1959 President Eisenhower refused to meet him. The USA cut all trade links with Cuba. Castro turned to the USSR for help. They agreed to buy Cuba's sugar, and by 1960, 80 per cent of Cuban trade was with the USSR and Eastern bloc countries.

The growing friendship between the USSR and Cuba prompted the Americans to take action to overthrow Castro. The **CIA (Central Intelligence Agency)** trained and armed anti-Castro Cuban exiles and made plans to invade the island. In April 1961, 1,500 exiles landed at the Bay of Pigs, in southern Cuba. Castro's forces overcame the invasion. For the USA it had been a complete failure and caused them great embarrassment.

After the Bay of Pigs, Castro turned to the USSR for military help. At first the Soviets sent advisors and military equipment.

On 14 October an American U2 spy plane took aerial photographs that proved that the Soviets were building missile bases in Cuba. These long-range ballistic missiles were capable of launching a nuclear attack on all the major American cities. There was also evidence that a fleet of Soviet ships, carrying nuclear weapons, were en route to Cuba.

The US president, Kennedy, demanded that the Soviets dismantle the missile sites immediately. He also ordered a naval blockade of Cuba to prevent the Soviets' delivery of nuclear weapons. He warned Khrushchev that all Soviet ships heading for Cuba would be stopped and searched.

Courtesy: Corbis

• President Kennedy meeting with army officials during the Cuban Missile Crisis, 1962.

The superpowers were on a collision course. Any wrong move by either side could have caused a nuclear war. For four days the world held its breath. The Soviet ships continued on course for Cuba. The US navy took position around Cuba and waited to see what the Soviets would do. The USA consulted with its NATO allies and kept them informed of developments. The Western military alliance was on alert, prepared to assist the USA if the Soviets attempted to break the naval blockade.

Eventually, on 24 October the Soviet ships turned back, before reaching the US blockade. Two days later Khrushchev wrote to Kennedy promising to remove the missiles if the USA agreed not to invade Cuba. The USA accepted the Soviet terms. The crisis was over. Both sides claimed victory. In Europe, as throughout the rest of the world, there was great relief that an armed clash between the superpowers had been avoided.

RESULTS

1. Both superpowers realised how close they had come to nuclear war over Cuba. They tried to improve East-West relations by setting up a 'hotline', or direct telephone line, between the White House and the Kremlin.
2. The superpowers also realised the need for arms control, and particularly the testing of nuclear weapons. In 1963 the two countries signed a Test Ban Treaty, banning nuclear testing. In 1969 they signed the **Treaty on the Non-Proliferation of Nuclear Weapons**.
3. The Soviets removed the missiles in Cuba, and the USA agreed to remove American missiles from Turkey.
4. After the Cuban Missile Crisis the superpowers avoided direct confrontation. The Cold War moved into a new phase. East-West relations became more stable and the nuclear threat became less urgent.

QUESTIONS

1. Explain why the USA wanted to overthrow Castro's government in Cuba.
2. How did the Cuban Missile Crisis provoke fears of nuclear war?
3. How was the Cuban Missile Crisis resolved?

DÉTENTE

In October 1964, following Khrushchev's resignation (see page 59), Leonid Brezhnev became leader of the Soviet Union. The nuclear threat and arms race caused a change in East-West relations and moves began to improve relations between the Soviet Union and the USA.

Richard Nixon became president of the USA in 1969. Like Brezhnev, he too was concerned about the arms race. Under these leaders a new phase in the Cold War emerged, known as **détente** – an easing of tensions between superpowers. This was a time when both sides made an effort to negotiate and co-operate with each other on a range of issues including arms control, trade and cultural links. Nixon, the first US president ever to visit the USSR, went to Moscow in May 1972 (he visited again in June 1974). The visit produced a series of agreements in which the two countries promised to improve commercial relations and to co-operate in scientific, medical and environmental areas. It also led to the signing of SALT I (Strategic Arms Limitation Treaty) in 1972. This treaty limited the construction and deployment of nuclear missiles, greatly reducing cold war tensions.

HELSINKI TREATIES, 1975

The high point of the détente came in 1975 when the USA, Canada and 35 European states (including the USSR) signed the Helsinki Treaties. These stated:

■ The West would recognise Europe's post-war boundaries (and Moscow's control of Eastern Europe).

■ The Soviet Union, in return, would uphold human rights and the free movement of people and ideas across frontiers.

The treaties also promoted further arms control and trade and cultural exchanges between East and West.

END OF DÉTENTE

In the late 1970s the détente ended when:

■ US President Jimmy Carter (1977–1981) supported human rights groups in the USSR and Eastern Europe (see charter 77, page 112).

■ The Soviet Union invaded Afghanistan in December 1979.

The USA boycotted the 1980 Moscow Olympic Games, abandoned arms limitation talks and increased military spending. Under Carter's successor, Ronald Reagan (1981–1988), East-West relations were at a very low ebb.

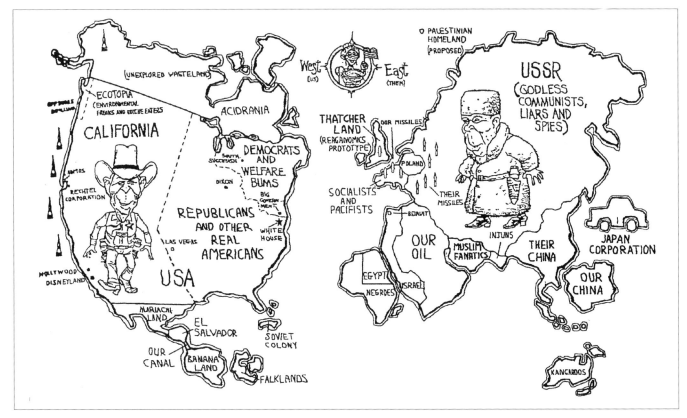

● How Ronald Reagan saw the world, from an American cartoon published in 1982.

GENERAL ESSAY QUESTIONS ON CHAPTER 2

1. Explain what is meant by the US policy of containment of Communism.

2. Write a short account of any of the main crises in the Cold War and show how that crisis affected relations between the superpowers.

3. Write a paragraph on the origins and aims of (a) NATO and (b) the Warsaw Pact.

4. "The dropping of the atomic bombs on Hiroshima and Nagasaki in 1945 were not so much the last military acts of the second World War as the first major operation of the Cold War." Discuss.

5. Why was NATO set up in 1949?

6. The American policy of containment led to US involvement in many conflicts during the Cold War. With references to crises in Europe and around the world, show how the USA 1945–1979 put containment into practice.

7. "Berlin … was increasingly seen by Khrushchev as a Western jewel tarnishing an Eastern crown." Discuss with reference to Berlin 1945–1991.

8. Give an account of the attempted revolts in Czechoslovakia 1945–1968, and show how the USSR reacted to them.

3

EMERGENCE OF REFORM MOVEMENTS IN EASTERN EUROPE

Words you need to understand

Cominform: The Communist Information Bureau set up in 1947 to link the Soviet Union with the other Socialist states of the Eastern Bloc.

Non-alignment: Marshal Tito's policy of not openly favouring either side during the Cold War.

De-Stalinisation: The policy adopted in the Soviet Union and the Eastern bloc states to move away from the rigid style of government pursued by Joseph Stalin.

Solidarity: The political reform movement that emerged in Poland in the early 1980s.

Partisans: In this chapter, irregular Yugoslav soldiers who fought against Nazi occupation.

3.1 THE YUGOSLAV-SOVIET UNION SPLIT

THE FIRST MOVES TOWARDS REFORM

As early as the summer of 1948 a challenge to Stalin's domination of the Eastern bloc had emerged from Yugoslavia. The Yugoslavs had successfully liberated themselves from Nazi domination in the second World War without assistance from the Soviet Union. This encouraged the Yugoslav leader, Josip Broz (**Marshall Tito**), to pursue an independent Communist programme. Stalin was so incensed by this development that on 28 June 1948 he expelled the Yugoslav Communist Party from Cominform (see page 14).

THE TITO-STALIN CLASH

By the summer of 1946 Tito had successfully overcome all opposition to Communism within Yugoslavia and had launched a programme of nationalisation of industry and agriculture. However, by the beginning of 1948 he clashed with Stalin over Greece. At this time the Communist Party in Greece was attempting to overthrow the democratically backed Greek government. In January 1948 Yugoslavia moved troops into Albania to defend Greek Communist bases there. Stalin intervened immediately because:

- Stalin had already agreed with Churchill that he would not seek control of Greece.
- America was committed to the democratisation of Greece. The Soviet Union did not want a military confrontation with a country that possessed atomic weapons.
- It now appeared that Tito was embarking on his own foreign policy.

Stalin could not allow his foreign policy to be undermined. In an era of the Cold War, the Soviet Union needed to pursue a very cautious line when dealing with the West.

Josip Broz (Marshall Tito) (1892–1980): Born into a Roman Catholic peasant family on 7 May 1892. In 1910 he joined the Croatian Social Democratic Party. Conscripted into the Austro-Hungarian Army in 1913, he was taken prisoner by the Russians in 1915. On release, he joined the Bolsheviks and fought on the side of the Red Guard in the Russian civil war.

When this ended he returned to Croatia and joined the Communist Party of Yugoslavia. By 1934 he had become a member of that party's Politiburo. Since the Communist Party was banned in Yugoslavia he was arrested several times during the 1920s and 1930s. To avoid being identified he adopted the pseudonym 'Tito'. In 1940 he became secretary general of the CPY. When Yugoslavia was invaded by the Nazis he formed an army of partisans who fought to free Yugoslavia. After the war Tito formed an exclusively Communist government, imprisoning and executing some of his opponents.

The split with Stalin led to the expulsion of Yugoslavia from Cominform in 1948. Stalin enforced economic sanctions on Yugoslavia and at that point Tito accepted Marshall Aid. In 1955 a reconciliation with the Soviet Union took place when he signed the Belgrade Declaration. It stated that all Communist-led countries were equal with each other. In the late 1950s he set up a bloc of neutral states which pledged non-alignment with either of the great powers in the Cold War. He promoted this policy of non-alignment until his death in 1980. He succeeded in keeping Yugoslavia an independent Communist state.

Courtesy: Corbis

YUGOSLAV EXPULSION FROM COMINFORM

On 10 February 1948 the Soviet Union warned the Yugoslavs against taking any foreign policy decisions without agreement from Moscow. The Yugoslav interpretation was that the Communist cause in Greece was being abandoned by Stalin. The Soviet Union's view was that its central role in the Eastern bloc was being challenged and Tito's Yugoslavia must go.

YUGOSLAVIA MOVES TOWARDS REFORM

Expulsion from Cominform did not shake Tito's commitment to the Communist cause. However, he did proceed to distance Yugoslav Socialism from that of the Soviet Union in a number of ways:

- In January 1949 the Communist Party of Yugoslavia (CPY) said that the split with the Soviet Union came as a result of Moscow's abandonment of the principles of Marxism. Tito claimed that the Yugoslavs were the true Marxists.
- In June 1950 Tito enacted a bill which set up workers' councils throughout Yugoslavia. These councils gave workers a say in the

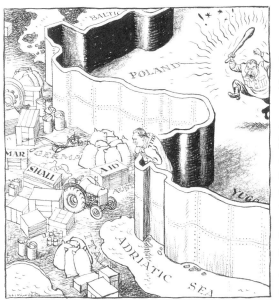

- Cartoon shows Marshall Tito pursuing an independent road to Socialism by looking beyond the Iron Curtain towards Marshall Aid while Stalin rages in the background.

Courtesy: The Centre for the Study of Cartoons and Caricature

management of industries. It was hoped that this would lead to workers eventually being responsible for the management of enterprises. This contrasted sharply with the highly centralised, tightly controlled and rigidly disciplined Soviet system of management.

■ At a congress of the Yugoslav Communist Party in November 1952 it was decided to change the party's name to the League of Communists of Yugoslavia to differentiate it from the other parties of the Eastern bloc.

■ Yugoslavia concluded a treaty of co-operation with non-Communist Turkey in February 1953.

By the time of Stalin's death in March 1953 it was clear that Yugoslav Socialism had its own identity. It had successfully distanced itself from Moscow, leaving Stalin's celebrated exclamation "I will shake my little finger and there will be no more Tito" looking extremely hollow.

Source Document

The Cominform Statement, July 1948

Inside Yugoslavia the Party does not have any internal Party democracy, elections are not held, there is no criticism or self-criticism. The Central Committee of the Party ... consists in its majority not of elected but co-opted members ... It is quite intolerable that in the Yugoslav Communist Party the most elementary rights of Party members are being trampled upon, that the slightest criticism of the incorrect way in which things are run in the Party is followed by grave repressions.

QUESTIONS ON THE DOCUMENT

1. Briefly describe the criticisms levelled by Cominform at the Communist Party of Yugoslavia.
2. Based on your knowledge of Stalin's rule in the USSR, do you find the accusations raised above ironic?

THE EAST GERMAN REVOLT, JUNE 1953

The next challenge to the centralised authority of the Soviet Union emerged in the German Democratic Republic (East Germany). In July 1952 the ruling Socialist Unity Party (SED), led by Walter Ulbricht, launched an intensified programme of nationalisation of industry and collectivisation of agriculture. The immediate effect of this was to increase the growing numbers of people who were disillusioned by the heavy emphasis on state control over the way they lived. They began to seek refuge in West Germany. Eastern German refugees rose dramatically in number from around 60,000 in 1950 to 297,000 in 1953.

REFORM PROGRAMME

Faced with this situation the SED was forced to revise its strict programme of state control and on 9 June 1953, with backing from Moscow, it announced the following reforms:

■ There would be a reduction in the quotas of produce which farmers had to pay to the state.

■ There would be less investment in heavy industries and more in consumer goods, of which there was a shortage.

■ There would be less state intervention in the affairs of the various Churches.

■ The state would interfere less in trade and traffic between East and West Germany.

WORKERS' REVOLT

The previous month, May 1953, the Party had passed a law insisting on a 10 per cent increase in work practices for all workers, but they did not reverse this ruling in its reform package in June. Buoyed by the new reform programme, workers took to the streets. By 17 June there were almost 400,000 workers on strike. They called for the abolition of the increased work rule, the resignation of the government and the institution of free elections. This challenge to centralised Socialism could not be tolerated and on the night of 17 June the Red Army ruthlessly suppressed the revolt. Official figures claimed that 21 people died, followed by 40 executions and nearly 20,000 arrests.

Courtesy: Getty Images

● Soviet tanks push back demonstrators in East Berlin on 17 June 1953.

The 10 per cent work increase was dropped and the Soviet Union cancelled the war debts owed to it by the GDR. In addition, a loan of 485 million roubles was issued by Moscow to rejuvenate the GDR economy.

QUESTIONS

1. By the summer of 1946 Tito had launched a programme of nationalisation of industry and agriculture. Explain what this means.

2. Outline four ways in which Yugoslav Socialism distanced itself from Soviet control between 1949 and 1953.

3. Explain why large numbers of East Germans sought refuge in West Germany after 1950.

4. List three reforms in the programme introduced by the SED in June 1953.

5. What effect did the reform programme have on East German workers?

3.2 THE CRISIS OF 1956: POLAND

THE POLISH REVOLT

The challenge to Soviet control of the Eastern bloc states received further impetus in the social and political crisis that shook Poland in 1956.

CAUSES

■ Since the Communist takeover in Poland, there was growing discontent over the continuing presence and influence of the Soviet Union in the country. Soviet troops still had bases in Poland in 1956 and the minister for defence was **Marshal Rokossowski**, a Soviet citizen.

■ Economic hardship was a major factor. Food rationing was introduced in 1951. There was a general shortage of consumer goods. Between 1949 and 1955 workers' incomes fell by 35 per cent in real terms, i.e. wage rises did not match inflation.

■ The purges of 1949–1953 ran contrary to the new dawn of a Communist Poland. The promise of a society built on the principles of equality and workers' rights had not materialised. The Roman Catholic Church was policed tightly by the ruling Communist Party, the Polish United Workers' Party (PUWP). **Cardinal Wyszynski**, the Catholic primate of Poland, was arrested and jailed in 1953.

■ In the more tolerant atmosphere that followed Stalin's death in 1953, student groups and the intelligentsia in general began to question where Communism in Poland was going.

■ Nikita Khrushchev's secret report to the 20th Congress of the Soviet Communist Party in Moscow, February 1956 was a crucial factor to the local and political crisis that shook Poland in 1956. Here, Khrushchev condemned Stalin's rule, denouncing his cult of personality leadership and the abuse of power that had brought terror and tragedy to so many people. Stalinism and the harsh regime imposed on Poland since 1945 was now open to question.

INITIAL REFORMS

Khrushchev's speech was followed by anti-Soviet demonstrations in Warsaw, Poland's capital city, in February 1956. The PUWP responded by releasing **Wladyslaw Gomulka** on 6 April. A former PUWP member, Gomulka was jailed in 1951 on the grounds that he was too much of a Polish nationalist. By the end of April over 30,000 political prisoners were freed, but workers' conditions did not improve.

THE POZNAN RIOTS, JUNE 1956

These riots were sparked by a directive issued to workers at the ZISPO plant in Poznan at the end of June. They were told to increase productivity by 25 per cent with no corresponding increase in pay. Having failed to get a hearing in Warsaw, the workers went on strike, chanting "Down with the USSR! Bread and Freedom! Russians Go Home!" The Polish army moved in and 53 people died and over 300 were wounded.

● The Polish national flag is carried by demonstrators in Poznan on 29 June 1956.

In mid-July 1956 the PUWP granted the following reforms:

■ There would be less investment in heavy industry and more emphasis on consumer goods.

■ Collectivisation of agriculture would be slowed down.

■ Wages would be increased, but no figure was set.

■ Gomulka would be readmitted to the Party.

THE OCTOBER CRISIS

Encouraged by these concessions the workers' demands grew louder during the late summer and autumn of 1956. One of their demands was that Gomulka should be made leader of PUWP. A full session of the Central Committee of the PUWP met on 19 October to deal with the social turmoil.

Concern was so great in Moscow that Khrushchev and Molotov attended, intent on influencing the outcome. The Polish army and Soviet troops in Poland were poised to intervene if no settlement was reached. On 21 October Gomulka became Party leader, having convinced Khrushchev that he would continue to pursue a Communist programme of government. Furthermore, Poland would remain within the Warsaw Pact. Khrushchev was placated and the crisis was defused.

● The cartoon shows the Soviet foreign minister complain that Imre Nagy (Hungary) and Gomulka (Poland) should not have been allowed back into the forefront of political life.

1. Why does he say this was 'a mistake'?

2. Why is the portrait of Stalin upside down in the cartoon?

Courtesy: Bettmann/Corbis

Courtesy: The Centre for the Study of Cartoons and Caricature

CONCESSIONS

- Gomulka promised further wage rises for workers.
- Cardinal Wyszynski, who had been jailed in the purges of 1953, was released and the government removed its control over ecclesiastical appointments.
- Soviet control of the Polish army ended and Marshal Rokossowski was removed as Minister for Defence.
- Collectivisation of agriculture came to an end.

SIGNIFICANCE

The programme of reform pursued by Gomulka never amounted to an attack on the ruling Party. He never wanted anything other than mild reform. There was the possibility, of course, that a demand for radical reform might lead to the occupation of Poland by the Soviet Union. However, the concessions won showed that Poland had exercised its separateness. Moscow had been confronted and, while Poland remained within the Warsaw Pact and the Comecon trading bloc, Poland had flexed its nationalist muscles with some success.

QUESTIONS

1. Give five reasons why a revolt against Communism took place in Poland in 1956.
2. Briefly explain why riots broke out in Poznan.
3. Do you think the Poznan riots were successful? Explain your answer.
4. What concessions did Polish reformers win as a result of the Polish revolt?
5. In what sense could the Polish revolt be seen as an expression of nationalism?

3.3 CZECHOSLOVAKIA 1968: THE PRAGUE SPRING

WHY DID THE PRAGUE SPRING HAPPEN?

- Khrushchev's public denunciation of Stalin in October 1961 (see page 59) stimulated calls for reforms.
- The Writer's Union called for a full programme of de-Stalinisation. An easing of censorship led to much more open debate on issues of public interest. News bulletins were less centrally controlled and some American soap operas, such as *Doctor Kildare*, were shown on television.
- The new spirit of reform extended to travel. In 1963, almost 47,000 Czechoslovaks visited the West. This figure increased to 154,000 in 1965 and 258,000 in 1967.
- A downturn in the fortunes of the Czech economy in the 1960s led to a fall in living.
- In the summer and autumn of 1967 the tide of discontent increased. In October students in Prague publicly demonstrated over living conditions and the lack of democracy in Communist youth organisations. This escalated into street violence and running battles between students and police.

Faced with the possibility of open revolt, Novotny (leader of the Czechoslovak Communist Party) invited the Soviet leader, Leonid Brezhnev, to address the Communist Party's Central Committee on 8 December. Novotny did not get the support he needed. Brezhnev said that the Czechoslovak Party would have to sort out its own problems. At a meeting of the Party's Central Committee on 5 January 1968 Novotny was removed as First Secretary and replaced by Alexander Dubcek. Novotny continued, for the time being, as president of the republic, but was eventually replaced by Ludvic Svoboda, an ex-general in the Czech army, on 21 March 1968.

Courtesy: Bettmann/Corbis

• Brezhnev (front left) beside Dubcek at a meeting of the Central Committee of the Communist Party, the National Front and the Czechoslovak government in February 1968.

DUBCEK'S ACTION PROGRAMME

Dubcek's Action Programme was published on 10 April 1968, setting out Czechoslovakia's own route to Socialism.

The Communist Party would continue to play the leading role in determining policy, but it would be much more open to new ideas coming from the National Front (an umbrella group of other political voices).

Dubcek's Programme promised freedom of speech, association and travel. All citizens would enjoy equality before the law. To avoid Soviet intervention, Dubcek insisted that only groups affiliated to the National Front could call public meetings or publish political and economic ideas.

A SUMMER OF REFORM

Socialism in Czechoslovakia was not under threat from Dubcek. What he attempted was to move Socialism forward, away from the rigid centralism favoured by Moscow, on to a more liberal, populist plane.

- The period from the end of April to mid-July 1968 saw significant reforms. As regards religion, the Catholic Church could control religious education and over 100 priests were released from prison.
- Students set up their own associations.
- Workers set up independent workers' councils on 1 July.
- There were calls for the revival of the Social Democratic Party outside of the National Front. This was a direct challenge to the Communist Party.

COMMUNIST CONCERN

On 23 March 1968 the Soviet Union offered military assistance to Dubcek if he felt that Communist Party control might be threatened. On 16 July the Warsaw Pact demanded that Dubcek stop the reform programme immediately. He refused.

Dubcek was now in an extremely difficult position – concessions to Moscow would arouse the anger of the reformists, while concessions to the reformists would subject him to the wrath of his Warsaw Pact allies. Brezhnev decided to act. The Brezhnev Doctrine stated all the Socialist states in the Eastern bloc had a responsibility to 'protect' Socialism.

Alexander Dubcek (1921–1992): Dubcek was born on 27 November 1921 in Uhrovec, Czechoslovakia. During the second World War he joined the underground resistance movement against the occupying German forces.

Dubcek became First Secretary of the Czechoslovak Communist Party on 5 January 1968. During the Prague Spring (March–August 1968) he attempted to liberalise the system and establish "Socialism with a human face". After the Soviet invasion on 27 August he publicly admitted that the great dawn of reform was over.

Dubcek supported the Velvet Revolution of 1989 and the new president, Vaclav Havel. He became speaker of the new Federal Assembly on 26 December 1989. He died on 7 November 1992 in a car crash.

Courtesy: Bettmann/Corbis

THE INVASION OF CZECHOSLOVAKIA

On the night of 20–21 August 1968 Soviet, Polish, Hungarian, East German and Bulgarian troops entered Czechoslovakia. The invading force was twice that used in Hungary in 1956. The Czechs and Slovaks did not fight the Soviets and the overall death toll numbered between 100 and 200.

A few weeks later censorship was reintroduced. When disturbances broke out in March 1969, Moscow intervened again and on 17 April Dubcek was removed as First Secretary of the Communist Party. In 1970 Alexander Dubcek was expelled from the Party.

Courtesy: Hulton-Deutsch/Corbis

● Soviet tanks and troops occupy a Prague street in August 1968, after invading the city to stop democratic reforms instituted during the Prague Spring.

Nearly half a million members were expelled from the Communist Party. The Soviet Union left nearly 70,000 Red Army troops on Czechoslovak soil. From the Soviet perspective the worrying fact was that the move towards reform could only be contained in Hungary and in Czechoslovakia by military intervention.

QUESTIONS

1. What changes in economic policy took place in Czechoslovakia in the mid-1960s?
2. List three reforms that followed the Writers' Union's demand for de-Stalinisation in 1963.
3. In your own words, summarise the main proposals of Dubcek's Action Programme.
4. List four reforms granted in the summer of 1968.
5. Explain the Brezhnev Doctrine.
6. Give two reasons why the Soviet Union invaded Czechoslovakia.

3.4 POLAND: THE 1970s AND THE SOLIDARITY CRISIS

INTRODUCTION

The response of the Soviet Union to events in Czechoslovakia was to tighten its control on the Eastern bloc.

Around this time the Eastern bloc countries announced that their programmes to establish Socialism were now complete. In effect they had entered a new phase, known as 'mature Socialism'. It was now envisaged that living standards would rise appreciably, that consumer goods would become much more plentiful and cheaper. Economic growth was generally lively up to the mid-1970s, but from there on it suffered a sharp decline. The result was yet more disillusionment, a drop in Socialist morale and ideological commitment and the re-emergence of dissident voices. While this pattern can be applied to all the Eastern bloc states, its effects in Poland were most profoundly felt.

Courtesy: Hulton-Deutsch/Corbis

• Two peasant women working on a farm in Poland in the 1950s. Would you say the method of farming seen here is backward or advanced? Explain your answer.

ECONOMIC PROBLEMS

The demand for reform that swept Poland in the late 1970s and culminated in the tumultuous events of the **Solidarity crisis** had its roots in a failing economy. Specifically, the problem lay in agriculture, which could not produce enough foodstuffs to meet demand. We have already seen that the programme of collectivisation of agriculture in Poland was dropped in the 1950s. This meant that Polish agriculture was based on small-scale peasant holdings. Peasants would only produce increased quantities of foodstuffs if prices were attractive. To achieve this, consumer prices had to be increased. This in turn led to waves of protests and strikes by industrial workers. As the 1970s developed these protests and strikes went beyond immediate economic concerns and included radical political reform.

THE BALTIC CRISIS

This was the first manifestation of the troubles of the 1970s. On 12 December 1970 the government, led by Gomulka, announced an increase in food prices of around 30 per cent. The public response was one of outrage. Two days later the workers in the Lenin shipyard in Gdansk went on strike. The following day the strikers clashed with police and between 70 and 80 demonstrators were killed. The industrial action spread to other Baltic ports and strikes in Szczecin (Stettin) demanded that free, independent trade unions be allowed. When strike action spread to Warsaw (within a week of the price rise) Gomulka was removed and replaced as First Secretary by **Edward Gierek**.

GIEREK'S RESPONSE

The new leader was more accommodating than Gomulka and abolished the price rises in February. He also granted the following reforms to peasants in an effort to improve agricultural production:

■ The practice of farmers being forced to sell produce to the state was dropped.

■ Farmers who agreed to sell produce to the state received grants and subsidies.

■ The ban on selling agricultural machinery to private farmers was lifted.

■ Pension and national insurance rights were granted to all private farmers.

On the broader economic front, Gierek decided to borrow substantial sums of money from the West and to import Western technology to boost the Polish economy. It was hoped that Poland could export enough manufactured goods to the West to repay the loans.

ECONOMIC SUCCESS

Between 1971 and 1975 the Polish economy prospered. In 1973 the Polish economy was the third fastest-growing in the world. By 1975 real wages were up by nearly 40 per cent. This brought a marked rise in living standards.

DOWNTURN

By 1975 it was clear that Poland's debt to the West was mounting because its exports could only pay for 60 per cent of its imports. The main reason for this was the oil crisis of 1973 (see Chapter 10), which made imported goods from the West more expensive. At the same time there was an economic depression in the West, which curtailed demand for Polish goods. Agricultural production did not meet consumer demand and agricultural imports increased.

1976 CRISIS

Faced with serious economic depression, Gierek's government repeated the mistake of 1970. In June 1976 price increases averaging 60 per cent were announced. There was immediate uproar and demonstrations took place in the Baltic ports of Radom and Warsaw. Gierek was forced to withdraw the increases.

CHURCH INFLUENCE

On 16 October 1978 the Polish cardinal, **Karol Wojtyla**, was elected Pope. As Pope John Paul II he visited his home country in June 1979. He urged the

Courtesy: Getty Images

• Solidarity members on strike in Gdansk in the late 1970s.

government to bring in reforms and tried to calm the rising tide of anger. He was greeted as a national hero and a symbol of freedom. The PUWP now faced a situation in which the economy continued to decline, the workers refused to accept the price increases and a majority of Poles looked to the new Pope as a kind of national leader. In 1980 all of these factors came together to produce the most powerful movement for reform yet seen in the Communist Eastern bloc.

THE BIRTH OF SOLIDARITY

The Solidarity movement that emerged in Poland in August 1980 was sparked by a price increase in the cost of meat on 1 July. The response of workers was to down tools (go on strike). By the end of the first week in August over 150 firms had been hit by strike action. On 14 August the Lenin shipyard at Gdansk went on strike. The leader of the workers there was **Lech Walesa**, a man who had persistently protested against the killing of workers in the 1970 crisis. From Gdansk the industrial action spread to other Baltic ports and the workers established **Inter-Factory Strike Committees** to co-ordinate their activities. The committee in Gdansk drafted a 21-point charter, which included the following demands:

Courtesy: Corbis

• Lech Walesa seen here addressing Solidarity supporters in Gdansk, 30 August 1980.

- ■ The right to establish free and independent trade unions.
- ■ An official recognition of workers' rights to engage in industrial action.
- ■ Pay increases and no work on Saturdays.
- ■ Censorship to be restricted.
- ■ Catholic mass to be broadcast.
- ■ A memorial to be built to the martyrs of 1970.

The Inter-Factory Strike Committees now adopted the name **Solidarity**, or **Solidarnosc**, the title of their newsletter.

INITIAL AGREEMENT

The tension was eased to some extent on 31 August, when Gierek agreed to workers' demands for independent trade unions. In return, Walesa and Solidarity had to recognise the dominant role of the PUWP. In other words, Solidarity was not challenging the Communist system. However, the agreement did not produce wage increases or work-free Saturdays and worker discontent continued.

Lech Walesa (1943–   ): Lech Walesa was born in 1943 in Popowo, Poland, the son of a carpenter. He began work in the Lenin Shipyards in Gdansk in 1967. In 1976 he was sacked because of his public opposition to rising food prices and his condemnation of the Polish government. When food prices went up again in 1980 Walesa was at the heart of the protests. In August 1980 more than 100,000 workers were on strike in Poland. Walesa became chairman of the Inter-Factory Strike Committee that same month and demanded economic and political reform. In September 1980 Solidarity was outlawed and Walesa was imprisoned. This gave him the status of a political and social martyr. By early 1989 unrest was so great that the government entered into talks with Solidarity in the famous Roundtable Talks. As a result Solidarity was made legal and democratic elections were held. Solidarity won every seat it contested. Walesa became president of Poland later that year.

Courtesy: Robert Maass/Corbis

SOLIDARITY REGISTRATION

Relations between the two sides worsened in the autumn because the government stalled the legal registration of Solidarity. The struggle for registration lasted from the end of August 1980 to 10 November 1980, when the movement was granted legal status. This was followed by the reluctant registration of Rural Solidarity, an organisation representing over one million landowners, in March 1981.

THE SHADOW OF THE SOVIET UNION

The Solidarity movement and the PUWP were aware that the discontent in Poland was being closely watched from Moscow. Leaders of other Eastern bloc states promised 'aid' to the PUWP if necessary. Neither Walesa nor the Polish government wanted Soviet-led military intervention. As a result, Walesa was careful to steer his Solidarity movement away from demands that might be seen as a direct challenge to the Communist system. Likewise, the PUWP sought peaceful settlement by offering reform.

Source Document

Extract from a letter from Erich Honecker, General Secretary of the ruling SED Party in East Germany, to Leonid Brezhnev, 26 November 1980:

According to information we have received through various channels, counter-revolutionary forces in the People's Republic of Poland are on the constant offensive, and any delay in acting against them would mean death – the death of Socialist Poland. Yesterday our collective efforts may perhaps have been premature; today they are essential; and tomorrow they would already be too late.

QUESTIONS ON THE DOCUMENT

1. Why was Honecker concerned by the Polish Crisis?

2. What kind of action do you think is implied in Honecker's phrase "our collective efforts"?

THE 9ᵀᴴ CONGRESS OF THE PUWP

Reform emerged at the Party Congress in July 1981. Elections at the Congress were held by secret ballot and 87 per cent of the Party's Central Committee were replaced by new faces. Only four of the 15-men Politburo retained office. It was also decided that no one could hold government or Party office for more than ten years. By Eastern bloc standards these changes were fiercely radical and encouraged some members of Solidarity to go beyond mere reforms for the workers.

THE FIRST SOLIDARITY CONGRESS

At the outset of the Congress in late September, Lech Walesa called for a moderate approach to reform. Specifically he wanted to steer Solidarity away from any ideas its members might harbour of pursuing political power for the movement. Neither did he want it to challenge Poland's involvement in the Warsaw Pact. However, the Congress opened with a call for a society free from "poverty, exploitation, fear, and allies". In itself, this amounted to an attack on the establishment. It became clear that elements within Solidarity were prepared to challenge the leading role of the Party. Demands were made for a national referendum to be called on the issue of free elections. The Party's response was to appoint Prime Minister General Wojciech Jaruzelski as First Secretary.

MILITARY INTERVENTION

The challenge now emanating from the ranks of Solidarity continued to cause tremors in Moscow and Jaruzelski decided to act in the interest of avoiding Soviet intervention. On the night of 13–14 December 1981 **martial law** was imposed on Poland. The army and riot police rounded up strikers and all leading figures in Solidarity and interned them. Thousands of people ended up in detention camps. The government was relieved of its authority and a **military council of National Salvation** was established to govern the country. A general strike planned by Solidarity for 17 December was now merely a dream. By Christmas Poland was under military rule. In October 1982 Solidarity was formally abolished and went underground. Martial law ended in July 1983 and the PUWP held on to power for the time being.

Courtesy: Peter Turnley/Corbis

● Lech Walesa makes his point at a Solidarity meeting, October 1989.

SIGNIFICANCE OF SOLIDARITY

- The primary role of the PUWP had been seriously undermined by the emergence of a movement that enjoyed such mass popular support.
- The idea that the PUWP championed the cause of the workers was virtually redundant. The need of their members to flock into the ranks of Solidarity proved that point.
- It was now clear that the PUWP had to rely on military intervention for survival. It could, of course, look to Moscow for backing, but by the late 1980s the Soviet Union was itself in troubled waters.

QUESTIONS

1. Identify the weakness in Polish agriculture in the 1960s.

2. What caused the Baltic crisis of 1970?

3. List four reforms granted to Polish peasant farmers in the early 1970s.

4. List five of the demands set out in Solidarity's Gdansk charter in August 1980.

5. Why do you think so many changes in personnel took place in the ranks of the PUWP at its 9th Congress?

6. Show how Solidarity had become a major threat to the Communist system in Poland by the time of its First Congress in September 1981.

GENERAL ESSAY QUESTIONS ON CHAPTER 3

1. Show how Marshall Tito steered Yugoslavia on an independent road to Socialism. Include references to Greece, Cominform, workers' councils and Marshall Aid in your answer.

2. Write a brief account of the life of Lech Walesa, outlining his aims, his leadership of Solidarity and his achievements.

3. Discuss the view that the period from the late 1940s to the 1980s was marked by continuous demands for reform in Eastern bloc countries.

4. Outline the reasons why reform movements emerged in Soviet-dominated Eastern Europe between 1948 and the 1980s.

5. Discuss the view that the demands made by the Polish Solidarity movement marked a new intensity in Eastern bloc calls for reform.

6. "Nationalism and a desire on the part of individual states to pursue their own routes to Socialism were the main driving forces of the reform movements in Eastern bloc states in the decades after the second World War." Discuss.

7. Outline the response of the Soviet Union to the demands for reform made by its satellite states from the expulsion of Yugoslavia from Cominform, 1948, to the Polish Solidarity crisis.

4

THE COLLAPSE OF THE SOVIET UNION

Words you need to understand

Samizdat: Literally 'self-publishing' – the underground publication of literature banned by the governments of the Soviet Union and other Communist states.

Apparatchik: A member of the Soviet government bureaucracy.

Glasnost and *Perestroika*: The policies of 'openness' and 'restructuring' introduced by Gorbachev in the late 1980s in an effort to reform the system of government in the Soviet Union.

4.1 STALIN'S FINAL YEARS, 1945–1953

EFFECTS OF THE SECOND WORLD WAR

The Red Army emerged victorious from the second World War, but at a huge cost to the Soviet Union. A few points will reveal the extent of that cost:

- Up to 40 million Soviet citizens, military and civilian, died in the war.
- Around 70,000 villages and 3,000 towns were destroyed, leaving over 25 million homeless.
- Road and rail transport suffered heavily in that 26 railway lines were knocked out of action and nearly 13,000 bridges were ruined.
- Food production fell dramatically because nearly 30,000 collective farms were devastated.
- An estimated 85,000 schools were flattened.
- The 1945 figures for coal production and electricity output show a fall of 25 per cent on the 1941 figures.
- Oil and steel production dropped by about 50 per cent in the same period.

THE FOURTH FIVE-YEAR PLAN, 1946

This was Stalin's response to the enormous task of rebuilding the Soviet economy. Heavy industry was given priority and agriculture got special attention too. Iron and steel production were transformed, exceeding the figures for 1940 by 29 per cent and nearly 50 per cent, respectively. Electricity output in 1950 was twice that of 1940. Railroad facilities increased by a remarkable 44 per cent over the same period.

● The Soviet Union 1917–1991.

Agricultural production fell well short of this success. One of the problems here was a shortage of labour caused by the awful upheaval of the war. During the war years the numbers working on collectivised farms fell by one-third. Another problem was that up to 1948 farmers on collective farms received no wages, but worked for their keep. As a result workers did not comply with the set number of working hours per day and gave more time to their own small private plots than to the collective farm on which they worked. The lack of a reward system for farm workers led to apathy and disillusionment.

A RETURN TO CONSERVATISM

During the second World War the Soviet Union witnessed a remarkable closing of ranks. Opposition to the Nazi invasion brought a temporary end to internal divisions. Relations between the state and the Russian Orthodox Church improved to such an extent that in January 1943 Stalin thanked the Church for its financial support of the war effort. Purges were abandoned and a greater level of tolerance came from the top.

The end of the war brought this liberal period to a close. **"Back to class vigilance"** was the slogan employed by the Communist Party of the Soviet Union (CPSU) to herald a return to the rigid Stalinist policies of the pre-war period. Harsh government and the 'cult of personality' that Stalin established before the war were well and truly restored.

CULTURAL UNIFORMITY

This was a feature of the return to rigid Stalinism. Writers, painters and composers were instructed to heap praise on the Soviet system. Stalin was frequently portrayed as the saviour of the state and glowing accounts were produced of the Soviet recovery from the ravages of the war. Literature became dull, functional and lacked imagination and creativity. **Socialist realism** is the name given to such a system, where art is made to serve the state. The man who supervised this conformity was **Andrei Zhdanov,** who was leader of the Communist Party in Leningrad. Up to his death in 1948 Zhdanov insisted that artists reflect the glorious progress of Soviet industry and the success of farm collectivisation in their work. Artists who opposed the official line were subjected to public ridicule. The most notable of these were the poet **Anna Akhmatova,** the

● 'Giving the Country a Triumphant Harvest!' A propaganda poster from 1945

writer **Boris Pasternak** and the composers **Dmitri Shostakovich** and **Sergei Prokofiev**. This policy did not end with Zhdanov's departure, but persisted until Stalin's death in 1953.

MORE PURGES

Another regrettable aspect of **"Back to class vigilance"** was a return to the policy of purging in 1949. A number of senior government personnel were executed for allegedly plotting against the state. The most notable victim was Voznesensky, Chairman of the State Planning Commission (Gosplan).

КООПЕРАЦИЯ

Courtesy: Bridgeman Art Library

● An artist's impression of uniformity of life in the Soviet Union. This painting is called 'The Co-operative Societies': on the left the range of urban dwellers conform and on the right the rural people bring their wares to distribute.

The Doctor's Plot of January 1953 was more serious. This was another alleged plot against the country's leadership. A group of doctors based in the Kremlin was accused of murdering Andrei Zhdanov in 1948 and of planning to kill other senior government figures. They were arrested and charged with plotting against the state. Stalin's intention was to implicate senior government figures in the plot and have them purged. His chilling threat to the Minister of State Security was: "If you do not obtain confessions from the victims we will shorten you by a head." The intended purge never took place because, ironically, Stalin fell ill on 2 March 1953 and died three days later.

Source Document

Official Announcement of the Doctor's Plot, *Pravda* (13 January 1953)

Some time ago, the agencies of state security uncovered a terrorist group of doctors who had made it their aim to cut short the lives of active public figures of the Soviet Union by means of sabotaged medical treatment …

The criminals confessed that they took advantage of Comrade A.A. Zhdanov's ailment by incorrectly diagnosing the illness and killed Comrade A.A. Zhdanov.

The criminal doctors sought, above all, to undermine the health of leading Soviet military personnel, to put them out of action and to thereby weaken the defence of the country …

… It has been established that all these homicidal doctors, who had become monsters in human form, tramping the sacred banner of science and desecrating the honour of scientists, were enrolled by foreign intelligence services as hired agents.

QUESTIONS ON THE DOCUMENT

1. What two charges are laid against the "terrorist group of doctors"?
2. On whose behalf are they accused of working?
3. Would you describe this article as straightforward reporting or do you think there is a strong element of propaganda in it? Explain your answer.

CONCLUSION

The achievements of the fourth Five-Year Plan were substantial in the areas of heavy industry, building programmes, transport and electrical output. Agriculture continued to struggle, unable to match industrial productivity. The fifth Five-Year Plan, initiated in 1950, did not really address the problem of agriculture. Stalin simply ordered more of the same, that is, heavy industry was given priority and collectivisation was rigidly enforced. The return to the purges emphasised Stalin's reliance on ruling by fear. His insistence on cultural uniformity hindered the work of artists and writers by stifling the imagination. And yet Stalin's death sparked a genuine outpouring of public grief. He was regarded at the time as a national hero, the man who successfully saw the USSR through the second World War. He was also the architect of the economic programme that brought the Soviet Union from a backward agrarian condition to the status of world power.

QUESTIONS

1. Which of the effects of the second World War do you think had the greatest impact on the Soviet Union? Explain you answer.
2. Identify the reasons why agricultural production lagged behind that of industry.
3. What do you understand the slogan "Back to class vigilance" to mean?
4. Write a brief paragraph summing up the policy of cultural uniformity.
5. Would you describe Stalin's final years as being successful or unsuccessful? Explain your answer.

4.2   THE KHRUSHCHEV ERA, 1953–1964

THE QUESTION OF LEADERSHIP

Prior to his death Stalin had not appointed a successor to take his place. The front-runners for the position were Lavrenti Beria, Minister of Internal Affairs; Georgi Malenkov, who was effectively in charge of the Communist Party; and Nikita Khrushchev, a high-ranking member of the Party and the Council of Ministers. Of these Malenkov was ranked highest, and on 6 March 1953 he was given Stalin's two posts of Chairman of the Council of Ministers (Prime Minister) and First Secretary to the Central Committee of the Communist Party of the Soviet Union (CPSU). Within a week the Central Committee of the CPSU ruled that Malenkov must step down from the office of First Secretary. Nikita Khrushchev took his place. It was clear that neither the Council of Ministers nor the CPSU wanted one person to dominate as Stalin had done. The path chosen was that of collective leadership, a situation that lasted for the next two years.

THE REMOVAL OF BERIA

As Minister of Internal Affairs, Lavrenti Beria was in charge of the state police and internal security. He had been very close to Stalin and had built up files on every senior member of the government, the CPSU and the army. Anyone of importance was under scrutiny. He was, therefore, a hated figure. Within a few weeks of Stalin's death he began building a popular image of himself by taking a softer line on policy than that of Stalin. For example, in early April 1953 he announced that the Doctor's Plot (see p. 55) was a fabrication and the jailed doctors were released. Furthermore, he sought to improve relations with

● Front cover of *Time* magazine, showing Malenkov as the boy on the father's (Stalin's) lap, 6 October 1952.

Yugoslavia, which was expelled from the Cominform in 1948 (see page 41). Beria may have been planning a bid for power and Malenkov and Khrushchev would not allow such a development. On 26 June 1953 Beria was arrested. He was charged with having been a spy for Britain for over 30 years and was executed in December of that year. This kind of justice belonged very much to the Stalin era, but more lenient times were at hand.

A POLICY OF RELAXATION

The collective leadership of Malenkov and Khrushchev now set about a programme of relaxing the stern system imposed by Stalin. Some of its features were:

- The Ministry of Internal Affairs, which had been such an organ of oppression, was dismantled and in 1955 replaced by a Committee of State Security (KGB), which was placed under the control of the CPSU.
- Thousands of political prisoners who were jailed under Stalin's rule were freed and cleared of guilt.
- Millions of people in the *gulags* (the forced labour camps) were set free.
- Soviet writers were encouraged to express themselves more freely as the policy of Socialist realism was played down.

● A front cover of Time magazine from 1952 shows Lavrenti Beria, one of Stalin's likely successors.

These reforms were welcomed by a Soviet Union that had been brutalised by Stalinism and the second World War.

KHRUSHCHEV BECOMES LEADER

Between 1953 and 1955 a keen rivalry developed between Malenkov and Khrushchev, which saw the latter emerge as the clear leader of the Soviet Union. By the summer of 1953 Malenkov was proposing a move away from the Stalinist emphasis on heavy industry to a concentration on lighter industry (consumer goods) and increased food production. He also proposed a 9 per cent cut in military spending for 1954. Senior army personnel were alarmed by any plan that might weaken the Red Army, especially in an era of Cold War. Older members of the CPSU (many of them Stalinists) were wary of reforms because they might spark a demand for wider freedom from the people. Khrushchev seized his opportunity and attacked Malenkov's policies. The Central Committee of the CPSU rallied around Khrushchev and on 8 February 1955 Malenkov was removed from his post of Chairman of the Council of Ministers and replaced by **Nikolai Bulganin**, a supporter of Khrushchev. Victory for Khrushchev seemed at first to be a victory for the old-guard Stalinists, but the new leader had no intention of returning to the harsh regime that had dominated the Soviet Union for so long.

THE 20ᵗᴴ PARTY CONGRESS OF THE CPSU

In a speech delivered to the Congress delegates in February 1956 Khrushchev clearly distanced himself from Stalinism. Entitled "About the Cult of Personality and its Consequences", the speech focused on the brutality of Stalin's methods in the following ways:

- Details of the 1930s purges were laid bare for the first time.
- Stalin was directly blamed for **Kirov's** murder in 1934 which set the purges in motion.
- His policy of 'annihilating the *kulaks*' was condemned, but Khrushchev did not condemn the policy of collectivisation.
- Stalin was accused of leaving the Red Army badly prepared on the eve of the second World War as a result of the savage purges carried out on senior army personnel.
- Blame for the break with Yugoslavia in 1948 was laid on Stalin.

● Khrushchev and Bulganin greeting delegates at the 20ᵗʰ Party Congress.

Khrushchev was careful not to condemn the Stalinist era completely and due recognition was given to the enormous leap forward made by the Soviet Union during that period. However, the thrust of the speech was that Stalin had become obsessed with self-image, that a 'cult of personality' had emerged. The result was that Stalin had wandered from the true principles of Socialism as set down by Marx and Lenin. The process of de-Stalinisation was now official policy.

EFFECTS OF THE SPEECH

- The most immediate effect was one of shock. Many of the delegates were astonished that a man of Stalin's reputation as a hero of the Soviet Union could be attacked like this.
- It sparked demands for a reduction of Soviet control in Eastern bloc countries, most notably Poland and Hungary (see pp. 43 and 73).
- In the long run it began a more tolerant period in the Soviet Union.
- In the short term it gave rise to a short-lived conspiracy against Khrushchev in 1957. This was led by Malenkov and Molotov, who were appalled by Khrushchev's treatment of their former leader. The outcome was that both men were removed from their posts. Unlike the Stalinist era, however, no trials or executions followed.

Khrushchev completed his sweep to power by taking Bulganin's position as Chairman of the Council of Ministers in March 1958.

Source Document

Extract from Khrushchev's secret speech to the 20th Congress of the CPSU, 1956

The 'Yugoslavian affair' contained no problems which could not have been solved through Party discussions among comrades . . . it was completely possible to have prevented the rupture of relations with that country . . . mistakes and shortcomings were magnified in a monstrous manner by Stalin, which resulted in a break of relations with a friendly country.

QUESTION ON THE DOCUMENT

1. Based on your reading of the Yugoslav-Soviet split, do you agree with Khrushchev's view?

CONSOLIDATION

Khrushchev now set about maintaining his hold on power. His first move was to decentralise industrial organisation. In February 1957 he set up economic councils throughout the Soviet Union. These councils were designed to give local CPSU leaders a greater say in planning and running the economies of their regions. Before this, all economic planning was centred in Moscow. It increased his popularity in the regions, but civil servants in Moscow were disgruntled. Next, he launched a huge housing programme which aimed at giving each family a home with modern conveniences such as refrigerators and televisions.

The Seven-Year Plan, launched in 1959, predicted that incomes would rise by 40 per cent by 1965. At that stage, he claimed, there would be a 40-hour week for workers. It was envisaged that the Soviet Union would become the greatest producer in the world of industrial and consumer goods.

RENEWED ANTI-STALINISM

At the 22ⁿᵈ Party Congress of October 1961 Khrushchev launched another fierce attack on Stalin. He told delegates that Stalin had wiped out millions during collectivisation and the purges. In an obvious fall from grace, Stalin's remains were removed from Lenin's mausoleum and buried in the Kremlin wall. Stalingrad was renamed Volgograd. Portraits of the former leader were removed from public places. The attack on Stalin was a diversionary tactic – an attempt to draw attention away from the fact that all was not as good as it seemed under Khrushchev. His addresses to the Congress were triumphant in tone, but Khrushchev's star was already in decline. One of the reasons for that was the continuing failure of agriculture.

• A change of image for the Soviet Union. Children stand beside a glittering Christmas tree, December 1965.

AGRICULTURAL POLICIES

From the outset, Khrushchev sought to improve agricultural production in a number of ways:

■ In 1954 he launched the **Virgin Lands Programme**. The target here was to produce about 60,000 acres of grain. The Virgin Lands were situated in Siberia, Kazakhstan, the Urals and the northern Caucasus and were so-called because they had never been cultivated before. At first the project enjoyed great success. For example, between 1953 and 1958 grain production for the Soviet Union increased by 70 per cent. In the long run the project proved to be a costly mistake because these areas were too dry and not suited to the growing of grain. Eventually it was abandoned.

■ He continued to increase the size of collective farms. By 1960 the Soviet Union had 44,000 collective farms averaging about 6,500 acres each. Farm workers could not be motivated to increase their output for the good of the state. They were only interested in tending to their own private plots. Therefore, increasing the size of collective farms simply increased inefficiency.

CRISIS

By 1962 agriculture in the Soviet Union was in severe difficulty. Shortages of meat and dairy produce meant that prices increased. Grain production could not satisfy demand, resulting in the Soviet Union having to import grain. By the summer of 1962 food shortages drove people onto the streets of towns and cities in protest. However, failure of the agricultural sector was not the only factor in Khrushchev's fall from grace.

• 1962 crisis in agriculture.

THE FALL OF KHRUSHCHEV

On 13 October 1964 Khrushchev was informed by the Soviet Praesidium that he was no longer in charge of the Soviet Union. He appealed to the Central Committee of the CPSU, but was out-voted there too. On 16 October 1964 his resignation was publicly announced. The reasons were "advanced age and the deterioration in the state of his health".

His position had been seriously weakened by the following:

- Between 1958 and 1964 the average annual rate of industrial growth had fallen to 7.8 per cent, compared with over 10 per cent for the previous ten years.
- His policy of setting up economic councils in rural regions was very unpopular with civil servants who were relocated from Moscow and had their lives seriously disrupted.
- Senior administrators in Moscow saw these councils as a reduction of their powers.
- The proposal in 1964 to make consumer goods a priority at the expense of heavy industrial goods was contradictory to what he had said previously and was seen to be a reversal of the tried-and-trusted policy that had made the Soviet Union great.
- His boasts that the Soviet Union would become the number-one producer in industry and agriculture did not become reality.

CONCLUSION

The Khrushchev era did see an improvement in living standards for the people of the Soviet Union. Wages went up by 18 per cent between 1959 and 1962. There was some improvement in housing and working conditions – for example, an eight-hour day had become the norm in the workplace. Significant improvement in agriculture was out of reach and the rate of industrial growth slowed down. However, the awful oppression of the Stalin era was gone. Khrushchev's removal was not followed by a trial, confession or execution. He was allowed to live out his retirement in peace. At least he had given Communism a human face, which was one of his great contributions.

QUESTIONS

1. Why was Malenkov not allowed to hold on to the two posts of Prime Minister and First Secretary in 1953?
2. What evidence is there that the period of collective leadership during 1953–1955 saw a relaxation of government?
3. List five criticisms made against Stalin in Khrushchev's secret speech.
4. Describe three ways by which Khrushchev attempted to consolidate his hold on power after 1958.
5. What factors, other than agricultural, contributed to Khrushchev's fall in 1964?
6. Overall, would you describe the Khrushchev era as successful or unsuccessful? Explain your answer.

4.3   THE BREZHNEV REGIME, 1964–1982

BREZHNEV AND KOSYGIN

Khrushchev's removal was immediately followed by a decision of the Central Committee of the CPSU not to allow any one person to acquire excessive power. Consequently, **Leonid Brezhnev**, who was president of the Party Praesidium, became First Secretary of the CPSU and **Aleksei Kosygin**, who was Deputy Chairman of the Council of Ministers, became Chairman of that body, or Prime Minister. Relations between the two men were generally good, mainly because Kosygin had no designs on Brezhnev's position. This was in stark contrast to the rivalry between Khrushchev and Malenkov in 1953. In time, Brezhnev would become the dominant figure in Soviet politics. His early years, however, focused on consolidating his position and distancing himself from what he called the "hare-brained schemes" of Khrushchev.

Courtesy: Bettmann/Corbis

● Brezhnev, 1966, at the 23rd Soviet Party Congress with a demand that the US pull out of Vietnam. Kosygin is seated on the right.

DISTANCING FROM KHRUSHCHEV

Brezhnev was a quieter, more even-tempered man than Khrushchev and immediately set about distancing himself from the boastful, fiercely energetic but unpredictable style of leadership of his predecessor. This policy showed itself in the following changes:

- In March 1965 Brezhnev announced that there would be no more highly adventurous and unsuccessful schemes like Khrushchev's 'Virgin Lands' project.
- Old-age pensions and sickness payments were granted to peasants.
- Labourers on collective farms would be paid every month instead of the yearly payment they received under Stalin and Khrushchev.
- In September 1965 the economic councils set up for industrial planning by Khrushchev were dissolved and planning was returned to Moscow.
- Peasants were allowed to keep more livestock on their private plots.

● Nixon and Brezhnev meeting in Moscow in 1972 after signing SALT I (see page 38). Occasions such as these sent out the message to the world that business could be done between the superpowers.

Courtesy: Wally McNamee/Corbis

Another departure from the Khrushchev line was to modify the overoptimistic view that full Communism could be established by 1980.

'DEVELOPED SOCIALISM'

This was Brezhnev's alternative to Khrushchev's unrealistic boast. **Developed Socialism** was the stage at which the Soviet Union had arrived by the late 1960s. The targets for the future were increased living standards for the people, continued industrial advances and the integration of all the nationalities under the Soviet Union.

To achieve these aims the period of Developed Socialism could last for a 'protracted period'. The realisation of full Communism would have to wait. Instead of the machinery of the state withering away, Brezhnev once again emphasised the role of the Party: "The leading and guiding force of Soviet society and the nucleus of its political system, its state organisations and public organisations is the Communist Party of the Soviet Union."

This highly centralised control by the state of the machinery of government and of people's lives gave rise to protests from artists, writers and scientists over the lack of human rights.

INTELLECTUAL PROTEST

Clamping down on dissidents was part of Brezhnev's growing control of power. The first demonstration of this took place in September 1965 when the KGB arrested two writers, **Andrei Sinyavski** and **Yulii Daniel**, on charges of producing anti-Soviet propaganda. Both men had written short stories in which they satirised the Soviet system. Sinyavski was given seven years and Daniel five years in the Gulag (forced labour camp). A new journal entitled *The Chronicle of Current Events* was published by dissidents in 1968 and continued thereafter to keep a record of the violations of human rights in the Soviet Union. The method of publication was known as *Samizdat* which translates as 'self-publishing'.

● A 1956 cartoon showing the ghost of Stalin gloating over the continued suppression of artistic freedom in the Soviet Union.

Courtesy: The Centre for the Study of Cartoons and Caricature

ANDREI SAKHAROV

His emergence as a protesting voice was a major embarrassment to the Brezhnev administration. He was one of the country's leading scientists and was a key figure in developing the atomic bomb. He began to question the whole rationale of the arms race and argued that Socialism and capitalism could be merged to everybody's benefit. Soviet Russia should therefore open its mind to external influences. In 1970 Sakharov was part of a group that formed the Human Rights Committee Campaign For Reform. Further embarrassment for the administration followed in December 1975 when Sakharov was awarded the Nobel Peace Prize. He went on to condemn the Soviet invasion of Afghanistan in December 1979. He and his wife, the writer Yelena Bonner, were exiled in 1980.

ALEXANDER SOLZHENITSYN

His publication of December 1973, entitled *The Gulag Archipelago*, highlighted the harsh treatment of political prisoners across the Soviet Union. In 1974 he was deported to the West.

Source Document

Extract from a letter from Andrei Sakharov to Anatoly P. Aleksandrov, president of the Soviet Academy of Sciences

I have learned of people who set themselves the goal of struggling for human rights by means of publicity, rejecting violence as a matter of principle, and of their cruel persecution by the authorities. I have been an eyewitness to unjust trials. I have seen the brazenness of the KGB, I have learned about terrible conditions in places of confinement. I have become one of those people you have called an "alien factor" and even accused of treason. But these are my friends and it is in them that I see the shining strength of our people.

QUESTIONS ON THE DOCUMENT

1. What violations of human rights does Sakharov describe as taking place in the Soviet Union?
2. What do you think he means when he says of his friends: "It is in them that I see the shining strength of our people"?

Another form of protest emerged from the 'guitar poets', of whom **Vladimir Vysotski** was the most famous.

The suppression of the voices of discontent remained a feature of the Brezhnev regime and demonstrated the great fear the administration had that opposition might emerge which they would find difficult to control. For once, the economy was not a source of that discontent. In the first ten years of Brezhnev's rule the economy prospered.

AGRICULTURE

The eighth Five-Year Plan 1965–1970 targeted greater production of agricultural produce. The motivation for this was increased government prices paid for agricultural goods, reduced taxes to be paid by collective farms, farm managers getting greater freedom in decision making with less interference from the state and state investment in agriculture would be doubled up to 1970. As a result of these reforms gross agricultural output increased by an average of 3.9 per cent for each of the years 1966 to 1970. However, during the 1970s this figure fell to an average of 1.2 per cent and the Soviet Union could not overcome the problem of a shortage of grain.

INDUSTRY

The eighth Five-Year Plan also included incentives for workers and managers in the industrial sector, e.g. increased bonuses were paid for greater production and greater profit. Priority was still given to heavy industry, but consumer goods did get increased attention. Gross industrial production increased by an impressive 50 per cent between 1966 and 1970 and by 43 per cent from 1970 to 1975. By 1980 this rate of increase had fallen to 24 per cent.

RELIGION

Religious freedom continued to be an issue during the Brezhnev years. The basic rule that applied was that religious communities could meet if their Church was registered with the state. They were not permitted to attempt to convert people to their beliefs, nor were they allowed to publish material. The Russian Orthodox Church generally enjoyed a reasonable working relationship with the state, but other denominations found it difficult to gain acceptance. Official government statistics for 1975 (which are probably conservative) estimated that just over 7,000 Orthodox Churches with around 6,000 clergymen were operating in the entire Soviet Union. Greater tolerance of the Orthodox faith continued throughout the 1970s. Roman Catholics and Protestants were subjected to closer scrutiny and some harassment.

The growth of the Muslim population in the Soviet Union was a cause for concern for the Party. By 1975 there were between 40 and 50 million Muslims in the USSR. The fear was that a fundamentalist movement might emerge which would fly in the face of Socialist principles. Such a development did not in fact take place because Muslims, like other faiths, learned to keep a low profile and practise their religion in relative peace.

A new anti-religion campaign was launched in 1981 and lasted until 1985. Over 300 places of worship were closed down as a result.

The overall picture during the Brezhnev era was that religious communities were closely monitored and viewed with suspicion, but were generally tolerated.

Courtesy: Corbis

● 1970s growth of the Muslim community in the USSR. Here the faithful are gathered for Eid prayer.

THE NATIONALITIES QUESTION

The Soviet Union consisted of 15 different republics and since Tsarist times nationalism had been a problem for successive regimes. For the Brezhnev administration this became another source of dissident activity. As early as August 1965, 18 Ukranian nationalists were jailed for expressing anti-Soviet Union sentiments. In the same year a nationalist demonstration in Armenia was broken up by the army. The invasion of Czechoslovakia in 1968 by the Red Army hammered home the message that nationalist attempts to break away from the central control of Moscow would not be tolerated. It was already clear that Brezhnev's policy was a continuation of that which existed before – national discontent would be suppressed, not solved.

● Map showing the 15 republics of the Soviet Union (including Russia).

● In this image from 1973, children play at being Communist officials.

RUSSIFICATION

While all of the republics had their own Communist Parties, Central Committees and First Secretaries, the non-Russian republics had a problem with what they saw as an official policy of 'Russification'. Basically this took two forms:

■ The promotion of the Russian language as the common language of the Soviet Union. All government publications, be they newspapers or books, were printed in Russian. The teaching of Russian was introduced in every state, from primary school to university level. By the mid-1970s fluency in Russian was essential for any kind of decent career.

■ Russians were employed by the central government in Moscow in administrative, industrial and agricultural positions throughout the other 14 republics. This reinforced the spread of the Russian language and was seen as a cultural threat in the republics.

In general, the Kremlin promoted the idea of unity between the republics. The fact that the Soviet Union was a multinational state was played down and national differences were papered over.

THE 1977 CONSTITUTION

This was the first constitution drafted since Stalin's constitution of 1936. It attempted to combine the rights of citizens and nationalities with the strict control exercised by the CPSU. Among the rights granted were:

■ Freedom of speech, of assembly and of the press.
■ Freedom to hold religious belief and worship.
■ Freedom of artists to exercise their creativity.
■ The right to privacy.
■ The right to work, health care, protection in old age, housing, and a proper education.
■ Each of the 15 republics "shall retain the right freely to secede from the Soviet Union".

These rights reflected the spirit of the Helsinki Accord 1975 but in Brezhnev's Soviet Union there were accompanying restrictions. The CPSU was in total control and no political opposition was tolerated. Article 39 allowed the government to suppress any activity it deemed inappropriate or dangerous: "Enjoyment by citizens of their rights and freedoms must not be to the detriment of the interests of society or the state, or infringe the rights of other citizens". Article 52 said that the right to freedom of expression could be overruled if that expression ran counter to Party policy.

● Brezhnev as 'cult' figure.

THE CULT OF BREZHNEV

Brezhnev's period of rule began with shared leadership with Kosygin and ended with Brezhnev as a kind of cult figure. One of his great weaknesses was his vanity. He showered honours on himself. He was conferred with the title "Hero of the Soviet Union" on no less than four occasions. In 1977 he created the title "President of the Soviet Union" so that he could meet President Jimmy Carter on an equal footing. In literature he took to setting an example for all Soviet writers by producing his own works. In 1979 he was awarded the Lenin Prize for Literature.

A PARTY IN DECLINE

By 1980 the political leadership of the Soviet Union had grown old. The average age of those in the Politburo was 69 years. The ruling body lacked energy, preferring to dwell on the achievements of Socialism since 1917; they had no appetite for change. This tired conservatism pervaded the CPSU from Moscow to the remote outposts of the Soviet Union. The system of *Nomenklatura* meant that Party members who had demonstrated continued loyalty were rewarded with secure posts. These Party loyalists, or *Apparatchiks*, did not have to possess any great level of ability and were allowed to grow old in their positions. When Brezhnev died on 10 November 1982 he was succeeded as General Secretary of the CPSU by Yuri Andropov, head of the KGB and a senior figure on the Central Committee of the CPSU.

● Yuri V. Andropov

1982–1984: ANDROPOV AND CHERNENKO

When Yuri Andropov became General Secretary of the CPSU on 12 November1982 he immediately targeted economic expansion as his priority. This was essential if the Soviet Union was to continue to match America as a world superpower. It was also fundamental to increasing the standard of living of Soviet citizens and keeping them happy. To achieve these goals, the most dynamic of these younger men was Mikhail Gorbachev, who was given overall responsibility for the economy.

POLITICAL CHANGES

Andropov set about restoring discipline on the country by the following measures:

- Government departments came under inspection to increase efficiency.
- Poor attendance and punctuality in the workplace would be subject to penalties.
- Police were ordered to arrest people found drunk in a public place.

● Konstatin Ustinovich
Chernenko

Andropov visited factories and spoke with workers about their daily lives and their concerns. This represented a huge change from the remote leadership of Brezhnev.

Already 68 years old when he became General Secretary, he died of kidney failure on 9 February 1984, after only 15 months in power.

CHERNENKO, 1984–1985

Konstantin Chernenko now became General Secretary. He was already 73 years old. Many of the older Politburo members voted for him because of his conservatism and resistance to change. His tenure of office ended when he died on 10 March 1985.

By this time the Soviet Union faced serious difficulties. The growth of the economy had slowed substantially, especially oil production. Agriculture, too, was in a state of decline. Too many senior figures in the Party had become complacent and inert. Soviet leadership needed ideology, energy and self-belief. Mikhail Gorbachev would provide all those qualities.

QUESTIONS

1. Show how Brezhnev distanced himself from the policies of Khrushchev.
2. What was Brezhnev's policy on nationalist movements within the Soviet republics?
3. Write a paragraph on the 1977 constitution, showing how it limited individual freedom.
4. Briefly show how the term 'stagnation' best describes the Brezhnev regime.
5. What measures did Andoprov take to improve economic performance?

4.4 MIKHAIL GORBACHEV AND THE FALL OF THE SOVIET UNION

When Mikhail Gorbachev became General Secretary of the CPSU on 11 March 1985 he was a relatively young man of 54 years. He was a lawyer by profession, energetic, intelligent and a committed Communist. As a senior figure in Andropov's government he was well aware of the problems facing the Soviet Union. Change was essential and Gorbachev began at the top.

Courtesy: Corbis

● Gorbachev and Yeltsin shake hands after a failed coup d'etat in 1991 (see page 71).

POLITICAL CHANGE

He proceeded to surround himself with supporters of reform. Boris Yeltsin, a Party leader, was promoted to the Secretariat of the Central Committee. Within a year of coming to power Gorbachev had removed most of Brezhnev's Politburo members as well as 45 per cent of Brezhnev's government and 40 per cent of the Central Committee of the CPSU.

ALCOHOL CLAMPDOWN

The new regime tackled the problem of drunkenness and alcoholism. In May 1985 the penalties for alcohol-related offences were raised. The number of outlets selling alcohol was reduced, while the price of vodka was trebled. Such a move was not popular, but was grudgingly accepted.

PERESTROIKA AND *GLASNOST*

In May 1985 Gorbachev told a gathering in Leningrad: "Everyone must adopt new approaches and understand that no other path is available to us". The concept of reconstruction, or *perestroika*, became central to Gorbachev's vision of the future Soviet Union. At the 27th Party Congress February–March 1986 he highlighted the need for *glasnost*, i.e. openness. The message was clear: mistakes, faults and deficiencies must be acknowledged, not hidden away. However, early signs of *glasnost* appeared in 1986 when the state newspaper, *Izvestiya*, carried an account of a serious accident on the Trans-Siberian railway. The traditional Soviet method of handling 'bad' news like this was to play down the scale and effect of the event or simply suppress it entirely. However, it took an accident of massive proportions to give *perestroika* and *glasnost* a real boost.

Courtesy: Corbis

● Reactor No. 3 of the Chernobyl Nuclear Power Station, before the 1986 disaster.

THE CHERNOBYL DISASTER

In the early hours of 26 April 1986 a major explosion rocked the nuclear power station at Chernobyl in the Ukraine. Due to lack of information and organisation, an evacuation of the immediate area (within a 10 km radius of the power plant) took place some 40 hours after the explosion. The slow reaction from the government was part of a policy to play down the disaster. Privately, however, Gorbachev was even more convinced that change in the Soviet Union was essential. Chernobyl proved that work standards had dropped, training was inadequate, complacency had filtered down to the workforce and management did not have its safety precautions in place. As the subsequent effects of Chernobyl emerged, the efficiency of the Moscow administration came into question. It would contribute to the eventual undermining of the Soviet Union.

GLASNOST AND PERESTROIKA IN PRACTICE

Between mid-1986 and the end of 1988 Gorbachev implemented the openness and restructuring that he believed was necessary to save the Soviet Union. Gorbachev wanted Socialism to survive. He was a dedicated Communist who believed that the problems of the Soviet Union could be solved.

MEDIA FREEDOM

The first big step in the policy of *Glasnost* came in June 1986 when state control over newspapers and journals was relaxed. Gorbachev's strategy here was to get journalists and writers on his side. The intelligentsia would be important in winning over public opinion. The release of Andrei Sakharov later that year was part of this strategy. We must also remember that media freedom was not complete: the Party still retained the power to set limits. Gorbachev now ventured to weaken the positions of the old guard in the Party by convening a special full session of the Central Committee.

Courtesy: Getty Images

● *Glasnost* at work: A larger range of media choice became available, importing national and international titles.

THE CENTRAL COMMITTEE CONFERENCE, JANUARY 1987

Opening the conference, Gorbachev attacked Stalin and criticised the Brezhnev era for its stagnation and its policy of keeping old Party members in secure position well into old age. He then succeeded in having the following resolutions passed:

- From now on senior Party officials should be elected by secret ballot within the Party.
- Non-members of the Party should be allowed to serve in important positions of public office.

ECONOMIC REFORM

In June 1987 the Law on the State Enterprise was passed, providing the following changes:

- The workers in each factory would have the right to elect the manager of the enterprise.
- Factories could decide their own wholesale prices.
- The tight control of wages by the state would be relaxed.
- Some degree of private enterprise would be allowed in light industries.

These reforms constituted an attack on the central planning authorities of the Soviet Union. The policy of *perestroika* was now in full flow, but one of its strongest advocates, Boris Yeltsin, had moved far too quickly.

THE REMOVAL OF YELTSIN

Boris Yeltsin embarked on *perestroika* and *glasnost* with fierce enthusiasm. He went on an anti-corruption drive within the CPSU, sacking many of the old guard. Yeltsin was gruff, undiplomatic, arrogant and impulsive. Gorbachev did not want to alienate the Party and in November 1987 he sacked Yeltsin. The removal of Yeltsin was not an indication that *perestroika* was weakening or slowing down. In fact, Gorbachev was about to make the process more radical.

A CONGRESS OF PEOPLE'S DEPUTIES

On 28 June 1988 at a specially convened conference of the CPSU, Gorbachev proposed that a two-tier system of government should be introduced, consisting of:

- A Congress of People's Deputies made up of 2,250 members, two-thirds of whom would be elected by the people of the country and one-third chosen by the CPSU.
- A Supreme Soviet of over 400 members to be elected by the Congress of People's Deputies and led by the General Secretary of the CPSU.

Courtesy: Getty Images

● Campaign material for the populist Boris Yeltsin, prior to the 1989 election.

Elections to the new legislature would take place in March 1989. Opposition to Gorbachev's proposal was led by his one-time ally, Yegor Ligachev, who, along with other senior Party members, believed that the General Secretary's reforms were going too far. Gorbachev's response was single-minded: he demoted Ligachev in October 1988 and promoted Aleksandr Yakovlev to his place. Yakovlev had already established himself as a loyal supporter of *perestroika*.

THE MARCH 1989 ELECTION

The election to the new legislature sparked public interest and 85 per cent of the electorate voted, with 85 per cent of the members elected belonging to the Party. Boris Yeltsin won nearly 90 per cent of the vote in his Moscow constituency. Later in the year he acquired one of the 400 seats in the Supreme Soviet.

PRESIDENT GORBACHEV

In March 1990 Mikhail Gorbachev was appointed president of the Soviet Union by the Supreme Soviet. He had executive power as head of state and commander-in-chief of the military forces. The CPSU had to share power with the Congress of People's Deputies. On the surface Mikhail Gorbachev seemed to have won, but in reality the Soviet Union was in deep trouble.

ECONOMIC DIFFICULTIES

By the close of 1989 Soviet technology had fallen substantially behind the West, except in armaments. Some of these problems were self-inflicted:

- The drive against alcoholism damaged the huge vodka industry and cut state revenue accordingly.
- Wages in industry rose by 9 per cent in 1988 and 13 per cent in 1989.
- *Glasnost* meant that issues such as price rises were known in advance by the public and this caused shortages of goods in shops because of panic buying.

Mikhail Gorbachev (1931–   ): Gorbachev was born into a peasant family in 1931. He studied law at Moscow University, graduating in 1953. In March 1985 he became General Secretary. He knew that substantial reform was needed in the Soviet Union. He introduced *perestroika* (restructuring) and *glasnost* (openness).

He wanted to end the conflict with the West and succeeded in ending the Cold War. Faced with opposition from all sides, Gorbachev survived an attempted coup in August 1991, but was forced to resign in December of that year. In 1990 he was awarded the Nobel Peace Prize.

Courtesy: Corbis

FOOD SHORTAGES

The agricultural problems that had plagued the Soviet Union had not been addressed properly by the Gorbachev administration. Furthermore, local Party officials disagreed with Gorbachev's reforms. This meant that supplies of agricultural produce did not always reach cities and towns. At the close of 1988 meat was rationed in the Russian Soviet Republic. A year later all major cities and towns suffered severe shortages of tea, coffee, meat, milk and cheese. A series of strikes occurred during 1989. These were settled by granting higher wages.

Courtesy: Corbis

● People queue for food during the shortage of the late-1980s.

OTHER DIFFICULTIES

To add to Gorbachev's problems, a huge earthquake hit Armenia in December 1988, leaving over 25,000 people dead. The war in Afghanistan had proven to be a considerable drain on the economy. Housing and public services were still inadequate and by 1989 most hospitals experienced shortages of medicines and facilities. With *glasnost* in place all of these issues were now discussed openly in the press and in the Congress of People's Deputies. Gorbachev's reforms were beginning to work against him. Not only was the president facing severe opposition in the Kremlin, but throughout the entire Soviet Union.

THE NATIONAL ISSUE

The weakening economy, the Chernobyl disaster and the shortage of food, proper housing and medical facilities all contributed to a reawakening of nationalism in all of the republics. *Glasnost* had played its part in this too since newspapers had revealed the horror of Stalin's purges and people were now sufficiently free to voice opposition.

The Baltic States, Estonia, Latvia and Lithuania led, the reawakening by forming nationalist movements. By mid-summer 1989 popular fronts had emerged in Ukraine, Uzbekistan, Moldova, Belarus and Georgia.

Gorbachev had no intention of allowing the union of Soviet Republics to disintegrate, however. He showed this in March 1990 when Lithuania declared its independence from the Soviet Union. Soviet tanks immediately entered Vilnius and on 30 June the Lithuanian government shelved its declaration.

GORBACHEV'S ACHIEVEMENT

By the spring of 1990 Gorbachev had applied *glasnost* and *perestroika* to an extent that would have been unimaginable five years before. The great achievement was the two-tier executive over which he presided. While in theory the CPSU was still in charge, in reality its position was seriously undermined and its future looked bleak.

Another blow to the old guard occurred in February 1990 when the Central Committee of the CPSU voted to end its own monopoly of power in the Soviet Union. Later that month Gorbachev won the support of the Congress of People's Deputies to introduce multi-party politics. Clearly, he was leaving Marxism-Leninism behind: some form of Socialist democracy now seemed to be the target.

GROWING OPPOSITION

As he pushed through his reform programme Gorbachev came under attack from two sides. Firstly, the old conservative element of the CPSU was dismayed by the changes. Secondly, the radical element within the CPSU argued that reforms were not sweeping enough and were coming too slowly. They wanted Gorbachev to set up a new political party. Boris Yeltsin was the driving force behind this group.

Courtesy: Novosti/Corbis

• Yeltsin emerges as leader, 22 August 1990.

THE RE-EMERGENCE OF YELTSIN

After his election to the Congress of People's Deputies and his appointment to a seat on the Supreme Soviet Boris Yeltsin formed an **Inter-Regional Group** of about 300 members to push for greater and speedier reforms. In March 1990 Yeltsin became chairman of the Supreme Soviet of the Russian Socialist Federal Soviet Republic (RSFSR). This provided him with a platform from which he could attack Gorbachev. In the summer of 1990 he announced the RSFSR's declaration of sovereignty. Yeltsin was intent on evening the score for his humiliating dismissal in 1987.

THE NATIONAL ISSUE AGAIN

The renewal of nationalist activity in Lithuania by Soviet troops led to the killing of 15 people in Vilnius on 13 January 1991. On 9 February 1991 Lithuania held a vote to sound out people's views on independence. Over 90 per cent voted in favour. The following month Estonia and Latvia voted 79 per cent and 74 per cent in favour, respectively. If this trend were to spread then Gorbachev would preside over the disintegration of the Soviet Union.

A NEW UNION TREATY

Gorbachev's response was to draft a new **Union Treaty** that would set up a new Union of Soviet Sovereign Republics. The main proposals were:

■ The sovereignty of each republic would be recognised.
■ Each could decide on its own form of government.
■ The republics could deal directly with foreign countries on issues such as trade, but not on foreign policy.
■ The central government in Moscow would retain the powers of foreign policy and defence.
■ The central government would retain control of taxation.

The new treaty was put to a referendum on 17 March 1991 and was overwhelmingly endorsed. However, six republics – the three Baltic States plus Georgia, Moldova and Armenia Yen refused to vote because they had lost interest in being part of a union under Moscow's control. Nevertheless, Gorbachev went ahead with the new Union Treaty for the other nine republics. This treaty would be signed on 20 August 1991.

MORE ECONOMIC DOWNTURN

In the meantime, the Soviet economy continued its downward trend, further undermining Gorbachev's position:

- In 1991 production of oil and coal fell by 10 per cent.
- Overall industrial production fell by 18 per cent.
- Agricultural production fell by 17 per cent.
- Shortages of goods meant that prices doubled.

A CONSERVATIVE *PUTSCH*

By the summer of 1991 the conservative old guard of the CPSU decided that it was time to intervene directly if the Soviet Union was to be saved.

It was obvious to them that Yeltsin wanted to dismantle the Soviet Union further. On 18 August Gorbachev was placed under house arrest at his holiday home in the Crimea.

On 19 August the conservatives announced that Gorbachev was too ill to continue in office. Tanks moved onto the Moscow streets on the same day.

Unwittingly, they had opened the door to power for Yeltsin. When Yeltsin learned of the attempted coup he occupied the building of the Supreme Soviet of the RSFSR and used this as a rallying point to counter the State Committee. Over the next couple of days he was supported by nearly 200,000 people. The army refused to act against the people. Yeltsin emerged as the new champion of reform. The leaders called off the *putsch* on 22 August.

YELTSIN TAKES CENTRE STAGE

When Gorbachev returned to Moscow on 22 August he found Yeltsin's popularity enormously enhanced. On 23 August Yeltsin made the CPSU temporarily illegal within the RSFSR. The following day Gorbachev stepped down as General Secretary of the CPSU, but retained his position as president. On 28 October Yeltsin told the Russian Congress of People's Deputies that he would introduce a new economic programme based on free markets. On 6 November he permanently banned the CPSU in the RSFSR.

● A rally in 1991 with placards of both Yeltsin and Lenin being held up.

Courtesy: Corbis

GORBACHEV'S LAST THROW

With Yeltsin's RSFSR behaving as though it were already an independent state, Gorbachev made one last effort to save the Soviet Union. His proposal was to set up a Union of Sovereign States with a substantial degree of independence for each state. It was too late. In September the independence of the Baltic States was recognised and the Soviet Union was on the way out.

FINAL BREAK-UP

On 1 December 1991 the Ukraine declared its independence. A week later Yeltsin, the new president of Ukraine, Leonid Kravchuk, and the leader of Belarus, Stanislav Shushkevich, met in the Belarusian capital Minsk. There they dissolved the Soviet Union and replaced it with a loose association of states called the Commonwealth of Independent States. The Baltic States and Georgia did not join. For Gorbachev there was no choice but to give way. On 25 December he made his parting speech: "I leave my post with trepidation. But also with hope, with faith in you, in your wisdom and force of spirit. We are the inheritors of a great civilisation, and now the burden falls on each and every one that it may be resurrected to a new, modern and worthy life."

The Soviet Union formally ceased to exist on 31 December 1991.

● Map of Russia after the break-up of the Soviet Union in 1991.

CONCLUSION

When Gorbachev launched his reform programme in 1985 he did not foresee the collapse of the Soviet Union. The policies of *perestroika* and *glasnost* eventually worked against him. *Perestroika* brought down the wrath of the old conservative Communists on him. *Glasnost* brought issues into the open, making the public aware of the deficiencies of government and generating open criticism. Economic failure left people with decreasing standards of living and food shortages that were simply unacceptable. All of these contributed to the wave of nationalism that swept the republics. What was surprising was the speed with which the Soviet Union folded.

QUESTIONS

1. Briefly explain what you understand the terms *perestroika* and *glasnost* to mean.
2. Why did Gorbachev relax state control over the media in June 1986?
3. Describe the two-tier system of government introduced by Gorbachev in June 1988. What was its significance?
4. What was Gorbachev's attitude to the move towards separatism in the republics?
    (a) Why did Gorbachev draft a new Union Treaty in the spring of 1991?
    (b) What were its main proposals?
5. Identify four factors that contributed to the collapse of the Soviet Union.

GENERAL ESSAY QUESTIONS ON CHAPTER 4

1. Write a brief account of Khrushchev's period of rule between 1955–1964. In your answer refer to his coming to power, criticism of Stalin, agricultural policy and fall from power.
2. Outline the problems experienced by the Soviet Union during the Brezhnev era.
3. Describe the role of Mikhail Gorbachev in Soviet affairs. Include references to *glasnost*, *perestroika*, the nationalities issue and conflict with Yeltsin.
4. Discuss the view that the energy and vitality that marked the last years of Stalin and all of the Khrushchev era disappeared towards the end of the Brezhnev regime.
5. Trace the development of the Soviet Union from 1945 to the end of 1991.
6. Discuss the reasons for the collapse of the Soviet Union in 1991.
7. "The rule of Mikhail Gorbachev contrasted starkly with that of Stalin, Khrushchev and Brezhnev." Assess the accuracy of this statement.
8. Discuss the view that Mikhail Gorbachev was responsible for bringing down the Soviet Union.

5

THE HUNGARIAN UPRISING – CASE STUDY

Words you need to understand

AVH: The Hungarian secret police.

Collectivisation: The Socialist policy of joining together privately owned farms into one large working unit.

Marxist doctrine: The Socialist ideas put forward by the 19th-century German thinker, Karl Marx.

Nationalisation: Placing all large industries under the ownership of the state.

Political asylum: Special protection given by a state to a person who has very serious political disagreements within his own country. An embassy is regarded as the territory of the foreign country.

Politburo: The committee of the Communist party.

Purge: Forcibly removing individuals from a political party.

Spontaneous: An act that is done without any planning.

5.1 BACKGROUND: HUNGARY 1945–1956

THE SOVIETS TAKE OVER HUNGARY

In April 1945 the Soviets and Romanians drove the Germans out of Hungary. The USSR army commander became president of a Communist-controlled provisional government. The Soviets reduced the size of Hungary and forced it to pay reparations to the USSR.

In the first post-war elections, the Communists won only 17 per cent of the votes. The Communist leader, Matyas Rákosi, was a loyal follower of Stalin. The Communists received only one ministry, that of the police. Using police powers, they harassed other parties.

In February 1947, Béla Kovecs, the leader of the largest party (called the **Smallholders Party**), was arrested on a false charge of plotting against the Soviets. Many opposition politicians were not allowed to take part in the 1947 elections. Rákosi described this policy of isolating the opposition politicians as "cutting them off like slices of salami".

The Communists gained full control after the election of May 1949. The new government nationalised the major industries and introduced the Soviet model of Five-Year Plans.

Imre Nagy (1895–1958): Imre Nagy emerged as the unlikely 'hero' of the 1956 Hungarian uprising. During the first World War, the Russians captured him as a prisoner of war. He joined the Bolshevik Party, fought in the Red Army and became a citizen of the USSR. During the 1920s he tried to organise an underground Communist movement in Hungary, but he had to flee the country. He stayed in the USSR between 1929 and 1944. After the second World War Nagy returned to Budapest and held several positions in the Communist government until he was expelled from the Communist Party's Politburo in 1949. In 1951 Nagy became Deputy Prime Minister under Communist leader Matyas Rákosi and was promoted to Prime Minister in 1953 because of the influence of the Soviet leader, Malenkov. Nagy was sacked and expelled from the party in late 1955.

Courtesy: Corbis

Courtesy: Getty Images

• An 11-year-old holds a rifle during the Hungarian uprising.

Rákosi ruled with an iron fist. The Communists began a purge of Party members whose loyalty was suspect. A series of **show trials** took place. Imre Nagy was expelled from the Hungarian Workers' Party Politburo after he asked for an easing of the collectivisation programme. In 1953, 30 Jewish Communists were removed from the ruling party.

NAGY PROMOTES REFORM IN HUNGARY

In June 1953 the new Kremlin leadership forced Rákosi to give up his premiership and to give it to Imre Nagy. Nagy criticised Rákosi: "We failed to realise the basic economic law of socialism – the constant raising of the standard of living."

Nagy set up the **Patriotic People's Front**. He hoped to combine Socialism, democracy and patriotism. He allowed more free speech and encouraged public discussion. Nagy also released anti-Communists from prison and spoke about holding free elections and withdrawing Hungary from the Warsaw Pact (see p. 27).

Nagy was safe once Malenkov was in charge in Moscow. Then Malenkov was dismissed in February 1955 and Nagy was sacked and expelled from the Party in late 1955. He had been dismissed for supporting important reforms, and this increased his appeal.

Nagy did not stay silent. He published his ideas under the title *On Communism*. He criticised the Soviet Socialist formula for relying too much on the use of force. He generally supported the Yugoslav position (see pp. 40–42), that all nations should follow their own road to Socialism.

He wanted less reliance on force and more emphasis on democratic reforms and freedoms: "Power is increasingly being torn away from the people and turned sharply against them." He also complained that "people's democracy" was being replaced by a "Party dictatorship".

Nagy followed a 'New Course', a new stage of Socialism. Unlike his political opponents in the Communist Party, Nagy appealed to the lower levels of the Party and the general public. He wanted to release political prisoners, slow down the forced move of industrialisation and allow peasants leave the collective, or state, farms. He wished to lower the price of food, to increase food supply and to allow farmers to use state machinery to produce crops for their own profit.

He was accepted back into the Party on 13 October 1956, without having changed his political views.

PUBLIC EXPRESSIONS OF HUNGARIAN NATIONALISM, 1956

The Petofi Circle supported Nagy's ideas. This new protest group was named after a 19th-century Hungarian poet and nationalist. In June 1956 their public meetings attracted crowds of over 5,000. On 27 June the Petofi Circle called for Nagy to be returned to power. Rákosi banned the Petofi Circle and called on Moscow to arrest Nagy and over 400 dissidents (protesters). However, in July 1956, Rákosi was dismissed and was succeeded by his second in command, Erno Gerö, under direction from Moscow.

The Hungarians took pleasure from the victory of their football team over the USSR in September 1956. Played in Moscow, the Hungarians won 1–0. The patriotism also showed in a massive demonstration on 6 October when the executed leader, Laszlo Rajk, was reburied in Budapest. Over a quarter of a million people attended.

Courtesy: Houser/Corbis

● A statue of Hungarian poet Petofi in Budapest.

QUESTIONS

1. How did Rákosi describe his policy of dealing with opposition parties?
2. What steps did Rákosi take to deal with opposition within the Communist Party?
3. What were the policies of Nagy's Patriotic People's Front?
4. How did Nagy criticise the Soviets in his book, *On Communism*?
5. Give one indication to show that Hungarians were prepared to support opposition to the existing government.

5.2   THE HUNGARIAN UPRISING: CAUSES

The Hungarian crisis emerged after a political crisis in Poland, during which the Soviets had parked their tanks on the Polish borders. The return to power of the popular Polish leader, Gomulka, ended the crisis. Many in Hungary saw the events as a sign of Soviet weakness. The Hungarian Communist Party, however, was less nationalistic and more loyal to Moscow than the Polish Party. Hungary would be a different experience.

WHY DID THE UPRISING BEGIN?

■ The heavy hand of Communism, directed by the Hungarian Communist Party under general direction from Moscow, fuelled massive resentment. The uprising began because the Hungarians were demanding more reforms than the Soviets were prepared to give them.

■ The Hungarian uprising followed purges and a terror more prolonged than in any other country under Soviet rule.

■ The uprising was a response to the policy of de-Stalinisation (see pp. 57–9) that Khrushchev had started in the Soviet Union after the death of Stalin. Khrushchev condemned Stalin in February 1956.

■ The government concentrated on heavy industry rather than producing consumer goods. This led to a shortage of clothing, footwear and household goods. The real earnings of workers fell by 18 per cent between 1949 and 1953.

■ In agriculture, the combination of collectivisation and (low) fixed prices for produce drove peasants from the land or into stubborn resistance.

- The Hungarians resented the Soviet presence, leading to a hidden sense of nationalism and patriotism. The USSR army stayed in Hungarian barracks. The Hungarian army wore a Soviet red star on their caps, not the Hungarian coat of arms. Students had to learn the Russian language.

- The government restricted freedom of speech. Writers, journalists and artists had to show awareness of Marxist doctrine. Those who refused attracted the attention of the **AVH**, or secret police, a much-hated organisation.

- The government did not allow religious freedom. Christianity provided an ideological alternative to Marxist ideas. The Communists jailed the Catholic cardinal Josef Mindszenty in 1949 to lessen the influence of the Church.

QUESTION

1. What do you consider to be the three most important causes of the Hungarian uprising?

5.3   THE HUNGARIAN UPRISING

THE UPRISING BEGINS

The 1956 uprising started on Monday, 22 October. It was sudden and unexpected, posing a great challenge to the Communist government and the USSR. The uprising was dealt with by force, not negotiation.

ANTI-RUSSIAN DEMONSTRATIONS: 23 OCTOBER

On Tuesday, 23 October, huge crowds, estimated at 200,000, demonstrated throughout Budapest. Demonstrators pulled down a large statue of Stalin. The statues of Hungarian kings and queens had been melted down to make Stalin's statue.

Nagy spoke to the excited crowds who marched to the parliament building. He addressed the crowd as "comrades", but the response was clear: "we are no longer comrades". He led the crowd in singing a banned song, "God Bless Hungary". The Prime Minister, Erno Gerö, criticised the demonstrators, calling them imperialists. But he was no longer in control of the situation and the crowd chanted, "Russians, go home."

Courtesy: Getty Images

• Hungarians jeer as the decapitated head of a statue of Stalin is shown to protesters.

As the demonstrations in the city became more serious, the police used tear gas and a number of students were shot dead. This action changed the nature of the protest. A spontaneous demonstration turned into a national revolution. The army and the police soon refused to disperse the crowds. Budapest was slipping into a civil war situation.

THE SOVIETS CONSIDER THE USE OF FORCE: 24 OCTOBER

After the Polish problem, Khrushchev wanted to stop any 'domino' effect and decided that the USSR should crush the rising. The Soviet ambassador to Hungary was Yuri Andropov, the future head of the KGB, as well as a future leader of the USSR. In co-operation with Moscow, he organised the Soviet response to the Hungarian crisis.

An emergency meeting of the Central Committee of the Hungarian Communist Party appointed Nagy as Prime Minister, a position he would hold for less than 11 days. Khrushchev and the Soviet

Politburo decided almost immediately to dispatch Soviet troops (based in Hungary and outside) to Budapest.

Demonstrators throughout the country set up 'Revolutionary committees' and 'national councils'. They asked for elections by secret ballot. Their demands were radical and included the withdrawal of Soviet troops from Hungary, as well as the disbanding of the security police.

The Soviets sent hundreds of tanks into Budapest during the next few days. Once the tanks were sent in to restore 'order', the Hungarians fought rather than went home. In four days of fighting, many of the tanks were destroyed. Demonstrators attacked the tanks using petrol bombs, nicknamed 'Molotov cocktails'.

Courtesy: Corbis

● Soviet tanks cross a Budapest street as they move in to crush the anti-Communist revolt.
Why do you think that ordinary people are allowed on the corner?

Source Document

Thomas Kabdebo, who emigrated to Ireland after the uprising, was a student in Budapest when the uprising started

Wednesday, 24 October

A small group of fighters runs up to the top storey of the house next door. They've been having it out with a tank down on the Little Ring Road. In the Square a teenage bus conductor lies face down in a pool of frozen blood. He must have been the rearguard, held back by his bag and ticket-punch. The moment the coast is clear the armed youngsters thunder down from the building and scurry off in the direction of Vörösmarty Square. I run with them as far as a handy doorway. "What are you doing?" I ask the leader. I see he is a lad of my own age: boiler-suited, roughened hands, a young worker. "We've got nothing to lose. We'll fight to the last man." There's only one *man* in the gang, himself. The rest are kids. Two of them are girls.

(Thomas Kabdebo, *A Time for Everything*, Maynooth, 1996, pp. 17–18)

QUESTIONS ON THE DOCUMENT

1. What explanation did the author give for the death of the bus conductor?
2. How does the young leader of the small group describe his mission?
3. The writer does not share the leader's opinion. How is this shown in the passage?

HOPE FOR REFORMS IN HUNGARY: 25–26 OCTOBER

From the start, Nagy was convinced that the Soviet leadership would grant a small number of concessions, as they had in Poland, to defuse the crisis at local level. He believed the Soviets would withdraw their troops from Hungary.

János Kádár replaced Erno Gerö as First Secretary of the Communist Party. Kádár promised that, once order was restored, negotiations would begin on the withdrawal of Soviet troops.

The Communist Party promised a wide-ranging series of reforms, including the corrections of 'past mistakes', an amnesty for all who had fought in the uprising and a new, democratically elected government.

At this early stage, according to the US embassy, the 'armed freedom-fighters' were hoping that the Western powers would send military support. The Hungarians realised that their struggle against the superior Soviet forces would fail without outside intervention.

Their hopes were raised by the reports from the American-funded **Radio Free Europe** that overstated the possibility of external assistance for the Hungarians rebels. They appealed directly to Western journalists and to diplomats in foreign embassies for political support and military intervention.

Source Document

Thomas Kabdebo describes the excitement of 25 October in the city

We run towards Kossuth Square. We are stopped outside. No procession, no organisation, no order, just a huge crowd, a whole lot of women, kids, old people. Looking over the mass of heads I make out, 30 to 40 paces ahead, that the dense mass of young people have surrounded a tank. It carries Hungarian flags, and inside – I take a look, and it's true – Russian soldiers. "*It's our sons who are fighting,*" the women chant. "*It's our sons they're shooting at,*" the men repeat to each other, hot with excitement. Then a noise like the crack of a whip ... Machine guns pour out round after round ... "God, God, oh! oh! Oh, my God, help!" Uproar, weeping, wailing, sounds of choking, coughing, screams, more shooting. Bursts of machine-gun fire. The crowd turns away, threatens to charge straight at us, but their sheer numbers trample one another instead. I'm too scared to stand ... We don't speak, just run, the choking terror in our throats. And behind us, the grunt of the tank's cannon.

(Thomas Kabdebo, *A Time for Everything*, Maynooth, 1996, pp. 19–20)

QUESTIONS ON THE DOCUMENT

1. Is there any evidence here to show that the demonstration has not been organised?
2. The protesters chant two slogans. What are they?
3. What is the reaction of the crowd when the gun battle started?
4. How would you describe the impact of the events on the writer? Explain your answer.

NAGY'S HUNGARIAN GOVERNMENT: 27–31 OCTOBER

27 October

Nagy headed a new government. Over 350 Hungarians had died in the fighting, while over 600 Soviet troops had also been killed.

28 October

The government called a cease-fire. Nagy arranged for the withdrawal of Soviet tanks. Within two days they had left Budapest, returning to their bases outside the city. The Hungarian Communist

Party collapsed. A new Hungarian National Guard was set up. Nagy ordered the Hungarian army not to fire on the insurgents.

However, the military setback was wrongly seen as a defeat for the Soviets. The Soviets had not left Hungary and their troops were still on Hungarian soil. Nagy demanded free elections as well as the removal of Soviet troops.

30 October

Nagy abolished the one-party Communist system and confirmed the return of multi-party democratic government. The hated AVH was abolished. Cardinal Mindszenty was released from house arrest. With this new sense of freedom, rioters invaded the security police headquarters and burnt down the Communist Party's offices as well.

Source Document

On 30 October, an armoured car approached the country castle in which Cardinal Mindszenty was being held by the police. John Horvath, head of the Communist government's Office of Church Affairs, entered the Cardinal's room. Mindszenty described what happened.

"Your life is not safe in this place," he almost shouted at me. "I have orders to move you!"

"I will not go," I told him. "You have everything from me there is to take. You can take nothing else."

Horvath left the room. He went to the telephone and called his superiors at Budapest, asking for help. By this time they needed it, for the people of the village had been attracted by his car. First came the children and young people, because they are always first in these things. After them, from the fields, from their homes, from the shops, came several hundred men and women from the village. Many of them carried hoes and other farming tools which they raised as their weapons.

These people had known I was in the castle. And on seeing the armoured car speed up to the building, were afraid for my life. They assumed the Russians were going to take me away. By this time the people had surrounded the castle and were raising their weapons, calling, "Freedom for Mindszenty and bread for the Hungarian people."

(Joseph Cardinal Mindszenty , "We Moved to Freedom",
New York Herald Tribune, 1 December 1956, pp. 1, 14)

QUESTIONS ON THE DOCUMENT

1. Why did the cardinal refuse to leave the castle?
2. Several hundred people from the locality came to the castle. Why?
3. The locals voiced a number of demands. What were they?
4. The story of the Hungarian uprising focused mainly on events in Budapest. What conclusions could a historian reach after studying this incident?

THE SOVIETS PREPARE TO TALK: 31 OCTOBER

On 31 October, an optimistic statement from Moscow encouraged the Hungarians. According to the official Soviet newspaper, *Pravda*, the USSR government seemed prepared to discuss some liberation issues with the Hungarians.

The Soviet Government said that it was "prepared to enter into the appropriate negotiations with the government of the Hungarian People's Republic and other members of the Warsaw Treaty on the question of the presence of Soviet troops on the territory of Hungary." It seemed that the Hungarians had won at least a small, if temporary, victory.

However, the Kremlin authorities decided to use violence to end the rebellion. Documents released after the collapse of the USSR showed that the Communist leadership in the USSR feared for its future if it did not act decisively. They believed that Communist rule in Hungary would not survive if they did not act.

THE SOVIETS 'INVADE' HUNGARY: 1–5 NOVEMBER

1 November

Many in Hungary had the mistaken belief that the Cold War division of Europe was a temporary settlement, and that the Western democracies would use the new situation in Hungary to end the Soviet control of Eastern Europe.

On the international scene, the Suez crisis (see pp. 32–3) began, when French and British forces attacked Egypt. This international crisis diverted attention away from the dramatic events in Hungary.

With the Suez crisis unfolding in the Middle East, the Soviet Politburo also believed that a Soviet defeat in Hungary would weaken Communist leaders in other countries. The Soviets consulted with the Communist leaders in East Germany, Romania, Czechoslovakia and Bulgaria. They all supported the Soviet policy of repression. The Czechs and the Romanians were willing to take part in an invasion of Hungary.

In November 1956 Khrushchev made clear his intentions to the US ambassador to the USSR, Charles Bohlen: "We will put in more troops – and more troops – and more troops – and more troops – until we have finished them" (*Time*, 6 January 1958).

The USSR set out to reassert its control in Hungary. By 1 November, 3,000 Soviet trucks had crossed into Hungary. They began to arrest Hungarian government officials in rural areas. Soviet soldiers began to occupy Hungarian airfields. Soviet tanks surrounded the capital city.

Once Nagy saw that he had been tricked by the USSR, he declared Hungary to be a neutral country and withdrew Hungary from the Warsaw Pact.

Nagy informed the Soviets: "The government of the Hungarian People's Republic wishes to begin immediate negotiations on the withdrawal of Soviet troops from Hungarian territory."

● A young boy and many adults observe the assaults by Soviet tanks on insurgent positions.

Courtesy: Corbis

He appealed to the UN to intervene. However, the Suez crisis continued to divert attention away from Eastern Europe.

2 November

Nagy's government protested to the Soviet embassy about the Soviet invasion. They also appealed to the United Nations, an organisation Hungary had joined in 1955. He asked for the major countries to protect Hungarian neutrality.

The rebel Hungarians, even at this stage, held on to the unrealistic hope that the Security Council or the General Assembly of the United Nations would be able to persuade the Soviets to find a peaceful resolution to the crisis.

3 November

In a final act of defiance, non-Communist ministers replaced Communist ministers who had resigned from Nagy's government.

Courtesy: Corbis

● Cardinal Mindszenty being escorted by Hungarian soldiers on 2 November 1956 after he was freed from house arrest. A few days later, he claimed political asylum in the American embassy in Budapest.

4 November

The Soviets began their direct assault on Budapest, supported by some Hungarians. Marshall Zhukov, the Soviet military leader from the second World War, led over 6,000 Soviet tanks. They took over the major communication centres and disarmed the Hungarian troops. János Kádár emerged as leader of the Hungarian Revolutionary Worker-Peasant Government, the new Soviet-approved cabinet.

Source Document

Cardinal Mindszenty seeks political asylum in the American Embassy, November 1956

On 4 November 1956, a Marine corporal and master sergeant were standing on the stairs at the entrance to the (American) Chancery. Cardinal Mindszenty and a monsignor walked up to the Chancery door. Through the Monsignor, who acted as the Cardinal's interpreter, they asked to come into the US embassy.

The corporal asked, "What should I do, Sir?"

"Do your duty," the sergeant replied. So the corporal, who had the keys to the building, unlocked the door and in walked Cardinal Mindszenty, who stayed for 15 years. A few moments later, a telex arrived from Washington instructing the embassy to extend every courtesy should the cardinal request asylum.

During his time in the embassy, the cardinal used the ambassador's office as his sitting room and he slept in the other smaller room to the side. The police outside the Chancery were ever watchful should he try to escape, and they ran their engines day and night, 24 hours a day, 7 days a week, just in case.

One Halloween, the embassy had a costume party, and as some employees still wearing their masks were leaving the building that night, they were accosted by flashlight-bearing secret police who pulled up their masks, looking for the cardinal. That was the last Halloween party in the building.

(A personal reminiscence of an unnamed American who worked in the American embassy at the time, from "The History of the United States Embassy in Budapest, Hungary", www.usEmbassy.hu/cardinal.htm.)

Monsignor: A priest.
Asylum: Protection given by a country to a person who has very serious political disagreements with his own country. An embassy is regarded as the territory of the foreign country, so the American embassy was regarded as American territory.

QUESTIONS ON THE DOCUMENT

1. "Do your duty." What duty did the corporal have to carry out?
2. How long did the cardinal remain in the American embassy?
3. Give one example to show that the Hungarian government was afraid of the cardinal's influence.
4. Why could the Hungarians not go near the cardinal once he remained in the American embassy?
5. This document was obtained from the Internet. What precautions would a historian have to take to ensure that this was a reliable document?

A NEW GOVERNMENT: 7 NOVEMBER

The Soviet military dealt with the remaining resistance in a matter of days. On 7 November, Kádár officially took up his role as the new Hungarian leader, replacing Nagy, who never formally resigned. Kádár ensured that Soviet influence would not be challenged.

He began a policy of 'normalisation', repressing reform and reformers and moving Hungarians towards tolerating rather than opposing the Communist government.

5.4   THE HUNGARIAN UPRISING: THE AFTERMATH

NAGY BECOMES A NATIONAL HERO

Nagy refused to support the new government of János Kádár. The Yugoslav embassy in Budapest gave political asylum to Nagy. Kádár's government promised Nagy that he could leave the embassy and that he would not be harmed. The Soviet Union failed to honour pledges of safe conduct. When Nagy left the Embassy on 22 November, the Soviets seized the Yugoslav bus and kidnapped him. Five days later, Nagy was flown to Romania.

Nagy refused to support the new government of János Kádár. He was held prisoner for almost two years. After a secret trial, he was executed on 16 June 1958, at the age of 62. His patriotic stance during the uprising had transformed this hard-line Communist leader into a nationalist hero for the Hungarian nation.

Hungarians could not openly discuss the 1956 uprising. To support Imre Nagy in public was to risk punishment by the Communist authorities.

TRIALS AND EXILES

Over 2,000 Hungarians died during the period of the uprising. Almost 35,000 Hungarians were placed on trial, and the new Communist government adopted the Stalinist model of show trials. Over 25,000 people were sent to jail. Over 400 people were executed.

Almost 200,000 political refugees left Hungary. Most went to the USA. Between them, the United Kingdom and Germany accepted almost 40,000 Hungarians. Ireland accepted a small number.

● Standing by a Hungarian Nationalist flag, one of the leaders of the uprising against the Soviet domination addresses a crowd.

Courtesy: Corbis

The period of 'retaliation' lasted until 1963. Internment (imprisonment without trial) was ended in 1960. In 1963, an amnesty was introduced for all Hungarians who had taken part in the revolution.

IMPACT ON EUROPEAN SOCIALISM

The Soviet use of force to deny the Hungarians any democratic say in their government shocked many Socialists in Western Europe. They had regarded the USSR as the ideal model for a future society. In the 1960s the Euro-Communist movement moved away from the Soviet model while still promoting Socialism.

It confirmed the Socialist satire of George Orwell. He criticised the Soviet view of Socialism in his book, *Animal Farm*. Clearly, the Soviets were not willing to allow any changes in their satellite states and would crush any threat to their control.

IMPACT ON THE SUPERPOWERS

The failure of the West to help Hungary confirmed the Soviet belief that the Western capitalist democracies would not interfere in Eastern Europe. The Western democracies accepted the unsatisfactory political map of the Cold War. The USA was not prepared to risk a global conflict to liberate Hungary. Relations between East and West in Europe, while critical, remained stable and borders were not changed.

The Hungarian crisis did not delay the move toward détente (negotiation instead of confrontation) after the death of Stalin. Soviet-capitalist relations improved during the late 1950s and the early 1960s.

● Khrushchev and Kádár during Khrushchev's visit to Hungary in April, 1958.

Courtesy: Getty Images

The Hungarian uprising had been a very important event in undermining the Soviet presence in Eastern Europe. The reburial of Nagy in 1989 in Budapest showed the weakness of the Hungarian Communist government, before it finally gave in to pressure and allowed democratic elections.

Source Document

An English view of the uprising

[The Hungarian people were] starved of what everyone must have a little of in the end if he is not to die – bread and liberty ... People for years were ill-fed, ill-clad, ill-housed, over-worked in the cause of headlong industrialisation and Russia's needs ... To judge from yesterday's reports the Budapest rising was the work of 'liberal' Communists, factory workers with Social Democratic traditions, Roman Catholics, the young and ordinary.

A land like Hungary, its frontiers sealed, its communications cut off, its population under martial law with Soviet troops in their midst and over their eastern borders, cannot hope to do other than fail in such a revolution. Yet as we write, shots are still being fired ... The fortunes of Eastern Europe hang by a thread.

Is resistance then useless?

As a way of winning back a decent life it is terribly painful. We dare not recommend it ... but we must salute people who are fighting their way back into Europe – a Europe that knows neither East nor West.

(*The Guardian*, 5 November, 1956)

QUESTIONS ON THE DOCUMENT

1. What did the writer suggest that the Hungarians had been "starved of"?
2. Who took part in the rebellion, according to *The Guardian*?
3. Why did the newspaper writer believe that the rebellion was going to fail?
4. How did the writer praise the Hungarians, even if they were likely to fail?

ROLE OF THE UNITED NATIONS

The events in Hungary showed both the strength and the limitations of the United Nations as an international body, showing that the United Nations could only act effectively if the problem to be settled did not involve a superpower or its allies.

A number of resolutions were passed in the United Nations calling for the USSR to take its troops out of Hungary. They were ignored.

The UN also issued a detailed report in July 1957. This concluded that the uprising was a spontaneous event showing the wish of the Hungarians for liberation. The USA raised the Hungarian issue until 1962 and used their influence to bring about the 1963 amnesty.

IMPACT ON THE USSR IN EASTERN EUROPE, 1956–1989

The Hungarian crisis showed the problem of loyalty that the USSR permanently faced in the satellite states. Clearly, nationalism remained as a powerful force in Eastern Europe.

The Hungarian uprising showed that the satellite states resented the USSR, as well as the determination of the USSR to hold on to its war gains. The failure of the Hungarian uprising guaranteed that the USSR would be the main force in Eastern Europe for the next three decades, and more. It also showed that no major change would take place in Eastern Europe without the consent of the USSR.

Reformers in the satellite states knew that any changes would only emerge from internal reforms, not external intervention from the Western states. The Communist parties in power needed the USSR to ensure their control. Tanks were dispatched to Poland and Hungary in 1956, into Prague in 1968 and once more massed on the Polish borders in 1980.

The threat of massive military retaliation kept Eastern Europe under control, until the USSR decided that it would no longer prop up the Communist governments. The events of the late 1980s convinced the Soviet leadership to remove its iron fist from Eastern Europe.

POSTSCRIPT: HUNGARY DEFEATS THE USSR AT THE 1956 OLYMPICS

The USSR and Hungary faced off during a water-polo match at the 1956 Sydney Olympics. The game descended into violence. Blood flowed in the pool as the teams traded kicks and punches. Hungary won the semi-final. The team went on to win the gold medal, and several members of the team claimed political asylum in Australia.

Source Document

"Ferenc Kocsis", a talented young filmmaker, described his role in the revolution

With 80 other film workers, Ferenc pooled funds and bought some red-white-and-green ribbons to wear as arm bands, and took a bus into Budapest. "At the head of the column were flags," remembers Ferenc. "An old woman waving a pair of scissors ran up. She reached up, grabbed a flag and cut the Red star out of the centre. It was a tremendous moment."

When Ferenc went out to Kilian barracks to get a rifle, he was told that it was more important for him to record what was going on in film. The director of his film company refused to give him a camera and film, but Ferenc broke into the warehouse, and commandeered both. From then on, until 3 November, he and his cameraman recorded the battle. He took pictures everywhere, in the streets, from the cellars, from speeding vehicles. Cursed film. They had 12,000 ft. of film in the can by the beginning of November and sent it to the laboratory, by that time under rebel control, for processing. Some rebel leaders wanted it sent out to the West to be developed, but Ferenc insisted on it being done under his supervision. He curses himself for that decision. On 4 November, the day the Soviet army came charging back into Budapest, one of the first places they captured was the film laboratory.

(*Time*, 7 January 1957)

Commandeered: Took control of.

QUESTIONS ON THE DOCUMENT

1. Why did the workers create a special badge?
2. Kocsis described a "tremendous act" by the old woman. What did the old woman do?
3. Kocsis filmed the events of the Hungarian uprising. What did he hope to achieve by using his filming skills?
4. Why was his film not shown to foreign audiences?
5. Ferenc Kocsis was not the real name of the film maker. Why did *Time* magazine not publish his real name?
6. What evidence is there to suggest that this was an eyewitness account of the Hungarian uprising?

Source Document

"Hungarian Freedom Fighter: Freedom's Choice"

In 1956, the American news magazine, **Time***, acknowledged the impact of the Hungarian uprising by nominating the "Hungarian Freedom Fighter" as its "Man of the Year".*

… the man who put his stamp on this particular year – the Man of the Year – was not on the roster of the world's great when the year began … he gave to millions, and specifically to the youth of Eastern Europe, the hope for an end to the long night of Communist dictatorship.

The Man of the Year had many faces, but he was not faceless; he had many names, but he was not nameless … history would know him by the name he had chosen for himself during his dauntless contest with Soviet tanks: the Hungarian Freedom Fighter.

(The Hungarian Freedom Fighter is one) of those anonymous thousands, many of them dead, who fought for their country's freedom against the most brutal tyranny on earth. Taken together, they epitomise the Hungarian Freedom Fighter, the man who made history leap forward in 1956 – the Man of the Year.

(*Time*, 7 January 1957)

Roster: List.

QUESTIONS ON THE DOCUMENT

1. What is meant by the following words: "he was not faceless … he was not nameless"?
2. Why would an American magazine choose the "Hungarian Freedom Fighter" as its "Man of the Year"?
3. What does this document tell us about the divisions in the Cold War period?
4. What evidence is there in this document to suggest that this was an editorial (or personal) comment by someone who did not take part in the Hungarian uprising?

Source Document

A Russian perspective

The following comment from Pravda, *the main Soviet newspaper, indicated the reasoning behind the Soviet suppression of the Hungarian uprising.*

When everything settles down in Hungary, and life becomes normal again, the Hungarian working class, peasantry and intelligentsia will undoubtedly understand our actions better and judge them aright. We regard the help to the Hungarian working class in its struggle against the intrigues of counter-revolution as our international duty.

(*Pravda*, 23 November 1956, from "United Nations Report of the Special Committee on the Problem of Hungary", January 1957)

QUESTIONS ON THE DOCUMENT

1. What groups in Hungary did the writer believe would eventually accept the need for the Soviet invasion?
2. Why did the writer say that the Soviets had to "help" Hungary?

GENERAL ESSAY QUESTIONS ON CHAPTER 5

1. The Hungarian uprising:
   (a) Why was Imre Nagy such an important figure before1956?
   (b) Why did the uprising start?
   (c) Outline three principle events of the Hungarian uprising.
   (d) Name three important results of the uprising.
2. What trend did the Hungarian uprising show most – the determination of the Soviet government to hold onto its satellite state or the determination of the Hungarians to campaign for independence?

6

MOVES TOWARDS EUROPEAN UNITY, 1945–1992

Words you need to understand

CAP: Common Agricultural Policy.

Collectivism: Acting together as one group.

Common Market: The name given to a free trade area set up in 1958, following the signing of the Treaty of Rome, 1957. The six original members of the EEC agreed to set up a common market, in which goods could be moved from one country to another without the charging of extra taxes.

EEC: European Economic Community.

EU: European Union.

EMU: European Monetary Union.

Federal Europe: With the establishment of the EEC in 1957, a new federal structure was introduced into Europe. While countries held onto their own independence, they co-operated with other countries in allowing a central commission based in Brussels to develop common policies in some areas, such as agriculture, fisheries and transport.

Integration by stealth: Promoting unity without telling people of the eventual aim.

Sovereignty: A country's right to control its own affairs.

Subsidies: Extra payments given to farmers and producers to make it worth their while to produce something that they could not sell unless they had an extra payment.

Supranational bodies: Groups who make decisions that cut across national boundaries.

Tariffs: A tax placed on goods going into one country from another, with the result that the imported product will be more expensive than the home-made product.

Veto: The power to stop a decision being made unless everybody agrees with it.

European Community Timeline

1950	Schuman Plan, proposes economic co-operation between France and Germany
1952	Paris Treaty, setting up the European Coal and Steel Commission
1957	Rome Treaties, setting up the European Economic Community
1985	Single European Act, setting the target of a single market in 'Europe'
1992	Maastricht Treaty, setting up the European Union

Titles for a Community in Europe, 1 January 1958–1992

European Economic Community, 1958–1967

The EEC was made up of three **communities**:

1. EEC (European Economic Community)
2. ECSC (European Coal and Steel Community)
3. Euratom (European Atomic Energy Commission)

European Community, 1967–1992

In 1967 the three communities of the EEC (ECSC, EEC and Euratom) were combined and became known as the European Community.

European Union, 1992, introduced in the Treaty of European Union, 1992

INTRODUCTION

After two world wars, after the years of Fascism and dictatorship and after the horrors of the Holocaust, nationalism for European countries had lost its appeal.

While Eastern Europe was run under the regulations of state Socialism, support for a federal union of democratic countries emerged in Western Europe.

On a continent divided by the Iron Curtain, influential Western European and US leaders supported the European idea. Many leaders in Europe tried to ensure that there would not be a third world war. Neighbours Germany and France had fought three wars in the previous 75 years.

European unity was not an original idea – the Romans, Napoleon and Hitler had tried to create a political unity by using force.

The USA supported the economic integration of Western European countries as a counterbalance to the Soviet dominance of Eastern Europe.

6.1 THE ROAD TO ROME: EUROPEAN INTEGRATION, 1943–1957

EARLY SUPPORT FOR EUROPEAN FEDERATIONS

During the war, a number of federal proposals emerged, suggesting different forms of co-operation between European countries.

Jean Monnet had suggested a political union between the UK and France. A 'European Union of Federalists' was formed in 1943. Winston Churchill, Prime Minister of the UK in 1943, called for a Council of Europe after the war. In 1944, the resistance movements that had fought against the Nazis met in Geneva: they called for a federal state of Europe.

In 1947, John Foster Dulles, the US Secretary of State, warned that Europe "must federate or perish". The Cold War convinced the USA that it had to provide financial aid to Europe and Marshall Aid trickled throughout Western Europe (see p. 22).

In 1948, the **OEEC** (**Organisation for European Economic Co-operation**) co-ordinated the distribution of Marshall Aid. The OEEC showed how difficult it was to agree on international budgets because national governments wanted their own interests looked after first. In 1948, a customs union between Belgium, the Netherlands and Luxembourg came into operation.

An influential meeting also took place at the Hague in 1948. Jacques Delors called it the "birth of a dream", when the "soul of Europe emerged". This **Congress of Europe** was attended by 750 representatives from throughout Western Europe, including Spaak (the Netherlands), de Gasperi (Italy), Churchill (Britain), Schuman (France) and Adenauer (FDR). The Congress supported political and economic union, a new European Assembly and a European Court of Human Rights.

● The first meeting of the Congress of Europe, held in the Hague in May 1948. Note the large E (for Europe) at the left side of the hall.

The federalist ideas eventually led to the creation of the **Council of Europe**. Set up in 1949, it had little power but it promoted the idea of European integration. It met in the city of Strasbourg, on the border of France and Germany, so that it would not be associated with any capital city. It set up a Court of Human Rights, a successful body that continues to adjudicate today.

Alcide de Gasperi (1881–1954): Prime Minister of Italy (1945–1953) who rebuilt Italy after the second World War. With Robert Schuman and Konrad Adenauer, he supported the establishment of the Council of Europe and the European Coal and Steel Community.

According to Paul Reynard, a French politician, "The Council of Europe consists of two bodies, one of them for Europe, the other against it." The Council of Europe was a step in the right direction for the promoters of European integration.

However, the idea of European integration seemed a distant dream after the chaos of war, as countries concentrated on rebuilding within their own areas. George Orwell, the author of *Animal Farm* and *1984,* wrote about the idea of 'European Unity' in 1947. The greatest difficulty, he stated, was the "apathy and conservatism of people everywhere", as well as "their inability to imagine anything new".

Source Document

Winston Churchill's speech on Europe, Zurich, 19 September 1946

This is an edited version of Churchill's speech, where he first spoke about the "tragedy of Europe"

… over wide areas a vast quivering mass of tormented, hungry, care-worn and bewildered human beings gape at the ruins of their cities and their homes, and scan the dark horizons for the approach of some new peril, tyranny or terror.

Yet … there is a remedy which … would … transform the whole scene, and would in a few years make all Europe, or the greater part of it, as free and as happy as Switzerland is today.

What is this … remedy? It is to recreate the European Family … and to provide it with a structure under which it can dwell in peace, in safety and in freedom. We must build a kind of United States of Europe.

I am now going to say something that will astonish you. The first step in the recreation of the European Family must be a partnership between France and Germany.

I must give you a warning. Time may be short. If we are to form the United States of Europe, or whatever name it may take, we must begin now. I say to you: let Europe arise!

(www.eurplace.org/federal/churdisco.html)

QUESTIONS ON THE DOCUMENT

1. How did Churchill describe the "tragedy of Europe"?
2. What remedy did Churchill put forward to make Europe "free" and "happy"?
3. Why did Churchill suggest that France and Germany should co-operate?
4. Churchill wanted to promote but not take part in the process of European integration. Is there any evidence in this speech that Britain would not join many of the new European institutions?

JEAN MONNET, THE 'FOUNDING FATHER' OF THE EUROPEAN IDEAL

The practical, workable idea of European unity came from Jean Monnet. Because of his promotion of European integration after the second World War, he is regarded as the 'founding father' of the European Union.

With the exclusion of the Socialist East, integration would be clearly confined to the capitalist West. Jean Monnet realised that Germany must become France's main partner, "however incredible it may seem". This radical new approach, in his view, "opened the door to the European integration".

Jean Monnet (1888–1979): Monnet is known as the 'founding father' of the European ideal. He convinced political leaders of the benefits of co-operating in international organisations. He was seen to rely on negotiation and consensus, rather than conflict, as the best way to promote European integration.

Courtesy: Hulton-Deutsch/Corbis

DEVELOPING INTERNATIONAL EXPERIENCE

Jean Monnet was born in 1888 in Cognac, France. He was a mild-mannered French wine producer who avoided party politics. On a sales trip to Canada, he asked a stranger in Calgary where he might rent a horse. He was told, "Take my horse. When you're through, just hitch it up here." It was a simple lesson in co-operation.

He soon turned to financial planning. Monnet became Deputy Secretary General in the League of Nations in 1920 and stayed for three years. He believed that the League of Nations would succeed because of its use of "moral force" and by "appealing to public opinion".

He used his international contacts to solve a major problem in his personal life. In 1929, he met and fell in love with an Italian woman. However, she was already married. She could not get a divorce, even in America, so Monnet took her to Moscow in 1934, used his connections to make her a Soviet citizen, arranged her divorce and remarried within days. He brought his new wife back to Paris and he immediately went to China to reorganise the Chinese railways.

HIS WORK DURING AND AFTER THE SECOND WORLD WAR

During the second World War, Monnet worked once more in the area of international economic co-operation. He suggested that the UK and France should unite into one country. In 1943, Monnet said that there would be no peace in Europe "if States re-established themselves on the basis on national sovereignty".

He worked in America on the wartime victory programme. He was so effective that Maynard Keynes, the economist, said that Monnet probably shortened the second Word War by one year because of his skills. He described America as the "arsenal of democracy", a phrase that was later used by the American president, Franklin D. Roosevelt.

After the war, Monnet was put in charge of French economic reconstruction and produced the Monnet Plan in 1947.

HIS IDEAS ON EUROPEAN INTEGRATION

He wrote and spoke constantly about the importance of the idea that he called 'Europe'. This was different from the geographical idea of Europe. Monnet was never a member of a political party. He insisted, "We are not making a coalition of States, but are uniting people."

He worked tirelessly for European integration until his death in 1979. He wrote out the plan for European integration: move forward sector by sector, promote integration and co-operate in economic areas.

He was the brain behind the 1950 **Schuman Plan**, as well as the European Coal and Steel Community (ECSC), of which he was president for three years. Monnet was not interested in the details of economic integration: when trade matters were discussed, he fell asleep or he left the room. "Nothing is possible without men," said Monnet, "nothing is lasting without institutions."

Monnet started with coal and steel, moved (unsuccessfully) to European security, then onto agriculture, nuclear energy, a united market and a common currency. His final aim was political union. He followed a policy of "integration by stealth", without people fully understanding the complete plan in its early years.

He believed that Europe could be united by a series of small steps, if countries agreed to give away small amounts of their independence to central commissions that worked for the good of all. His achievement was formally recognised in 1976, when the European Council made him an "honorary citizen of Europe".

THE SCHUMAN PLAN, 1950: THE FIRST SUCCESSFUL MODEL OF ECONOMIC INTEGRATION

Monnet convinced Robert Schuman, the French Foreign Minister, that peaceful co-operation could achieve major results, even between traditional enemies such as France and Germany.

In 1950 Schuman and Monnet, after consultation with Konrad Adenauer, the West German leader, and the Americans produced the **Schuman Plan**. Adenauer saw the proposed co-operation

Robert Schuman (1886–1963): Born in Alsace when it was German territory, he fought in the German army during the first World War. When France reclaimed Alsace in 1918, he became a French citizen. He was elected as Prime Minister in 1947 and acted as Foreign Minister between 1948 and 1953. He put forward the Schuman Plan that set up the ECSC. He supported Jean Monnet's economic ideas for closer economic co-operation between European nations.

Courtesy: Hulton-Deutsch/Corbis

between France and Germany as a way to bring his country back into the international community.

The Schuman Plan was negotiated in great secrecy. The United Kingdom, for instance, was only given a few hours' notice of its publication. A new **supranational** body was to be set up to control the production of coal and steel in France and Germany.

"IT'S JUST A QUESTION OF MAKING AN 'ARRANGEMENT' TO FIT THE BAND"

SCHUMAN SYMPHONY

Courtesy: The Centre for the Study of Cartoons and Caricature

- Schuman (France) conducts Adenauer (West Germany) and Bevin (Britain). The cartoonist shows Bevin trying to play a saxophone while holding two babies ("Socialist Planning" and "Commonwealth").
  1. What details suggest that Schuman and Adenauer co-operate with each other?
  2. How does the cartoonist suggest that Britain has difficulties co-operating with France and Germany?

Source Document

How Jean Monnet tried to persuade people

I put forward ideas: if they were accepted, so much the better. (I) always followed the rule of doing only one thing at a time … People knew that I wanted nothing for myself, and that I was not looking for a job. My efforts were not always successful, and they rarely succeeded at the first attempt. I was satisfied if there was a chance of succeeding.

Since I did not bother the politicians, I could count on their support. When they are short of ideas, they are glad to accept yours, so long as they can claim the credit. Since the risks are theirs, they need the laurels. In my work, one has to forget about laurels. Whatever others may say about it, I have no liking for the shade … (but) I choose the shade.

(Jean Monnet, *Memoirs*, London 1978)

Laurels: Praise.

QUESTIONS ON THE DOCUMENT

1. Monnet regarded himself as an 'ideas' man. What do you understand by this statement?
2. Monnet did not worry if his efforts did not succeed. What satisfaction did he get from his work?
3. How did Monnet try to get the support of politicians?
4. Monnet states that he "chose the shade". What did he mean by this?

Source Document

Jean Monnet on the Schuman Declaration

The Schuman proposals are revolutionary or they are nothing. The … first principle of these proposals is the abnegation of sovereignty in a limited but decisive field. A plan which is not based on this principle can make no useful contribution to the solution of the major problems which undermine our existence.

(Jean Monnet, *Memoirs*, London 1978)

Abnegation: Surrender.

QUESTION ON THE DOCUMENT

1. What reason does Monnet give for saying the Schuman proposals are "revolutionary or they are nothing"?

Source Document

The Schuman Declaration, 9 May 1950

Europe will not be made all at once, or according to a single plan. It will be built through concrete achievements.

The coming together of the nations of Europe requires the elimination of the age-old opposition of France and Germany.

With this aim in view, the French government proposes that action be taken immediately on one limited but decisive point. It proposes that Franco-German production of coal and steel as a whole be placed under a common High Authority, within the framework of an organisation open to the participation of the other countries of Europe.

The pooling of coal and steel production should immediately provide for the setting up of common foundations for economic development as a first step in the federation of Europe.

(The English translation (above) of the Schuman Declaration is found at http://europa.eu.int/comm/publications/booklets/eu_documentation/04/txt06_en.htm#FAC)

QUESTIONS ON THE DOCUMENT

1. Which course does the Schuman Declaration favour, a "single plan" or a series of "concrete achievements"?
2. The French government wanted to concentrate on "one limited but decisive point" to improve relations between France and Germany. What solution did it offer?
3. According to Schuman, how would the new body improve life in Europe?

THE EUROPEAN COAL AND STEEL COMMUNITY, 1952

The Treaty of Paris, signed on 18 April 1951, formally set up the European Coal and Steel Community (ECSC). The ECSC began its work in August 1952.

Belgium, Luxembourg and the Netherlands (known as the Benelux countries) and Italy also joined France and Germany in the ECSC. This core group of six countries would drive the move towards the Common Market.

Jean Monnet understood the political importance of the ECSC – it was an essential step towards a broader united Europe: "Our Community is not a coal and steel producers' association – it is the beginning of Europe."

The ECSC encouraged industrial growth and removed tariffs on coal and steel. Over the next five years, the production of steel increased by 42 per cent. The ECSC project was an economic success.

The ECSC succeeded because leaders in positions of authority accepted the new structures. It became the model for later, more successful European projects. The ECSC included a council of ministers, a civil service, an assembly of national parliamentary representatives and a Court of Justice, all based in Luxembourg.

• A Welsh steel mill of the 1950s, showing the vastness of production. Britain did not join the ECSC. Note the woman working in the foreground.

Courtesy: Hulton-Deutsch/Corbis

MONNET'S FAILURE: THE CAMPAIGN FOR A SINGLE EUROPEAN ARMY

Monnet's idea of European integration included the formation of a new European army. In a new European Defence Community (EDC), German soldiers would join a new European army. Germany had not been allowed to have an army after 1945 and was also not allowed to join NATO. However, popular fears in France about a rearmed Germany defeated the proposal.

It was one of the few failures associated with Monnet's promotion of European integration. Security and defence matters would stay at the bottom of the list of priorities for those supporting European integration.

THE TREATY OF ROME CREATES A COMMON MARKET, 1957

The success of the ECSC experiment encouraged further economic expansion. In 1955, at a conference in Messina, Sicily, the ECSC countries decided to expand the ECSC model and to create a 'common market' area.

In 1956, the ECSC countries decided to use the ECSC's **supranational** model, with countries surrendering some of their authority to a central commission.

Once again, the United Kingdom and the Northern European countries were not willing to join. A community was possible without the UK, but it was not possible without France or Germany.

The Treaty of Rome was signed in March 1957, setting up the European Economic Community. A separate treaty set up **Euratom** (European Atomic Energy Commission) to promote the non-military use of nuclear power.

Courtesy: The Centre for the Study of Cartoons and Caricature

• **French salute.** A French soldier stands on the podium as a European army (composed of different countries) marches by. How does the cartoonist show French opposition to a European army?

● West German Foreign Minister and Chancellor Konrad Adenauer (centre) signing the treaty setting up the European Economic Community, March 1957, in Rome.

The new treaties spoke of the need to "lay the foundation of an ever closer union among the peoples of Europe".

The new EEC began its operation in January 1958. It promoted four basic freedoms: the free movement of people, goods, services and capital. It set up a customs union and placed common external taxes for the movement of goods between member countries.

Things did not happen immediately, in line with Monnet's belief in the gradual growth of the community. A **European Assembly** was formed in 1958. Robert Schuman was elected as its first president. This later became known as the **European Parliament**. Robert Schuman's important role in supporting the European Union is celebrated annually on 9 May.

The Treaty of Rome showed the major progress made since 1945. Not all Western countries were in favour of it. The UK was concerned about the power of the new EEC and did not join. It formed EFTA (European Free Trade Association) with Denmark, Austria, Norway, Sweden, Switzerland and Portugal. The setting up of EFTA coined the joke that Europe was at sixes and sevens.

QUESTIONS

1. Why was the Hague meeting of 1948 important?
2. What new path was followed by the new leaders in Western Europe after the second World War?
3. What lesson in co-operation did Monnet learn in Canada?
4. How did Monnet's idea of European integration differ from the 'geographical' idea of Europe?
5. Indicate one economic success of the ECSC.
6. Why did the idea of a European army prove to be unpopular?
7. Name the four freedoms encouraged by the European Economic Community.

6.2   FROM ROME TO MAASTRICHT: THE EVOLUTION OF THE EUROPEAN ECONOMIC COMMUNITY, 1957–1992

From 1957 until the mid-1980s, little progress was made on the idea of European integration. The biggest difficulty came from the slow pace of reform within the EEC during the 1960s and the 1970s. When Jacques Delors became president of the European Commission in 1985, major reforms were introduced by the **Single European Act** (1986) and the **Treaty on European Union** (1992), also known as the Maastricht Treaty.

PROBLEMS DURING THE 1960S AND THE 1970S

France, under President de Gaulle, would not allow the expansion of the community. When de Gaulle resigned in 1969, the new French president, Georges Pompidou, supported the expansion of the community.

The economic difficulties of the 1970s meant that countries were more concerned about their own affairs than those of the community. The Oil Crisis of 1973 (see chapter 10) slowed down the move towards integration, with countries eager to protect their home markets.

THE COMMON AGRICULTURAL POLICY (CAP)

The EEC placed great stress on agriculture. **The Common Agricultural Policy** (CAP) set out to produce more food in Europe, to create a large market and to guarantee prices to the producers. It also tried to lessen food imports, to keep farmers on the land, to give them a steady income and to modernise agriculture.

The CAP system (finalised in 1962) protected European farmers against non-EEC imports. It made imports more expensive than food produced within the community.

AFTER THE BALL WAS OVER ...

Courtesy: The Centre for the Study of Cartoons and Caricature

• Harold Macmillan (British Prime Minister) sits in a chair, surrounded by pro-French slogans.
1. Identify the flags in the background.
2. Why is Macmillan unhappy?

In the mid-1980s, the CAP payments and subsidies took up over 60 per cent of the EEC budget. Countries such as France strongly opposed any major reform of the system, as it was of great advantage to its farmers.

By guaranteeing fixed prices, the CAP system led to unwanted surpluses (such as 'wine lakes' and 'butter mountains'). In 1991, the EU had to store 450,000 tons of beef and 600,000 tons of dairy produce. The CAP system was reformed during the 1980s. Farmers were to be paid lower prices, but they were also given other income supports.

ENLARGEMENT OF THE EUROPEAN COMMUNITY – FROM SIX TO 12

After its creation with six members in 1957, the community took in new members on four occasions between 1957 and 1990. The original nations in 1957 were France, Germany, Italy, Belgium, the Netherlands and Luxembourg.

The United Kingdom applied three times for membership of the EEC, starting in 1961. The French president, General de Gaulle, twice refused to let the UK in.

The United Kingdom, Ireland and Denmark joined in 1973, Greece in 1981, Spain and Portugal in 1986.

Spain, Portugal and Greece were allowed to join after the end of military dictatorships in their countries. East Germany joined the EEC in 1990 after the reunification of Germany.

Courtesy: Getty Images

• Jean Monnet was featured on the cover of *Time* magazine on 6 October 1961.
1. How is Monnet linked with developments in "Europe"?
2. The Union Jack is one of the featured flags. Why was it unusual to link the UK with the Common Market?

Courtesy: Corbis

● The 12 stars of the European Union flag.

SYMBOLS OF THE NEW EUROPE

The design of 12 gold stars against a blue background was agreed in 1985. Even the enlargement of the Union after 1992 did not change the number of stars on the flag. A European Union anthem (Beethoven's "Ode to Joy") and a common format for a Burgundy-coloured **European passport** were also introduced.

The role of sport in building a European identity was shown by the success of the Ryder Cup, a golf trophy contested between golfers from the USA and Europe after 1979.

A COMMUNITY WITHOUT INTERNAL FRONTIERS

The idea of *Europe without Borders* became a reality in 1985. The Benelux countries, France and Germany signed the **Schengen Agreement**. This removed customs barriers at their national frontiers. However, the pressures from illegal immigration, fear of terrorism and drug smuggling delayed the dismantling of national borders throughout the rest of the community.

Source Document

The leaders of the EEC countries did not always agree on the idea of Europe. These two documents show the different approaches of the leaders of France and the United Kingdom.

Helmut Schmidt, Chancellor of the Federal Republic of Germany from 1974 to 1982, explains why he supported the idea of European integration

European integration struck me as necessary, less for economic than political reasons. After the disastrous wars of the past 100 years, in which Germany had played a key role … I believed it desirable to bind my country into a greater European entity to prevent the recurrence of such conflict.

I became a proponent of the French political economist Jean Monnet's step-by-step approach that would tie France as well as Germany into the European Economic Community.

(Helmut Schmidt, "Miles to Go: From American Plan to European Union", *Foreign Affairs*, May/June 1997)

QUESTIONS ON THE DOCUMENT

1. Why did Schmidt support European unity?
2. What part of Jean Monnet's ideas appealed to Schmidt?

Source Document

Margaret Thatcher was Prime Minister of the United Kingdom from 1979 to 1990

Speaking at the College of Europe in Bruges (Belgium) on 20 September 1988, she criticised the trend towards centralising power in Brussels, the capital of the European Community

To concentrate power at the centre of a European conglomerate would be highly damaging. We certainly do not need new regulations which raise the cost of employment and make Europe's labour market less flexible and less competitive with overseas suppliers.

And certainly we in Britain would fight attempts to introduce collectivism at the European level – although what people wish to do in their own countries is a matter for them.

(www.historiasiglo20.org/europe/acta.htm)

QUESTIONS ON THE DOCUMENT

1. Why did Thatcher oppose the concentration of power at the centre of Europe?
2. How would the British people react to the introduction of "collectivism at the European level"?

THE EUROPEAN PARLIAMENT: A DEMOCRATIC VOICE FOR REFORM

In 1962 the EEC Assembly was renamed the European Parliament. Direct elections to the European Parliament began in 1979. The European Parliament kept alive the debate about reforming the EEC and published a **Draft Treaty on European Union** in 1984.

THE HOUSE THAT JACQUES BUILT: EUROPEAN INTEGRATION, 1985–1992

1. Jacques Delors

Jacques Delors, president of the European Commission from 1985 to 1995, set out to revitalise the EEC and to make it more competitive in world markets. He took a long-term view on the needs of the EEC and introduced major reforms. He became the most important president of the European Union, although he did not achieve all of his aims.

He was elected to the European Parliament as a Socialist candidate in 1979.

In 1985, French president Mitterrand sent him to the EEC to represent France as president of the European Commission.

Delors had a keen sense of history and wanted to unite "Europe behind its common values". He promoted a unified European approach to any problems. He believed that community-wide changes could eventually lead to political union.

He said that Europeans would not fall in love with a "common market". He provided that "something else", the **Single European Act** (1986) and the important **Maastricht Treaty**, signed in 1992.

Jacques Delors (1925–): President of the European Commission from 1985 to 1994, he was the main mover behind the idea of the single market and he also promoted the single currency. Between 1981 and 1985, he was French Finance Minister before he started his term as president of the Commission of the European Union.

Courtesy: Corbis

He improved the EEC and laid the foundations for a new currency (the euro). When his presidency ended in 1995, the structure of the EEC had changed – it had all the appearance of a state, but it was not a state

2. The Single European Act (1986)

The Single European Act (SEA) marked the first major change since the 1957 Treaty of Rome. Governments were prepared to give more power to the central authority.

It laid down a final date of 1992 for a single, or common, market throughout the EEC. Delors called this "the great market without frontiers". After 1992, countries could not set up national trading barriers or give subsidies to local industries.

Until 1986, single countries could veto (block) any proposals that they disagreed with. Under the SEA, a new way of majority voting was introduced. It helped to speed up decision making within the EEC.

The powers of the European Parliament were increased.

Source Document

Europe on the eve of the Maastricht Treaty

Statement on the European Community and German reunification by the Federal Chancellor, Helmut Kohl, Brussels, March 1990

We Germans now have the chance to find ourselves back in a newly unified Germany … because our compatriots in the GDR have found the road to freedom in what was without doubt the most peaceful revolution in history.

Konrad Adenauer rightly said, 35 years ago, "German unity is only possible under a European roof."

We do not want a Fourth Reich. We do not want to run over anyone. We will not act like a bull in a china shop. I want to say exactly what I feel and what is felt by many of my compatriots, including those in the GDR. We want to be European Germans and German Europeans. And to achieve this we need the help of our friends in the Community and in the Commission.

(European Document Series, No. 23, Spring 2000)

Compatriots: Fellow countrymen.
GDR: East Germany.
Reich: A German empire.

QUESTIONS ON THE DOCUMENT

1. Why did Helmut Kohl believe that Germans could form a "newly unified Germany"?
2. What link did Konrad Adenauer (a former chancellor of West Germany) make between European unity and German unity?
3. How did Kohl address the fears of other Europeans that a unified Germany might be too powerful?

3. The Treaty on European Union: the Community becomes the Union

The **Treaty on European Union** (TEU) became known as the Maastricht Treaty because it was signed in the Dutch town of Maastricht.

The TEU revised three existing treaties (Paris in 1952, Rome in 1957 and the SEA in 1986). The EEC would now be called the EU (or European Union). It dealt with more than economic issues.

The Treaty, according to Article 2, marked "a new stage in the process of creating an ever closer union among the peoples of Europe." It also introduced the idea of a "citizenship of the Union".

The creators of TEU concentrated on three main areas, called **pillars**, as follows:

Courtesy: Corbis Sygma

i) Economic and social aspects:

The new institutions would be more democratic and have more responsibilities. A single currency would be regulated by a new Central Bank, and countries would agree to co-ordinate economic activities.

● A French parliamentary assembly debates the Maastricht Treaty in 1992.

ii) A common foreign and security policy:

The new EU would promote its identity in international affairs. It was hoped that countries would follow a common foreign and security policy and eventually agree on a common defence policy for the EU area.

iii) Co-operation on home affairs and justice:

The TEU looked for closer co-operation between countries on immigration policy, fighting international crime, drug smuggling and the free movement of people across internal frontiers.

The TEU introduced a Cohesion Fund to help less-developed regions, such as Spain, Portugal and Ireland. However, the CAP policy continued to use over half of the EU's finances, slowing changes in other areas.

The Maastricht Treaty promoted **EMU** (**European Monetary Union**) – the creation of a 'common' currency. Local currencies, such as the Irish pound or the French franc, would be replaced by a single currency known as the 'euro'.

Courtesy: Corbis

The Maastricht Treaty set 1999 as the deadline for the common European currency.

It introduced the idea of **subsidiarity**: decisions should be made in Brussels only if it is better to do so than at local level.

● Spanish demonstrators in 1992 during an anti-Maastricht march; the banner says that they are "against the death of Spain".

The single market came into being on 1 January 1993, marking the first major move towards economic and political integration in Europe.

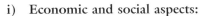

QUESTION

1. Why are these protestors against the Maastricht Treaty?

4. Assessment of the Maastricht Treaty

The TEU was a triumph for Delors in the short term, but he was unable to guarantee its implementation because of the economic difficulties of the time.

• In France, extreme right-wing leader Jean Marie Le Pen (of the National Front Party) stands in front of a large curtain, with the word 'NON' (French for 'no'). His party was against European integration.

However, the TEU was the most ambitious European project. While economic reform was acceptable to most European leaders, it was more difficult to drive forward the political and defence parts of the TEU.

The continuing debate over European unity

European integration was an unfinished project in 1992. The emergence of democratic countries in Eastern Europe after the collapse of Communist governments gave a new impetus to the ideal of economic unity.

Monnet's notion of "integration by stealth" no longer worked. The expansion of the EEC and the need for greater openness and democracy meant that the promoters of European unity had to work openly rather than behind the scenes.

The Maastricht Treaty did not finish the debate on the development of the EU. In the words of Helmut Schmidt, former chancellor of West Germany, writing in 1997, "The European Union still has far to go."

Helmut Schmidt (1918–): West German statesman and chancellor (1974–1982), he was Minister of Finance (1972–1974) and created a firm basis for Germany's continued economic growth. As chancellor, he described his aim as the "political unification of Europe in partnership with the United States".

CONCLUSION

The founding fathers of the European ideal would have been satisfied with the progress of the new Europe less than 50 years after the second World War.

The process of unity was not reversed during the period. Those who opposed one European experiment were called **eurosceptics**. The Danish people, for instance, were given a special 'opt-out clause' on the common currency because of local concerns.

Critics of European integration said that countries were losing their national identity and their independence to write their own laws. Countries might accept regulations about food (good standards, etc.), but were less inclined to change their defence policies, to support a common foreign policy or to agree to a single currency.

The difficulty of member countries acting as one in foreign affairs was shown by the conflict in former Yugoslavia (Croatia, Bosnia, Kosovo). Intervention by the USA and NATO countries brought the dispute to an end, where the EU was simply ineffective.

The voluntary sharing of sovereignty by nation-states since 1945 had brought the EU into the life of ordinary people. The gradual manner of the integration process also ensured that the European experiment was unfinished in 1992.

European integration brought peace and prosperity to the EU. No wars have been fought between member countries since 1945 – when Europe was on the verge of total collapse.

QUESTIONS

1. Why did the CAP system take up so much EEC money?
2. What major change did Delors try to introduce in the Single European Act?
3. Why is one treaty of the European Union known as the Maastricht Treaty?
4. Name three things that the TEU (Treaty on European Union) set out to do.
5. Suggest two reasons why the movement for European unity was successful.
6. Give one indication of opposition to the idea of European integration.

GENERAL ESSAY QUESTIONS ON CHAPTER 6

1. Jean Monnet was called the 'founding father' of European integration. Write a brief description of his achievements under the following headings:
   (a) His ideas on European unity.
   (b) His role in the Schuman Plan and the ECSC.
   (c) His failure to introduce a European army.
   (d) A brief assessment of his success in promoting European unity.

2. Jacques Delors introduced two major reforms, the Single European Act and the Treaty on European Union (known as the Maastricht Treaty). Write a brief description of his achievements under the following headings:
   (a) The Single European Act.
   (b) The Treaty on European Union.
   (c) A brief assessment of his work as president of the European Commission (was he successful?).

3. "The experience of the war convinced many Europeans that unity was more desirable than conflict, and that European structures would have to be set up to promote unity." How true is this statement for the period 1945 to 1957?

4. "Despite many obstacles, the promoters of European Union could claim that the progress towards integration had been very successful by 1992." Discuss this in relation to the period 1957 to 1992.

7

FRAGMENTATION AND REALIGNMENT IN EUROPE

Words you need to understand

Realignment: To leave one group in favour of another. In this chapter, used to describe states changing from a Communist system to democracy.

Privatisation: To place factories, businesses and farms in the hands of private owners.

HSWP: The Hungarian Socialist Workers' Party, i.e. the ruling party in Communist Hungary.

Abgrenzung: The policy adopted by Erich Honecker in East Germany claiming that East and West Germany were completely different states economically, socially and culturally.

Velvet Revolution: The move from Communism to democracy in Czechoslovakia – so-called because of the smooth, bloodless manner by which it took place.

INTRODUCTION

In this chapter we will look at the collapse of Communism in the Eastern bloc states and how they fared in the wake of that collapse up to the end of 1992.

INTERNATIONAL REALIGNMENT

One of the major outcomes of the collapse of Communism was the break-up of the Warsaw Pact, which was formed in 1955 and dominated by the Soviet Union. In November 1990, NATO and Warsaw Pact leaders met in Paris and signed a treaty which introduced a "new era of democracy, peace and unity in Europe". In February 1991 in Budapest, the member states of the Warsaw Pact agreed to dissolve the organisation on 31 March 1991. The economic alliance which had tied these states together, Comecon, was dissolved in June 1991.

ECONOMIC REALIGNMENT

The new governments of Eastern Europe now embraced a **market economy**. In other words, they proceeded to dismantle the state control of the economy and to take on a policy of **privatisation**. Under Socialism these economies had gone into serious decline and they now turned to international financial institutions for help. These institutions set down conditions accompanying financial loans. The new governments would have to rigidly control their spending and bring to an end the practice of funding businesses or factories that were not making a profit.

POLITICAL REALIGNMENT

This meant an end to totalitarianism. The leading role of the Communist Party in Eastern Europe was over. Multi-party systems, open elections, freedom of the press and democratic parliaments emerged. It also meant that the use of secret police units was severely restricted or simply abolished. The first state to experience this process was Poland.

7.1 POLAND

As we have seen in Chapter 3, the Solidarity crisis presented a serious challenge to the ruling Communist Party of Poland, the PUWP. Faced with Brezhnev's threat of Soviet intervention, General Jaruzelski established martial law in 1981. The PUWP was still in place, but the fact that it had to rely on military rule to remain in control was a sign of its weakening power.

Source Document: A

Extract from a telegram from Brezhnev to Jaruzelski on 21 November 1981

The anti-Socialist forces not only are gaining sway in many large industrial enterprises, but are also continuing to spread their influence among even wider segments of the population [...] The direct consequences of this hostile activity is the dangerous growth of anti-Sovietism in Poland.

Source Document: B

A Polish priest challenges the State

Fr Jerzy Popieluszko organised a series of "patriotic masses" between 1982 and 1984, after the declaration of martial law. State policemen murdered him on 19 October 1984 and over 300,000 people attended his funeral.

One Sunday a group of miners travelled several hours to Warsaw to hear his sermon. He said openly what they really felt but could not say. "You will rise again after any humiliation for you have knelt only before God. Solidarity means remaining internally free, even in conditions of slavery."

(G. Sikorski, *Jerzy Popieluszko*, London, 1999, p. 34)

QUESTIONS ON THE DOCUMENTS

1. To whom is Brezhnev referring in the phrase "the anti-Socialist forces" in Document A?
2. In Document B, why did the miners travel to hear Fr Popieluszko speak during this Sunday mass?

Courtesy: Getty Images

● Lech Walesa with shipyard workers after his release from prison in 1982.

● 1988 – coal miners down tools in Gdansk shipyard.

Courtesy: Corbis

MARTIAL LAW ENDED

In an attempt to improve relations with workers, Jaruzelski's government released Lech Walesa from prison in 1982. The following year martial law was ended. Opposition and unrest continued, however, largely because of the poor state of the economy.

ECONOMIC DIFFICULTIES

By 1987 the Polish economy had shown no significant signs of improvement. The reliance on foreign borrowing continued to grow, from $26.3 billion in 1983 to $39.2 billion in 1987. In 1988 food prices increased by nearly 40 per cent and this sparked a new wave of protests and strikes, once more led by Solidarity.

THE REVIVAL OF SOLIDARITY

The ban on Solidarity did not make it go away. It simply operated secretly. By the summer of 1986 it was still producing newspapers and periodicals and **Radio Solidarity** was widely listened to. The strikes of 1988 reached a crisis point in August when coal miners downed tools in protest at rising prices. Faced with widespread opposition Jaruzelski decided to enter into negotiations with the discontented workers throughout the country.

THE ANTI-CRISIS PACT

The result of these negotiations was the **Anti-Crisis Pact** between the government and Walesa and his followers. On 6 February 1989 roundtable negotiations began between the two sides. By 6 April the following agreement was reached.

■ Solidarity was once more recognised as a legal organisation.

■ The trade unions would support the government's reform package, both economic and political.

■ A general election would be held in the summer with 35 per cent of the seats in the parliament's lower house being openly contested by both sides; the other 65 per cent were reserved for the PUWP.

■ All of the seats in the Senate, or upper house, would be openly contested.

■ The Roman Catholic Church was made legal.

The PUWP believed that it could hold on to its position of power by conceding reforms from the top. The Party had no idea that this pact was setting in motion a series of events that would bring Communism down in Poland.

ELECTION RESULTS

The elections were held in June and produced startling results. Solidarity won 92 of the 100 seats in the Senate. Of the 161 seats that were openly contested in the lower house, Solidarity won 160. In July Jaruzelski was elected to the presidency. He was supported by Solidarity because Walesa did not want to cause panic in the army or bring about Soviet intervention.

A NEW GOVERNMENT

On 20 August a new administration was formed with Tadeusz Mazowiecki, a Solidarity member, as Prime Minister. By the end of 1989 this broadly based government had made the following sweeping changes:

■ The leading role of the PUWP was removed from the constitution.

■ Poland ceased to be a People's Republic and was renamed The Republic of Poland.

■   The existing police force, the Citizen's Militia, became a regular police force.

■   Henceforth the army would have no political leaning.

At the end of January 1990 the PUWP dissolved itself and re-emerged as the **Social Democratic Party**. The Communist system in Poland simply folded.

NO SOVIET INTERVENTION

One of the most notable aspects of this momentous event was the Soviet Union's refusal to intervene. Gorbachev had decided that the Soviet Union would no longer impose its will on its Eastern bloc satellite states. Within 12 months of the collapse of Polish Communism, the other Communist states would follow suit.

ECONOMIC CHANGE

On 1 January 1990, Poland's Finance Minister adopted a policy of "shock therapy" for the country:

■   Most of the state's price controls on goods were lifted.

■   State subsidies to enterprises were severely cut back.

■   In July 1990 nearly 7,600 state enterprises were put up for sale to private bidders.

This was a radical policy and had the immediate effect of driving prices up in some cases by as much as 500 per cent. In 1992 inflation fell to 43 per cent and then to 20 per cent in 1995. It also caused an initial rise in unemployment, which reached 12 per cent in 1991. However, in March 1991 America wrote off over 70 per cent of the $3 billion owed to it by Poland, and 17 other countries agreed to remove 50 per cent of Poland's debt to them. Poland had adopted capitalism and by 1996 talk of Poland joining the European Union had begun.

POLITICAL CHANGE

In the summer of 1990 Solidarity split into two factions, the **Democratic Union Party** led by Mazowiecki and a **Citizens' Central Alliance** led by Walesa. These two opposed each other for the presidency, which was vacated by Jaruzelski in November 1990. Walesa became president of the Republic of Poland in December 1990. A general election followed in October 1991 based on proportional representation. No fewer than 67 political parties took part. In the coalition government that followed, Jan Olszewski of the Central Alliance became Prime Minister. In July 1992 he was replaced by a female Prime Minister, Hanna Suchocka. There remained within the Polish parliament a substantial number of the old Communist guard, but they never threatened to overthrow the new democratic system.

Courtesy: Corbis Sygma

● Hanna Suchocka, who became Prime Minister of Poland in July 1992.

QUESTIONS

1.   What two steps did Jaruzelski take in the early 1980s in order to improve relations with workers?

2.   What evidence is there that the Polish economy was doing badly by the mid-1980s?

3.   List five points of agreement arrived at as a result of the roundtable negotiations in February 1989.

4.   Briefly describe the economic "shock therapy" introduced in January 1990. How did it differ from the Socialist economic system?

5.   What effect did Gorbachev's non-intervention policy have on the fall of Socialism in Poland?

7.2 HUNGARY

From the suppression of the Hungarian uprising to the early 1980s Hungary had survived quite well under the leadership of János Kádár. The period was dominated by economic issues. Up to the mid-1970s the country enjoyed reasonable prosperity and as a result economic reform was limited. A downturn in the economy in the late 1970s changed that policy. By 1979 Hungary's foreign debt stood at $9 billion and growing. The following year saw the 12th Congress of the Hungarian Socialist Workers' Party (HSWP) agree to encourage a greater degree of privatisation. As a result small private businesses emerged. Since the Soviet invasion of 1956, political dissent remained muted, but the introduction of economic reform brought a new call for political reform.

POLITICAL DISSENT

By the end of 1981 democratic opposition to Communist rule was publishing a regular journal, *Beszelo*, which called for substantial political reform. The HSWP responded in 1983 by making multi-candidate elections compulsory. Some of these candidates were independent of the Party, but their nominations had to be sanctioned by the Party. It was a small concession, but one that proved that reform was possible.

THE FORMATION OF OPPOSITION PARTIES

By 1987 the economy was performing badly and living standards were stagnant. This raised the voices of democratic opposition and *Beszelo* began to demand a multi-party political system. In September of that year the first opposition party, the Hungarian Democratic Forum, was formed. The following March saw a second opposition party, the Alliance of Young Democrats, emerge. The HSWP called a special Party conference in May 1988. Here, Kádár was removed from his position of First Secretary and replaced by Karoly Grosz. The old guard of the HSWP had to give way to a young, pro-reform generation of Communists. This development spurred the democratic opposition and the Smallholders' Party re-emerged in November 1988, followed by the return of Hungary's Social Democratic Party in January 1989. In March all of these opposition parties formed a loose association called the Opposition Round Table. The HSWP agreed to meet with them in September 1989.

THE EMERGENCE OF DEMOCRACY

Following the September talks the following momentous changes took place:

- The leading role of the Communist Party in Hungarian politics came to an end.
- Hungary was formally declared a republic instead of a People's Republic.
- The HSWP changed its name to the Hungarian Socialist Party.
- From now on elections would be democratically based.

A DEMOCRATIC GOVERNMENT

Elections to the new parliament took place in March and April 1990. The Hungarian Democratic Forum emerged as the largest party, led by **Jozsef Antall**. He formed a coalition government with the Smallholders' Party and another new party, the Christian Democrats. This coalition lasted in government until 1994. On 3 August, **Arpad Goncz** became president of the new Hungarian Republic. The new government survived a wave of strike action by lorry and taxi drivers in October 1990, but had to climb down on a proposed petrol price increase of 60 per cent.

MORE REFORMS

In June 1991 the democratic government passed a Compensation Law for all those who had lost land and property to the state since 1948. In July, Churches were allowed to reclaim any properties taken over by the state during the Communist regime. The move towards privatisation continued and by the end of 1990 the government had announced that 20 leading state-owned companies would be offered to private bidders. Overall, reforms emerged slowly as the Antall-led government adopted a conservative approach to change. This conservatism undoubtedly contributed to the defeat of Antall's government in 1994 and its replacement by another democratic coalition.

• Private second-hand car market in an Hungarian suburb, 1987.

QUESTIONS

1. What was *Beszelo*?
2. What reform did the HSWP make in 1983?
3. In your opinion, why was Kádár removed as First Secretary in May 1988?
4. List four enormous changes that took place following the roundtable talks in September 1989.
5. Describe three reforms of the new democratic government in 1991.

7.3   THE GERMAN DEMOCRATIC REPUBLIC AND WEST GERMANY

From the foundation of the German Democratic Republic (GDR) in the summer of 1949 it struggled with the problem of being recognised internationally as a separate nation. The attitude of the Federal Republic of Germany (West Germany) was that there were two German states, and these were part of one German nation. The attitude of **Walter Ulbricht** was that East Germany should be recognised as a separate entity. The Berlin Wall, built in 1961, became a concrete symbol of that separateness.

RECOGNITION ACHIEVED

The process of recognition was accelerated when Ulbricht was replaced as First Secretary of the SED by **Erich Honecker** in May 1971. Ulbricht had always stated that the goal of East Germany was to make West Germany Socialist. When Honecker came to office he dropped that objective and adopted a policy of *Abgrenzung*, i.e. separate development. In other words, the Communist idea that Germany would one day be reunited as a Socialist country was set aside. There were now two German nations, each with its own cultural and historical identity. The dropping of Socialist designs on West Germany paved the way for the following developments:

• Erich Honecker (German).

■ The Basic Treaty between the two countries was signed in December 1972, by which they agreed to recognise each other's sovereignty.

■ In September 1973 both countries joined the United Nations.

■ In April 1974 East Germany set up diplomatic relations with America.

This formal recognition of the GDR as a separate nation made the possibility of the reunification of Germany all the more remote. However, as in the other Eastern bloc states, a failing economy would have profound effects.

ECONOMIC DIFFICULTIES

Throughout the history of Comecon, the GDR's economy remained strongest. From the mid-1970s the economy suffered a downturn which resulted in major foreign debt. In 1977 that debt was $6.6 billion, but by 1981 was nearly $12 billion. This pattern continued into the 1980s as economic growth slowed to 5.2 per cent in 1985, to 3.3 per cent in 1987 to 2.1 per cent in 1989. While East Germans enjoyed a higher standard of living than their Eastern bloc allies, they tended to gauge their standard by that of West Germany. It was all too clear to East Germans that they were worse off. For decades this discrepancy had motivated East Germans to seek refuge in the West.

EAST GERMAN EXODUS

On 3 August 1989 Hungary announced that it would accept East German migrants. On 11 September 1989 Hungary opened its border with Austria and allowed over 125,000 East Germans access to Western Europe. This drift from the country was an embarrassment for Honecker. On the other hand, it was a boost to the growing voice of popular discontent in East Germany.

Courtesy: Corbis

• One of the Monday meetings in Leipzig, organised by Neues Forum to protest against the Communist government in East Germany.

DISSENT TAKES SHAPE

On 11 September 1989 **Neues Forum**, a group of intellectuals opposed to the Communist system, was formed. This gave rise to organised protest meetings throughout East Germany. At one such meeting in Leipzig at the end of September the police attacked demonstrators. From then on a meeting was held every Monday in Leipzig, drawing ever larger crowds each week.

THE REMOVAL OF HONECKER

The SED planned to mark the 40th anniversary of the East German state with suitable celebrations. Honecker criticised Gorbachev's reform programme in the Soviet Union as a sign of weakness. Earlier in the year Honecker praised the Chinese government for its ruthless handling of student protests in Tiananmen Square in Peking (Beijing). It was becoming more obvious that Honecker was prepared to suppress revolt in East Germany by force. To prevent the country from slipping into anarchy the SED decided to remove Honecker, which they did on 18 October 1989. He was replaced as General Secretary of the Party by **Egon Krenz**.

Courtesy: Corbis Sygma

• A scene at the Berlin Wall on the night of 9 November 1989, when thousands of people crossed into the West.

THE FALL OF THE WALL

Honecker's removal served as renewed encouragement for popular revolt. In an effort to calm the situation Krenz, on 8 November, dismissed the entire Politburo. On 9 November Krenz announced that private trips to West Germany could be requested "without fulfilling requirements". That night thousands of people filed past armed guards at the Berlin Wall and crossed into the West. It was a memorable moment, and highly significant. It not only opened a route to the West, but it suggested that sweeping fundamental change might be on the cards.

THE FALL OF EAST GERMAN COMMUNISM

The breaking down of the Berlin Wall forced the government into reform. A new, pro-reform Prime Minister, **Hans Modrow**, was appointed on 18 November. The SED renamed itself the **Party of Democratic Socialism**. Elections were set for 18 March 1990. The short notice did not allow parties within East Germany to organise themselves and the vacuum was filled by political parties from West Germany. They campaigned on the issue of reunification of Germany and received a huge groundswell of support from the people. As a result the **Christian Democratic Party** emerged with a greater number of seats.

● East German troops stand guard just before the fall of the Wall.

REUNIFICATION

On 9 April 1990 a new coalition government was formed, led by the Christian Democrats. In addition to promising unification, the Christian Democrats offered a one-to-one exchange for the East and West German marks (the Ostmark and the Deutschmark). On this basis the two states formed one economic unit on 1 July 1990. On 3 October 1990 Germany became one nation again. Economic union meant the opening of East Germany as a market for the West. Shops in the former East Germany were swamped by goods from the West. In the short term this caused greater economic hardship in the East.

By now the Communist system in the Eastern bloc was disappearing quickly and with little resistance.

QUESTIONS

1. How did the policies of Ulbricht and Honecker differ on the attitude of West Germany?
2. What three developments between 1972 and 1974 gave recognition to East Germany as a separate nation?
3. How did Hungary contribute to Honecker's problems?
4. Do you agree that East German politics were hijacked by West German politics in the March elections of 1990? Explain your answer.

7.4   CZECHOSLOVAKIA

THE 1970s

Following the Soviet invasion of Czechoslovakia in 1968 the Communist Party pursued a policy of **normalisation**, that is, everything would be placed under rigid Party control. Normalisation began in 1969 and largely consisted of clearing the Party of reformists. On 17 April 1969 Dubcek was replaced as First Secretary by **Gustav Husak**, an old Stalinist who defiantly resisted reform. The purges that followed removed 327,000 from Party membership. Nearly 2,000 journalists were sacked. Around 900 university staff lost their posts.

● Gustav Husak (Czech).

The government made consumer goods more plentiful and the 1970s generally saw a steady rise in standards of living. In 1971 one in every 17

Czechoslovaks owned a car; by 1979 this rose to one in eight. Some films, television soap operas and music were allowed in from the West, but strict control was maintained. This combination of coercion and reform did not, however, completely suppress the desire for reform.

CHARTER 77

This was the name given to a group of intellectuals led by **Vaclav Havel**, a Czechoslovak playwright. Charter 77 did not seek the removal of the Communist Party from power or the dismantling of the Communist system. It called on the Party machinery to stop abusing its power and to uphold basic human rights. The movement published instances of harsh treatment of citizens, and between 1977 and 1980 over 60 of its members were given long prison sentences. Husak's severe form of government survived very well as long as the economy stayed strong, but in the 1980s difficulties arose in that sector.

• Victor Havel, one of the founding members of Charter 77.

Source Document

Extract from Charter 77's manifesto

Tens of thousands of our citizens are prevented from working in their own fields for the sole reason that they hold views differing from official ones, and are discriminated against and harassed in all kinds of ways by the authorities and public organisations. Deprived as they are of any means to defend themselves, they become victims of a virtual apartheid.

1 January 1977, Prague

QUESTION ON THE DOCUMENT

1. What does the Czechoslovak government stand accused of in this extract?

ECONOMIC DOWNTURN

By the mid-1980s the growth of the Czechoslovak economy had slowed to 2 per cent. An increase in foreign debt from $3.3 million in 1985 to $5.1 million in 1987 also indicated that not all was well. As living standards stagnated the people grew impatient. Gorbachev's policies of *Perestroika* and *glasnost* did not appeal to Husak, and in December 1987 he resigned his post as First Secretary.

PUBLIC DISCONTENT

The 20th anniversary of the invasion by the Soviet Union gave thousands of people the opportunity to demonstrate against the system. This was followed by a spate of demonstrations in 1989:

■ In January the commemoration of Jan Palach's death (he burned himself to death in protest against the Soviet Union's invasion) attracted a crowd of 4,000 demonstrators.

■ 10,000 marched on 28 October to celebrate the foundation of the Czechoslovak state.

■ Just over a week after the breach of the Berlin Wall, over 30,000 demonstrated in Wenceslas Square in Prague; the police attacked the crowd and sparked public outrage.

Courtesy: Bettmann/Corbis

Two days later, on 19 November, Havel formed **Civic Forum**, an umbrella organisation for all those who opposed the system. In Slovakia a similar organisation called **Public Against Violence** was set up. The aim of both groups was to co-ordinate pro-democracy activity.

GOVERNMENT RESPONSE

In an attempt to save itself the Communist Party forced the entire leadership to resign and to adopt a reformist policy. On 27 November a two-hour general strike confirmed that the workforce now supported the reformists. In response to this the Communist Party removed all mention of its primary role from the constitution. On 3 December the new Communist leadership proposed a new government consisting of 16 Communists and five non-Communists. It was rejected by the people. Another government was formed on 10 December, this time with a majority of non-Communists. That same day Gustav Husak resigned as president. The Communist regime was at an end. Vaclav Havel was elected President on 29 December. Aleksandr Dubcek was appointed Chairman of the National Assembly. This completed the **Velvet Revolution**.

Vaclav Havel (1936–   ): Vaclav Havel was born in Prague on 5 October 1936. Although he trained as a laboratory technician, his first love was literature, specifically the theatre. His first plays were written in the 1960s and during that decade he became openly critical of the Communist regime in Czechoslovakia. In 1977 he helped to found Charter 77, a group of intellectuals who attacked the Communist Party over the violation of human rights. He was imprisoned on three separate occasions. In 1989 he formed Civic Forum, an organisation that campaigned for a democratic system of government. As leader of this group he played a central role in the Velvet Revolution. He became president of Czechoslovakia on 29 December 1989.

● **Velvet Revolution.** Havel being elected in 1989.

Courtesy: Getty Images

DEMOCRATIC ELECTIONS

In a celebration of democracy, 23 parties contested the elections of 8 June 1990. Before this, in April, the country was renamed the Czech and Slovak Federal Republic, governed by a Federal Assembly and two local parliaments, the Czech and Slovak National Councils. Civic Forum and Public Against Violence won a majority of seats. They now proceeded to complete the democratic process on 17 September 1990:

- State control of prices was dropped.
- Privatisation of industry was announced.
- The secret police were abolished.
- Agreement was reached with the Kremlin that all 75,000 Red Army troops would be withdrawn by July 1991.

THE VELVET DIVORCE

The setting up of a federal republic in March 1990 was seen by most Slovaks as the first step towards ultimate independence. By 1992 it was clear that Slovakia would not compromise on the issue. On 20 July 1992 Slovakia declared its sovereignty and in November 1992 the federation was dissolved. The following year the Czech Republic joined the United Nations and became a member of the World Bank and the IMF (International Monetary Fund). In 1996 it made a formal application to join the European Union.

QUESTIONS

1. What was the policy of normalisation?
2. What was Charter 77?
3. List four examples of discontent in Czechoslovakia in 1989.
4. What was the Velvet Revolution?
5. What changes were made in September 1990 to complete the shift to democracy?
6. Explain the Velvet Divorce.

7.5   YUGOSLAVIA

A Communist takeover of Yugoslavia was established in January 1946 with the setting up of the Federative People's Republic of Yugoslavia. It consisted of the republics of Serbia, Croatia, Slovenia, Bosnia-Herzegovina, Montenegro and Macedonia. Each of these had its own regional government, ruled over by the federal government in Belgrade. Within Serbia lay the province of Kosovo, which had been incorporated into Yugoslavia at the end of the second World War. Kosovans resented their status as a mere province being ruled by Serbia and demanded that Kosovo be made a separate republic within the Yugoslav federation. This was refused, but Kosovo became a "Socialist autonomous province" of Serbia in 1968. Up to the end of the 1960s Yugoslavia survived quite well as it pursued its own road to Socialism.

Courtesy: Corbis

● Heavily armed Croatian soldiers in 1988.

● Eastern European borders as at June 1993, showing the division of Yugoslavia after the break-up.

INTERNAL TENSION

The first major threat to the Yugoslav state came in the early 1970s from Croatian nationalism. Croatia's economy was prosperous, due mainly to its thriving tourist industry. In 1970 Croatia complained that 45 per cent of its total revenue was going to the central Yugoslav treasury. This gave rise to demonstrations in November 1971. Marshall Tito immediately clamped down on the unrest, arresting over 400 Croat nationalists.

In 1981 the Kosovans once again demanded a separate republic within the federation. This time public demonstrations were so vehement that martial law was imposed on the province in April 1981. In the meantime, Tito had died in 1980 and had arranged that the presidency of Yugoslavia would be shared by all six republics on a rotating basis.

ECONOMIC DIFFICULTIES

Throughout the 1970s the Yugoslav economy experienced steady decline because:

■ Wages had risen to such a level that enterprises had to borrow to stay in production.

■ Investment in business projects was ill advised and poorly planned.

■ Enterprises that were doing badly were subsidised in order to prop up employment.

As a result inflation rocketed in the mid-1980s, going from 88 per cent in 1986 to 157 per cent in 1988, to a disastrous 300 per cent in 1989. This economic crisis created the atmosphere in which nationalism would dismantle the Yugoslav federation.

KOSOVO

In October 1987 **Slobodan Milosevic** had become leader of the **Serbian Communist Party**. He believed that Kosovo should always remain part of Serbia and was prepared to impose that belief ruthlessly if needed. In July 1989 the Serbian government voted to remove the status of "autonomous province" from Kosovo and in September it was formally incorporated into Serbia. His aggressive action was a clear demonstration of Serb nationalism rather than an attempt to keep the Yugoslav federation together.

Courtesy: Corbis

● President Slobodan Milosevic at peace talks.

THE EMERGENCE OF MULTI-PARTY POLITICS

In the course of 1989 political parties opposed to Communism emerged. The **Croatian Democratic Union** was formed in June and by the end of the year the **Slovene Democratic League** was formed. Similar groups were established in the other republics. Faced with this development, the League of Communists of Yugoslavia held an Extraordinary Congress in January 1990 and agreed to allow multi-party elections to take place. By the end of 1990, multi-party elections had been held in all of the republics and it was only in Montenegro and Serbia that the League of Communists retained their control. No election to the Federal Parliament in Belgrade took place, nor would it, because the Yugoslav federation fell apart.

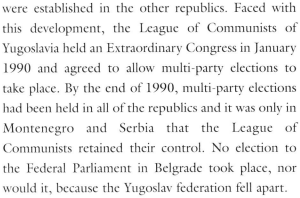

● Kosovan youth demonstrating at a Serbian nationalist rally, 1989.

Courtesy: Corbis Sygma

ETHNIC TENSION

Yugoslavia plunged into civil war in 1991.

- In August 1990 Serbs in Krajina (in Croatia) fought with Croatian police and announced their intention of breaking away from Croatia.
- In February 1991 Slovenia announced its intention to secede from the Yugoslav federation.
- The same month saw Croatia declare that its laws were more important than Yugoslav law.
- At the end of February 1991 the Serbs of Krajina declared their independence from Croatia.
- In April Croatia established its own republican army.

Courtesy: Corbis

● Yugoslav Federal Army soldiers burn a Croatian flag after taking the Croat stronghold, Jasenovac, 1991.

By this time the Yugoslav National Army, which was dominated by Serbia, was already on the streets. It seemed now that only direct military action could stop Yugoslavia from fragmenting.

CIVIL WAR

On 8 May, Slovenia announced its intention to leave the Yugoslav federation.

On 19 May Croatia voted in favour of leaving the federation, and open warfare developed between the Yugoslav army, dominated by Serbia, and the Croatian republican army. By the end of 1991 Croatia had lost almost one-third of its territory to Serbia. The United Nations arranged a ceasefire there in December 1991. In January 1992 the European Union formally recognised Croatian independence. Yugoslavia was disintegrating by now. The real issue was not the preservation of Yugoslavia, but how much territory would fall to Serbia and Croatia.

YUGOSLAVIA COMES TO AN END

By the end of 1991 four of the six republics of the Yugoslav federation had gone their own separate ways.

THE BOSNIAN WAR, 1991–1995

The independence of the republic of Bosnia-Herzegovina was recognised by the European Union in the spring of 1992. This republic contained sizeable Serb, Croat and Muslim communities. The Serb community objected to independence because they wanted to be linked to Serbia and did not want to belong to a multi-ethnic state. Led by **Radovan Karadzic** and supported by Slobodan Milosevic, the Bosnian Serbs staged an armed revolt in the early summer of 1992. Their target was to **ethnically cleanse** a whole area of Bosnia and establish the Serb Republic of Bosnia. After three months of bitter fighting they controlled almost two-thirds of Bosnia-Hercegovina. The war then dragged on for three years, with the Croats and Muslims fighting to preserve their territories.

THE DAYTON ACCORD

This was the deal that ended the war. It was signed in December 1995 and gave 49 per cent of the territory of Bosnia-Hercegovina to the Bosnian Serbs. The other 51 per cent was given to a Croat-Muslim federation. The Bosnian War left over 200,000 dead and nearly two million people were uprooted from their homes.

Courtesy: Corbis

● Wanted poster of Radovan Karadzic.

QUESTIONS

1. The first threat to Yugoslavia's unity came from Croatia. Why were the Croats discontented?
2. Why was martial law imposed on Kosovo in April 1981?
3. Give three reasons why Yugoslavia experienced economic decline in the 1970s and 1980s.
4. What was Slobodan Milosevic's response to Kosovo's demand for a separate republic in 1989?
5. List five developments that contributed to the outbreak of civil war in Yugoslavia in 1991.
6. Briefly explain the roles of nationalism and economic problems in the collapse of Communist Yugoslavia.

CONCLUSION

The collapse of the Communist system in Eastern Europe between 1989 and 1991 was a remarkable development. Given that the regimes were based on rigid control and discipline, their collapse is all the more remarkable. The Communist Party controlled the army, the police, the media, the legal system, education and the economy. The dismantling of this powerful structure of government demands a few observations:

- Gorbachev's accession to power in the Soviet Union in 1985 had a massive influence on the collapse of Communism in the Eastern bloc. He overturned the Brezhnev Doctrine, adopting a policy of non-intervention on the part of the Soviet Union and the Red Army. The Communist leaders of the Eastern bloc states could no longer rely on Moscow to keep them in power.

- Economic decline played a major role in the demise of Communism. The rigid Socialist economic systems of Eastern Europe did not keep pace with the capitalist West.

- Increased access to Western media, especially television, revealed the discrepancy in standards of living. A relaxation of travel restrictions in the Eastern bloc played a significant role.

- Finally, too many of the Communist leaders had grown old. Many of them had been in power for too long and represented stagnation, aversion to change and corruption. For the generation born since 1945 the horrors of the second World War were part of history. They were better educated, more open to new ideas and certainly more adventurous. They were attracted to the concepts of freedom of expression, multi-party politics and a market economy.

Source Document

Extract from Gorbachev's address to the United Nations in December 1988

It is obvious that force and the threat of force cannot be and should not be an instrument of foreign policy … Freedom of choice is a universal principle, and it should know no exceptions … This applies to both the capitalist and Socialist systems.

(Robert Harvey, *Comrades – The Rise and Fall of World Communism*,
John Murray Publishers, 1992)

QUESTIONS ON THE DOCUMENT

1. How did Gorbachev apply the above policy to the Eastern bloc of Communist states?
2. In your view, did the Communist leaders of Eastern Europe agree or disagree with Gorbachev's statement? Explain your answer.

GENERAL ESSAY QUESTIONS ON CHAPTER 7

1. Discuss the reasons why the Communist regimes of Poland and Hungary fell in 1989.

2. Trace the development of the German Democratic Republic from the accession of Erich Honecker to power in May 1971 to reunification with West Germany in October 1990.

3. Compare and contrast the fall of Communism in Czechoslovakia and Yugoslavia.

4. Assess the importance of economic factors and the Soviet Union's policy of non-intervention in the collapse of Communism in Eastern Europe.

5. Discuss the view that the limitations of the Communist system made its downfall in Eastern Europe inevitable.

8

THE WESTERN ECONOMIES 1945–1990

Words you need to understand

Balance of payments: The difference in total value between payments into and out of a country over a specific period.

Bloc: A group of countries that joins together for a common purpose.

EFTA: European Free Trade Association (1959).

EPU: European Payments Union (1950).

ERP: European Recovery Programme, the official name for the Marshall Aid programme.

GDP: Gross Domestic Product – the GDP is the total value of all goods and services produced in a country during a particular period.

Monetarism: An economic policy based on the idea of controlling the supply of money.

Nationalisation: A government takes control of either all or part of a business or industry, taking it out of private ownership.

OEEC: Organisation for European Economic Co-operation. Set up in 1948, it grew out of the Marshall Aid programme.

OECD: Replaced the OEEC in 1961 and included members not in Europe, such as America and Canada.

Recession: A decline in economic well-being.

Stagflation: A combination of rising unemployment, high inflation and stagnant demand in that country's economy.

INTRODUCTION

The rebuilding of Europe was so successful that the period from 1950 to the oil crisis of 1973 has been called the 'Golden Age' of Western Europe. After 1945, countries set out to build their infrastructure and to hasten economic recovery.

The Americans insisted that Europeans should co-operate more on economic matters. They promoted the idea of free trade. The **American European Recovery Program** (called **Marshall Aid**) contributed to this growth.

By 1970, European production accounted for 41 per cent of all world trade. Over two decades of prosperity led to an average 5.5 per cent growth in Western Europe's **GDP** (**gross domestic product**) between 1953 and 1973, before slowing to half that rate between 1973 and 1992.

WHY DID THIS SUPER-GROWTH TAKE PLACE IN WESTERN EUROPE?

- The political and territorial stability after the war in Western Europe was important. No wars broke the spell of peace.
- The idea of reconstruction proved more attractive than revenge for the victorious Allies in Western Europe. Major investment in transport and industrial infrastructure stimulated the economy.
- The division of Europe by the Iron Curtain meant that US Marshall Aid was spent only in Western Europe.
- Governments concentrated on long-term growth rather than short-term needs. The European governments feared that any return to the poor economic conditions of the early 1930s would lead to an increase in Communism.
- The trend towards international co-operation on economic and political matters also promoted prosperity. The European Economic Community played a major role in co-ordinating trade policies.
- The consumer society created demand for mass-produced goods, such as cars and television.

RECONSTRUCTION IN EUROPE, 1945–1951

The immediate economic task was clear: repair the transport structure, replace the damaged housing and rebuild industry. European countries would need outside assistance. After 1945 the USA became an economic support for Western Europe and assisted its economic reconstruction.

Western Europe recovered very quickly. Because of the armaments industry, Europe had a larger industrial base in 1945 than in 1939. By 1951, excluding Germany, industrial output was 43 per cent up on pre-war figures.

8.1   MARSHALL AID

President Truman in America had concerns about the possible triumph of Communism in Western Europe. He gave Western European countries a huge cash injection between 1948 and 1951. This policy contributed to the financial and political stability of Western Europe.

Courtesy: Corbis

● George Marshall (4th left) with Josef Stalin (3rd right) in Moscow in 1947. After this conference, Marshall was convinced that the USSR still posed a major threat to the countries of Western Europe.

AMERICAN FEARS ABOUT EUROPE

In March 1947 George Marshall, the American Secretary of State, met Stalin in Moscow. He believed that Stalin had no intention of helping Europe out of its post-war economic difficulties. Viewed from America, Europe looked open to a Communist takeover. The Cold War encouraged the USA to consider a massive investment programme for Western Europe.

GEORGE MARSHALL SUGGESTS A MAJOR NEW AMERICAN INITIATIVE

George Marshall realised that a prosperous and stable economy was essential for political stability and the survival of free institutions in Europe. The USA also wanted to develop capitalist economies that would oppose Soviet expansion and the Communist threat.

George Marshall (1880–1959): Head of the US army until 1945, in 1946 he became Secretary of State. He launched the American aid plan for Europe, known as the Marshall Plan. He resigned in 1949 and was awarded the Nobel Peace Prize in 1953.

Courtesy: Bettmann/Corbis

Source Document

The Marshall Plan speech, June 1947

The American Secretary of State, George C. Marshall, outlined the need for American aid to Europe, at Harvard University, Cambridge, Massachusetts, USA, on 5 June 1947.

The truth of the matter is that Europe … must have substantial additional help or face economic, social and political deterioration of a very grave character.

The manufacturer and the farmer throughout wide areas must be able and willing to exchange their product for currencies, the continuing value of which is not open to question.

Our policy is directed not against any country or doctrine but against hunger, poverty, desperation and chaos. Its purpose should be the revival of a working economy in the world, so as to permit the emergence of political and social conditions in which free institutions can exist. Any government which manoeuvres to block the recovery of other countries cannot expect help from us.

The initiative, I think, must come from Europe. The program should be a joint one, agreed to by a number, if not all, European nations.

(*www.marshallfoundation.org*, under the heading "The Marshall Plan")

Manoeuvres: Attempts.

QUESTIONS ON THE DOCUMENT

1. In Marshall's view, what would happen if Europe did not receive a major injection of funds?
2. Why did Marshall believe that currency stability was essential for Europe?
3. How would the American government respond to those who tried to block Europe's recovery?
4. Why did Marshall insist that the US government should consult with the Europeans before implementing the plan?

Courtesy: Getty Images

Ernest Bevin (1881–1951):
English politician. As Foreign Secretary for the Labour Government (1945–1951) he co-operated with the USA in rebuilding Western Europe.

THE START OF THE MARSHALL PLAN

The Marshall Plan, known as the **European Recovery Program** (ERP), grew out of Marshall's speech at Harvard University.

The USA had clearly learned a lesson from the experience of Europe between the two World Wars – do not punish the loser with heavy financial penalties. The errors of the Treaty of Versailles were avoided.

This time, the defeated nations were not humiliated or saddled with enormous sums of reparations. Jacques Delors later described the inclusion of Germany as a "masterpiece".

Ernest Bevin, the British Foreign Secretary, called the Plan "a lifeline to sinking men, bringing hope where there was none."

LAUNCHING THE MARSHALL PLAN

The European countries received grants and loans to buy US goods and services. The receiving countries had to co-ordinate their approach to economic recovery.

The USSR would not agree to any economic co-operation, refusing to let its Eastern European satellites take part.

Between 1948 and 1951, the USA invested over $13 billion in Western Europe. The Americans spent as much on Marshall Aid as they had given to the USSR during the war. In contrast, between 1948 and Stalin's death in 1953, the USSR took almost $14 billion out of Eastern Europe.

Sixteen countries attended a conference in Paris in July 1947 that set up the **Committee of European Economic Co-operation** (**CEEC**). The CEEC quickly released a report on the needs of the European economies. Another body, the **Organisation for European Economic Co-operation** (**OEEC**), decided where the money went.

The following countries received some form of assistance: Austria, Belgium, Denmark, France, Greece, Iceland, Ireland, Italy, Luxembourg, the Netherlands, Norway, Portugal, Sweden, Switzerland, Turkey and the United Kingdom. West Germany was soon added to the initial group of 16.

MAKING THE EUROPEAN RECOVERY PROGRAM WORK

The Marshall Plan set out to increase industrial production, to expand European trade, to promote economic co-operation and integration and finally, to control inflation.

Courtesy: Hulton-Deutsch/Corbis

According to Roy Jenkins, the ERP "enabled Europe to plan more securely and to embark on an essential programme of fixed investment."

The situation in Europe was critical. Helmut Schmidt recalled that during the winter of 1946 "we stayed in bed because there was nothing to eat and nothing to burn for warmth." Some German cities had been shelled or bombed to rubble. Before the winter of 1946, thousands of graves were dug in advance for the many who were expected to starve or freeze to death.

Roy Jenkins (1920–2002):
British Labour politician, he served as president of the European Commission from 1976 to 1981. On his return to the UK, he left the Labour Party.

In Paris every second streetlight was unlit. A shortage of petrol kept cars off the streets. Vernon Walters, an American who helped to administer the Plan, remarked, "The business sector did not exist, pretty much everywhere. Very little was left of the pre-war structure."

SOME OF THE SUCCESSES OF THE MARSHALL PLAN

- In France, American wheat meant the return of white bread.
- British children drank American orange juice.
- Greek families were given hens to start a poultry industry.
- The future German chancellor, Helmut Kohl, recalled how American troops brought soup to his school.
- The Otis Elevator Company from the USA helped to modernise British factories.
- New cranes were purchased for the important Dutch port of Rotterdam.
- Over $50 million was used to buy medicine to fight the widespread incidence of tuberculosis.
- Over 3,000 people visited America to see the latest industrial techniques.
- Marshall Aid revived Renault in France, Fiat in Italy and Volkswagen in Germany. In Berlin, American aid rebuilt a power station that had been dismantled by the Russians for war reparations.

● Hunger Week, March 1946. Citizens of Hamburg queue among the ruins for their soup rations. They have pails and buckets as each recipient is allowed rations for five people.

HOW IMPORTANT WAS THE MARSHALL PLAN FOR EUROPEAN RECOVERY?

Europe's GNP rose by one-third between 1947 and 1951 to almost $160 billion. The ERP helped Europe to regain its economic viability and moved countries towards free trade. Within ten years, 3,000 American companies had set up in Europe.

Marshall Aid was not solely responsible for the economic recovery of Europe. While the ERP was economically significant, it was also important in political terms.

American historian Charles Maier described the ERP as the "lubricant in an engine – not the fuel – which allowed a machine to run that would otherwise buckle and bind".

Historian John Lukacs described the Marshall Plan as a milestone, but not a turning point.

RESULTS OF THE EUROPEAN RECOVERY PROGRAM

A principal American aim was to integrate the new state of West Germany into a healthy international economy. This objective was so successful that German products soon replaced many American imports in Europe once the funding finished.

● France and Argentina signing a commercial treaty (Eva Perón is standing in the foreground). Deals like these became more numerous because of the ERP.

But despite, or maybe because of, the scale of aid, a significant level of resentment against the Americans existed in Europe. In France in 1950, 40 per cent of the people believed that the aid was an insult to French independence.

The Marshall Plan also limited the spread of Communism. After 1947, no Western European country voted for the Communist system of government, a demonstration of the political influence of Marshall Aid.

Ultimately, the Marshall Plan helped to increase the standard of living in Europe, stimulated the pattern of international trade and promoted political stability as well as economic growth.

QUESTIONS

1. What evidence is there to show that the Americans were concerned about the spread of Communist influence at this time?
2. What lessons had the Americans learned from the settlements of the first World War?
3. How did the USA and the USSR differ in their attitude to investing money in Europe?
4. Give some examples of the problems faced by Europe before the Marshall Plan was introduced.
5. Indicate two effective ways in which Marshall Aid improved the economy in Western Europe.
6. Suggest three long-term results of the Marshall Plan.

8.2 THE NEW ROLE OF THE STATE IN ECONOMIC MATTERS, 1945–1973

State control of the economy was a feature of the post-war economies in Europe. France and Britain rationed bread after 1945 so that they could control the use of wheat.

Western governments played a greater role in economic and social life, promoting investment, funding the public sector and providing more social welfare services.

After 1945 Jean Monnet drew up economic plans to renew France's economic infrastructure. This included nationalising major industries such as coal mining, gas, electricity and businesses such as Air France and the Bank of France. The French government provided 30 per cent of the money invested in their economy between 1947 and 1951.

The British government widened its control over major industries (such as coal) by nationalising them. In Italy, the Institute of Industrial Reconstruction owned and ran large sections of major industries such as transport and chemicals.

By the early 1970s the Scandinavian countries, the UK and the Netherlands were spending over 50 per cent of their national income on the public sector, mainly on social welfare supports.

TWO DECADES OF PROSPERITY

The decades of the 1950s and the 1960s were periods of almost constant economic growth in Western Europe. Conservative governments, not Socialist ones, were responsible for this economic triumph.

Industrial growth was helped by a stream of innovations. Developments took place in the new plastics industry, nuclear energy, electronics and chemicals, as well as in modern consumer durables such as colour televisions and cars.

Different countries grew at different rates. French industrial output rose by 100 per cent between 1948 and 1958. It almost doubled again between 1959 and 1970. The Italian 'economic miracle' started in 1958, when Italy joined the new common market.

The demand for workers was constant. The rate of unemployment fell in the advanced industrial countries as the 'Golden Age' developed. The millions of refugees after the war, the migration of peasants from the farms to the cities and the millions of

Harold Macmillan (1894–1986): Harold Macmillan, UK Prime Minister, said in July 1957, "Most of our people have never had it so good." British Conservative Prime Minister (1957–1963), he presided over a period of prosperity for the British economy.

Courtesy: Hulton-Deutsch/Corbis

non-European migrants provided a willing labour force for the new industries. Between 1945 and 1990, the number of people working in agriculture fell from 30 per cent of the labour force to just 5 per cent.

This growth was not constant, though. There were setbacks to progress, such as the brief downturn in industrial output after the end of the Korean War in 1952. A fall in output took place every four or five years. In 1958 GDP in Western Europe even slipped to less than 2 per cent growth. It actually dropped in Belgium, Norway and Ireland. Further falls occurred in 1963 and 1967.

GERMANY'S 'ECONOMIC MIRACLE'

Because of the military occupation of West Germany after the war, its economic recovery took longer than in the rest of Western Europe. In 1947 the Americans finally realised that an economically strong West Germany would provide a balance against the Soviet Union's influence. West Germany was then included in the list of Marshall Aid countries.

The introduction of the new Deutschmark in 1948 provided an incentive for businesses to innovate, as it removed the uncertainty of currency reform. Germans exchanged one Deutschmark for ten of the older Reich marks. The new currency highlighted the partition of Germany into two countries.

The three zones occupied by the Americans, the French and the British were joined to form the new German Federal Republic in September 1949. Under its new president, Konrad Adenauer, and his economic minister Ludwig Erhard, the German Federal Republic experienced an 'economic miracle'.

The West German government was not allowed to invest in military equipment, which released more money for industrial investment. West Germany reached its pre-war levels of production in 1951. It prospered during the 1950s and the 1960s. Like Britain, the Germans combined state intervention with the 'free market' approach.

Courtesy: Bettmann/Corbis

● Italian workers shopping in Wolfsburg, West Germany in 1962. As "guest" workers, they often had to buy winter or heavier clothes when they arrived in their new homes.

Courtesy: Bettmann/Corbis

● The Volkswagen Automobile Company built this "village" for 4,000 Italian workers. The houses can be seen at the back, while the hall at the front was used as a canteen, recreation centre and a church.

North Sea

Baltic Sea   **USSR**

Hamburg

Gdansk

NETH.

Berlin

Potsdam ■

■ Warsaw

FEDERAL

GERMAN

P O L A N D

REPUBLIC

DEMOCRATIC

Bonn ●

REPUBLIC

OF

GERMANY

■ Prague

C Z E C H O S L O V A K I A

FRANCE

Munich ●

Vienna ■

AUSTRIA   **HUNGARY**

SWITZERLAND

British zone	Territory incorporated in Poland
French zone	Territory incorporated in USSR
American zone	

Twelve million refugees came to West Germany between 1945 and 1960. This new source of labour kept German wage costs down.

West Germany was the most successful economy of the 1950s.

- Inflation was low and between 1950 and 1960 six million extra people were employed.
- Almost five million housing units were built during the 1950s.
- Germany had 10 per cent unemployment in 1950. This fell to 1 per cent by 1960.
- By 1970 a West German worker had four times more money to spend than in 1950.
- German exports rose from 9.3 per cent of GDP in 1950 to 17.2 per cent in 1960 and to 23.8 per cent in 1970.

QUESTIONS

1. Give two examples of industries that were nationalised.
2. How did car ownership grow during this period?
3. Why was currency reform important in Germany?

Source Document

Helmut Schmidt was Chancellor of the Federal Republic of Germany from 1974 to 1982. He recalls the changes brought about by the Marshall Plan between 1948 and 1951.

In June 1948 the American, British and French occupation authorities replaced the hopelessly inflated Reichmark with a new currency, the Deutschmark. Until then, we had lived on the meagre rations our cards got us, and money did not really matter, except in the shadows, where one paid six Reichmark for a single cigarette.

Now money became all-important. The ration cards slowly disappeared over the next two years and shops began to fill with goods we had only dreamed about: bread, butter, fruit, even coffee and cigarettes.

This monetary and economic revolution would never have transpired had it not been for the Marshall Plan. The American aid program became operational in Germany in the summer of 1948, about the time the Deutschmark was put in place.

The American, British and French zones of occupation in Western Germany merged in 1949 to become the Federal Republic, and the new state was a success within a decade. Over the course of the 1950s the United States became my most favoured nation.

(Helmut Schmidt, "Miles to Go: From American Plan to European Union", *Foreign Affairs*, May/June 1997)

QUESTIONS ON THE DOCUMENT

1. Why did money become all-important in June 1948, according to Schmidt?
2. What role did the Marshall Plan play in bringing about this economic revolution?
3. What effect did the American aid have on Schmidt's attitude towards the USA during the 1950s?

8.3 MOVES TOWARDS FREE TRADE

AMERICAN SUPPORT FOR FREE TRADE IN EUROPE

Western European countries increasingly took up the idea of free trade and international co-operation during the 1950s and 1960s. When Marshall Aid was given, countries had to agree to move towards free trade, as well as to co-operate on economic matters. The ERP encouraged countries to remove import duties on goods made elsewhere.

EUROPE'S PROGRESS TOWARDS FREE TRADE

An important economic conference at Bretton Woods in 1944 had set up the **International Monetary Fund (IMF)**. In 1947, 23 countries signed the **GATT** agreement (**General Agreement on Tariffs and Trade**). Both the IMF and GATT promoted free trade between countries.

Despite initial reluctance, Western European countries gradually eliminated most trade barriers by the end of the 1960s.

Starting with the **European Payments Union** (1950), the restrictions on free trade began to disappear. By 1955 the OEEC had succeeded in removing 84 per cent of the trade restrictions that had been in place at the start of the 1950s.

The new trading groups, such as the EEC (set up in 1957) and EFTA (set up in 1959), led to closer economic co-operation among the countries of Western Europe.

The EEC set the standard for removing customs duties. By 1968 it had abolished duties on non-agricultural goods, and set up a common import tax for goods coming into the EEC bloc.

Courtesy: Bettmann/Corbis

● The 1944 Bretton Woods conference discussing programmes of economic co-operation that helped Western Europe.

The impact of the removal of duties was seen very quickly. Between 1955 and 1969, the volume of trade between the six countries that formed the EEC increased from 25 per cent to 33 per cent – a major achievement.

The EFTA group included Austria, Denmark, Norway, Portugal, Sweden, Switzerland and the UK. It had a narrower scope than the EEC, concentrating only on trade matters. However, most of the customs duties payable between these countries had been removed by 1965.

American multinationals in Western Europe encouraged the transfer of managers and technical specialists between countries, creating a European working space that did not depend on national boundaries.

Improvements in technology, especially in the area of consumer durables and engineering, were shared across national borders. The growth of trade stimulated the transfer of goods as tariff barriers were gradually reduced between countries.

Charles de Gaulle (1890–1970):
French president in 1958, de Gaulle encouraged economic growth, developed nuclear energy and blocked the entry of the UK into the EEC.

Small companies found it hard to compete in this new free trade market, which led to state-approved mergers in important industries to protect employment. In France during the 1960s, Charles de Gaulle supported the creation of "national champions" in industry. France had no business listed in the top 500 industrial firms in 1963. The creation of large corporations meant that France had 23 firms on that list by 1970.

CONCLUSION

The economic progress experienced in Western Europe until 1973 led people to believe that recessions were temporary and that prosperity was permanent. The post-war generation had generally lived in a stable economic period, in an age of affluence and generally knew far less about poverty than their parents. The 1973 oil crisis changed all that.

QUESTIONS

1. How did American companies contribute to economic growth?
2. How did de Gaulle improve the performance of French companies?

Source Document: A

Giovanni Agnelli founded the Fiat motor company, based in Italy. In an interview, he recalls the importance of the Marshall Plan.

Well, in 1947, in Europe and in Italy especially, we thought of America as all-powerful. The generosity of their foreign policy, and the generosity of their foreign policy at that moment was expressed through the Marshall Plan.

And the Marshall Plan, to us ... was part of that very strong pro-American feeling that was created in Italy in those days. In the immediate post-war years, the whole of Europe was in a recession. So first of all, it helped us step out of a recession; it gave a certain amount of speed to the economy. But that was the first step.

The second real step was that it (brought us closer to) this European Community ... It brought us toward what has been considered the Atlantic community, it brought [us] toward NATO and it brought the European countries toward a European integration.

(Interview transcript, from CNN documentary on Cold War
www.cnn.com/SPECIALS/cold.war/episodes/03/interviews/agnelli/)

Source Document: B

Nokia trades with the Soviet Union

Nokia, the Finnish company, became linked with mobile phones during the 1990s. However, Nokia was originally a cable company and traded with the Soviet Union, among other countries.

Björn Westerlund had been in charge of the cable business since 1956. As Nokia's managing director, he ... built new business relationships with the Soviets.

The problem, as Westerlund saw it, was that the Soviet Union, as a significant and demanding customer, was developing and building Nokia ... yet the Soviet economy was not market-driven. When Nokia's business reached 20 per cent of ... total revenues, Westerlund warned the senior management: "We must be cautious and not allow the proportion of Soviet business [to] grow too much ... If one day they'll say *nyet*, we'll lose our business overnight."

Some of his managers thought this attitude too cautious. If the Soviets wanted to pay, why avert the flow of business? ... True, argued Westerlund, the world had changed, but the Soviet command economy had not.

(D. Steinbock, *The Nokia Revolution*, New York, 2001, p. 27)

Avert: Change.
Nyet: No.

QUESTIONS ON THE DOCUMENTS

1. In Document A, Agnelli admired America. Why did he believe that many Italians admired America in 1947?
2. What was the first immediate impact of the Marshall Plan, according to Agnelli in Document A?
3. What was the second, long-term impact of the Marshall Plan, according to Agnelli in Document A?
4. In Document B, how did the Soviet Union contribute to Nokia's financial success?
5. Why was Westerlund concerned about the amount of business that they got from the Soviets?
6. Why did Westerlund believe that the Soviets would not be able to change their approach to financial matters?

8.4   THE 1970s

The Oil Crisis of 1973 brought the optimistic era of 'super-growth' to an end for Western Europe. Economic growth slowed down, unemployment rose and inflation ran out of control. International trade co-operation suffered as trade restrictions returned as a means of protecting national economies. The recession that followed was the worst since the depressions of the 1920s and 1930s.

The term coined by economists to describe this crisis was 'stagflation', a combination of rising unemployment, rapid inflation and stagnation of demand. A second oil crisis occurred in 1979 which damaged economies even further. The early years of the 1980s brought no improvement and Western Europe struggled to keep inflation down, to keep balance of payments steady and to cope with serious unemployment. In the second half of the 1980s the situation improved. The rate of inflation came down and GDP increased, oil prices fell dramatically and consumer spending grew.

DECLINE IN ECONOMIC GROWTH IN WESTERN EUROPE
1974 was the first year of economic decline.

■ In West Germany, gross domestic product fell from an average growth of 4.4 per cent for the 1960s to 0.2 per cent for the year 1974.
■ A similar comparison for the United Kingdom shows a decline from 2.9 per cent to 1.7 per cent and for France from 5.6 per cent to 3.1 per cent.
■ The overall average GDP growth for Western Europe was only 1.3 per cent in 1980.

DECLINE IN INDUSTRIAL PRODUCTION
The dramatic price rises imposed by OPEC (Organisation of the Petroleum Exporting Countries) put a severe check on industrial output, as the following examples show:

■ The average industrial growth for Western Europe fell from 5.4 per cent for the 1960s to 2.6 per cent for the 1970s.
■ The decline in West Germany was from 5.3 per cent for the 1960s to 1.9 per cent for the 1970s.
■ The same comparison showed a fall from 2.4 per cent to 1.0 per cent in the United Kingdom and from 5.1 per cent to 3.2 per cent in France.

Increased oil prices drove up the cost of production, which meant that consumers had to cope with a sustained rise in the cost of living.

INFLATION AND PRICE RISES
One of the most notable features of the economic recession of the 1970s was the steep and lasting price rise in consumer goods. In Western Europe the average rise in consumer prices jumped from 3.8 per cent for the 1960s to 10.7 per cent for the 1970s. Of the three bigger economies, West Germany fared best in this sector:

■ In the 1970s West German price rises never went above 7.5 per cent in any year.
■ France recorded a price rise increase in 1974 of 14.8 per cent and of 13.3 per cent in 1980.
■ The inflation rate for the United Kingdom went from 8.5 per cent in 1973 to 17.1 per cent in 1974 to 23.3 per cent in 1975, tapering off to 16.1 per cent in 1980.

Ten states in Western Europe had inflation rates above 10 per cent. The severe rise in the cost of living led to a reduction in consumer spending and, therefore, a fall-off in demand for consumer goods. The downturn in demand led to lay-offs in the workforce.

UNEMPLOYMENT

The average rate of unemployment in Western Europe went from 2 to 4 per cent between the 1960s and 1970s. However, rising unemployment in the 1970s varied within European states.

• Unemployed man looking after the baby in 1973, England.

- ■ West Germany's unemployment increase was relatively low, going from 0.7 per cent for the 1960s to 3.2 per cent for the period 1974–1979.
- ■ The French increase over the same periods was from 1.7 per cent to 4.5 per cent.
- ■ The United Kingdom experienced a rise from 2.6 per cent to 5.1 per cent.
- ■ Ireland had the highest unemployment rate for the 1970s, recording 7.6 per cent (5 per cent for the 1960s).

This level of unemployment continued into the 1980s.

WAGE DEMANDS

As the cost of living developed throughout the 1970s, so too did the wage claims. Trade unions acquired more muscle and increased their demands for higher wages. The tendency towards the end of the 1970s was for governments to give in, but as the economic crises developed into the 1980s, governments took a firmer line. This was particularly true of Britain, where a major confrontation developed between the conservative government, led by Margaret Thatcher, and the trade unions.

• Unemployed docker presents a lonely image at London's docklands.

QUESTIONS

1. The economic crisis of the 1970s and 1980s has been described by economists as 'stagflation'. What does this term mean?
2. Give two reasons why GDP fell in Europe in the 1970s.
3. What was the extent of decline in industrial output in Western Europe between the 1960s and 1970s?
4. What were the rates of inflation in West Germany, France and the United Kingdom during the 1970s?
5. What evidence is there that unemployment had become a significant problem by the close of the 1970s?

8.5   THE 1980s

The second oil crisis that broke in 1979 made matters even worse for Western Europe. As a result, the general economic trend showed a decline up to the mid-1980s with a slow recovery during the second half of that decade.

Courtesy: Tweedie/Corbis

● The recession of the 1970s–1980s increased the numbers of homeless people.

ECONOMIC GROWTH

The overall growth of GDP for Western Europe in the 1980s was 2.4 per cent, compared with 3 per cent for the 1970s and 4.7 per cent for the 1960s. A few individual examples show that there was little variation in GDP growth during the 1980s:

■ West Germany experienced a growth rate of 2.2 per cent, compared with 2.7 per cent for the 1970s.

■ GDP in France grew by 2.4 per cent, compared with 3.3 per cent for the 1970s.

■ Growth in the United Kingdom reached 2.7 per cent, compared with 1.9 per cent for the 1970s.

INDUSTRIAL PRODUCTION

Growth of industrial output across Western Europe fell to 1.8 per cent during the 1980s, compared with 2.6 per cent for the 1970s. A look at some specific performances in this sector shows that:

■ West German industrial output grew by 1.9 per cent in the 1980s, the same as the 1970s.

■ Industrial production grew by 1.1 per cent in France, compared with 3.2 per cent for the 1970s.

■ In the UK industrial output grew by 2.1 per cent, compared with only 1 per cent during the 1970s.

THE DECLINE OF INFLATION

By 1980, however, curbing inflation had become the priority for most European states. The outcome was that rates of inflation went into steady decline throughout the 1980s. The reasons why this occurred were threefold:

1. Governments introduced strict monetary policies. This meant that high interest rates were used to discourage borrowing and government spending was cut back.

2. By the mid-1980s oil prices had fallen substantially. The second oil crisis that broke in 1979 and the Iran–Iraq War of 1980 pushed the price of oil up to $36 a barrel in 1981. By 1986 this price had fallen to $16 a barrel.

3. Governments and employers put a strict curb on increasing wages for the labour force. By 1986 the average inflation rate for all of Europe was only 4 per cent, compared with 12.2 per cent for 1981. In the same period the inflation rate in France fell from 13.4 per cent to 2.5 per cent.

UNEMPLOYMENT

In the 1980s unemployment levels remained high. The level of unemployment stayed at 6 per cent in West Germany, France experienced an average 9 per cent, while the UK level averaged 9.6 per cent.

The overall trend shows that unemployment in Western Europe continued upward from an average 5.4 per cent in 1980 to 7 per cent in 1990.

CONCLUSION

In general, the 1980s began badly with slow economic growth, high inflation and rising unemployment, but by the close of the decade things had improved. The rate of inflation was severely reduced, GDP was recovering, consumer spending increased and prices of oil and raw materials fell. Despite these improvements the levels of unemployment remained high. Of all the Western economies Britain suffered most from the scourge of unemployment.

Courtesy: Corbis Sygma

• The economic crisis in Britain was seized upon by Australia to increase its labour force.

QUESTIONS

1. What evidence is there of a decline in economic growth in the 1970s?
2. Give three reasons why the rate of inflation went down during the 1980s.

8.6   RECESSION AND THE RISE IN UNEMPLOYMENT: THE BRITISH EXPERIENCE

THE GROWING POWER OF THE TRADE UNIONS

In 1972 the number of unemployed in Britain reached one million. The rising cost of living resulted in demands for wage increases from workers.

In November 1973 the National Union of Mineworkers (NUM) and electricity engineers began industrial action in support of their claim for a wage increase. The Conservative government, led by Edward Heath, decided to place British industry on a three-day working week because of coal and electricity shortages. In early February the NUM called an all-out strike. Mr Heath responded by calling a general election for 28 February on the issue "Who governs Britain?" The Conservatives were voted out of power and replaced by a Labour government, led by Harold Wilson. The election result confirmed the power of the trade union movement in the UK.

Courtesy: Corbis Sygma

• Striking coalminers seen here walking out of their colliery in January 1974.

Edward Heath (1916–): British Prime Minister (1970–1974). Elected leader of the Conservative Party in 1965. After a confrontation with the miners' union in 1973, he narrowly lost the two elections of 1974 and in 1975 was replaced as leader by Mrs Thatcher.

Courtesy: Corbis

Source Document

On the miners' strike Mrs Thatcher said:

We had to fight the enemy without in the Falklands. We always have to be aware of the enemy within, which is always more difficult to fight and more dangerous to liberty.

(P. Wiolenius, "Enemies Within: Thatcher and the Unions", www.bbc.co.uk.)

QUESTIONS ON THE DOCUMENT

1. Who do you think Mrs Thatcher saw as "the enemy within"?
2. Why did she see that enemy as "more dangerous to liberty"?

FALL OF THE LABOUR GOVERNMENT, 1979

Mr Jim Callaghan became Prime Minister in 1976. He placed a 5 per cent upper limit on wage rises. The trade unions disagreed and Britain was plunged into the infamous 'winter of discontent', which ran for the first three months of 1979. The government granted the unions a 9 per cent increase. Once again union power was demonstrated. In the general election of May 1979 the Conservatives, led by Margaret Thatcher, came to power.

Courtesy: Corbis

• Margaret Thatcher, seen here rallying Conservative Party supporters during the 1979 general election campaign.

CONSERVATIVE ECONOMIC POLICY

Margaret Thatcher took over the leadership of the Conservative Party from Edward Heath in 1975. She fought the 1979 general election on the issues of reducing inflation, curbing the power of the trade unions and restoring law and order to the streets of Britain. The problem of inflation was given priority. Mrs Thatcher's government adopted a monetary policy to counter it.

MONETARISM

The policy of **monetarism** was formed by an American economist, Professor Milton Friedman, in the 1960s. Monetarists believe that inflation can be controlled if the supply of money is restricted in two ways:

1. By placing high interest rates on borrowing money.
2. By cutting back on government spending.

Courtesy: Bettmann/Corbis

Margaret Thatcher (1925–   ): British Prime Minister (1979–1990). In 1959 she was elected to parliament and was Minister for Education and Science in Edward Heath's Conservative Government (1970–1974). In February 1975 she succeeded Heath as leader of the Conservative Party.

The victory of the Conservatives in the general election of May 1979 made her the first female Prime Minister of Britain. She won a second term in power because of Britain's defeat of Argentina in the Falklands War in 1982. Thatcher finally broke the power of the unions when the government defeated the National Union of Mineworkers in a year-long strike that started in March 1984. She consistently supported NATO and backed the decision to place Pershing and Cruise missiles in Europe to counter the Soviet threat.

Thatcher was elected Prime Minister for a third time in 1987. By then the British economy had recovered to some extent, but unemployment continued to be a problem. In 1990 her popularity dwindled dramatically as a result of the poll tax. She resigned as Prime Minister in November 1990 and was succeeded by John Major. She was given a seat in the House of Lords in 1992.

MONETARISM IN PRACTICE

The economic policy of Thatcher's first government put into practice the following measures:

- Income tax was lowered.
- Government expenditure was cut back – strict cash limits were placed on most government departments.
- The minimum lending rate was raised to 17 per cent to discourage borrowing.

The short-term outcome of this was a lack of investment, a fall in GDP and an increase in unemployment and inflation. In 1980 unemployment rose by 836,000 and inflation was running at 18 per cent. Despite these poor figures, Thatcher persevered with her monetarist policy, refusing to consider any other course of action. Addressing journalists who suggested she might do a U-turn, she famously told them: "You turn if you like, the lady's not for turning." She now focused her attention on the nationalised industries.

PRIVATISATION

Selling off nationalised industries became part of Conservative policy in 1981 under the Secretary of State for Industry, Sir Keith Joseph. One government member, Nigel Lawson, summed up the policy thus: "No industry should remain under state ownership unless there is a positive and overwhelming case for it so doing. Inertia is not good enough. We simply cannot afford it."

THATCHER AND THE TRADE UNIONS

By the end of 1982 the Conservative government had put in place a set of laws that diminished the strength of the unions:

- Strike ballots were made compulsory.
- Secondary strikes were declared illegal.
- The power of unions to impose a 'closed shop' system in the workplace was curtailed.
- Employers were given more freedom to dismiss employees.

● People's March for Jobs reaches London, May 1981.

Courtesy: Hulton-Deutsch/Corbis

UNEMPLOYMENT

The monetarist policy of reduced government spending and high interest rates resulted in a sharp decline in investment. During Thatcher's first term of office from 1979 to 1983, industrial output fell by over 10 per cent. In the same period unemployment went from 1,253,000 to 3,021,000. Unemployment reached a peak of 3.3 million in 1986.

The Conservatives won a second term in power in 1983. Britain's victory over Argentina in the Falklands War had boosted Thatcher's popularity enormously. The other major factor was the government's success in bringing the rate of inflation down from 18 per cent in 1980 to 4.6 per cent in 1983. By the close of Thatcher's first term in government, unemployment had seriously weakened the unions. However, one last major set-to was about to take place.

THE NATIONAL UNION OF MINEWORKERS' STRIKE, 1984–1985

The miners' strike began on 12 March 1984 and ended on 5 March 1985. In March 1984 the Conservative government announced a plan to close 20 coal mines with a loss of 20,000 jobs.

• Arthur Scargill leads a NUM rally, Nottinghamshire, 1984.

NUM OPPOSITION

The leader of the NUM, Arthur Scargill, called a national strike of mineworkers without holding a ballot. Nevertheless, a majority of miners went on strike and presented Thatcher with a long, violent and bitter dispute.

GOVERNMENT STRATEGY

Thatcher took the following steps:

- Building up massive coal stocks at coal-burning power stations.
- Road haulage companies were urged to employ non-union drivers to collect and deliver coal.
- 140,000 specially trained police were employed to keep the coal pits open – often resulting in outright battles with the miners.

In the end the government was victorious. The defeat of the NUM added to Thatcher's growing stature.

• In 1990 anti-poll tax riots fired up all around Britain. Here police charge demonstrators in Trafalgar Square, April 1990.

ECONOMICS

Thatcher continued her programme of cutting back on government expenditure, restricting borrowing, privatising state enterprises and reducing income tax. By 1987 Britain's economy showed signs of recovery and Mrs. Thatcher was returned to power for a third time. The recovery was shortlived, however, and by the close of the 1980s the economy was once more in decline and headed for another recession. In 1990 Thatcher's government introduced a 'poll tax', a community charge to be paid by everyone over the age of 18. Massive public hostility resulted, and faced with growing opposition from within her Cabinet, Thatcher resigned on 22 November 1990.

QUESTIONS

1. Why did the Conservative government fall from power in 1974?
2. What happened during 'the winter of discontent' in 1979?
3. Explain monetarism.
4. List three pieces of legislation introduced by the end of 1982 to curb trade union power.
5. What caused the miners' strike in 1984?
6. Who was Arthur Scargill?
7. Give four reasons why the Thatcher government defeated the NUM.

GENERAL ESSAY QUESTIONS ON CHAPTER 8

1. Write a paragraph on each of the following:
   (a) The reconstruction of Europe.
   (b) Marshall Aid.
   (c) The recovery of Germany, 1948 to 1973.
2. Write a brief essay on prosperity in Europe, 1945 to 1973 (You may include some points about the rebuilding of Europe, Marshall Aid, industries during the 1950s and the 1960s).
3. Assess the contribution that the European Recovery Plan made to the recovery of Europe, 1947 to 1951.
4. Why did Western Europe have such economic success between 1950 and 1973?
5. Discuss the view that the OPEC Oil Crisis of 1973-74 sparked a prolonged and damaging economic recession in Western Europe.
6. Describe the effect of the economic recession of the 1970s and 1980s on industrial production, inflation and employment in Western Europe.
7. Assess the Thatcher Government's handling of the problems of inflation, unemployment and trade union power.

9

THE COMMUNIST ECONOMIES: PROBLEMS AND OUTCOMES 1945–1990

Words you need to understand

Nationalisation: To bring the means of production, both economic and agricultural, under state control.

State Planning Commission: The body set up in all the Communist states to plan their economies.

Balance of payments deficit: Occurs when the value of imports to any one country is greater than its value of exports.

9.1 THE COMMUNIST ECONOMIES, 1950–1970

NATIONALISATION OF INDUSTRY AND AGRICULTURE

By the end of 1949 almost all industry was under state control within the Eastern bloc states. This process of nationalisation was extended to banking, retailing and all aspects of commercial life.

The nationalisation of agriculture took longer to implement. By 1960 most of the land was organised under the collective system. Less than 10 per cent of the land was made up of state farms (farms completely under the control of the state).

INTRODUCTION

The Communist economies of Czechoslovakia, East Germany, Poland, Hungary, Bulgaria, Romania, Yugoslavia and the Soviet Union enjoyed considerable growth between the late 1940s and the close of the 1960s. The structure of the economic system in these states differed considerably from that of the Western economies. The Western economies were based on a capitalist system which encouraged individual enterprises, private ownership and free markets. The economies of Eastern Europe were built on the principle of state ownership of the means of production.

STATE PLANNING OF ECONOMIES

The overall planning of economic programmes was conducted in each state by the State Planning Commission. The primary aim of all the Eastern economies was industrialisation.

Courtesy: Corbis

• Comecon (Council for Mutual Assistance) building in Moscow. It was dissolved in 1991.

The Communist economies sought to develop heavy machinery, transport vehicles, chemicals and electronics. Agriculture and the production of consumer goods did not enjoy the same level of importance.

GROWTH OF GROSS DOMESTIC PRODUCT

The rate of growth in GDP for the whole Socialist bloc of Eastern Europe during the 1950s and 1960s was 7 per cent per annum. The top performer was the Soviet Union with 7.6 per cent. The poorer achievers were Czechoslovakia with 5.2 per cent and Hungary with 4.8 per cent. By the early 1960s the rate of growth began to slow down except in Bulgaria and Romania.

EMPLOYMENT

This movement from agriculture to industry was reflected in employment figures. The following increases of employment in industry for the period 1950–1967 show the trend: Bulgaria went from 7.9 per cent to 28.3 per cent, Czechoslovakia from 27.9 to 38 per cent.

On the other hand, employment figures in agriculture for the same period show a downward trend: Bulgaria went from 82.1 to 41.8 per cent, Czechoslovakia from 36.9 to 19.1 per cent.

INCOMES

Economic growth in the 1950s and 1960s brought an improved standard of living. In East Germany wages tripled and workers in Yugoslavia, Romania and Bulgaria did well with increases in the region of 150 per cent. However, they still fell well short of incomes in Western Europe.

PROBLEMS IN COMMUNIST ECONOMIES

Spending on personal consumption was held back by the shortage of consumer goods such as domestic products, processed food and textiles. This led to rationing and queueing in shops and stores and contributed to social unrest and disillusionment with the system.

INEFFICIENCY OF INVESTMENT

- The Socialist states believed that by providing large quantities of workers and money they could achieve rapid economic growth.
- They generally tended to waste resources. It is believed that for the 1950–1970 period, investment costs in the Communist economies were 25 per cent greater than in Western Europe.
- Productivity rates lagged behind the West. By the early 1960s productivity in the Soviet Union achieved 40 per cent of the US level.

These problems meant that change had to come.

Courtesy: Corbis

● Visitors to the Moscow Exhibition of Economic Achievement in 1964. This massive show gave the impression to citizens and the rest of the world that Soviet technological advances were every bit as progressive as those of the USA.

ECONOMIC REFORM

The changes that were introduced to the Communist economies in the 1960s were first applied to industry and then to trade and agriculture:

- The role of the Central Planning Commission in each state was relaxed. Greater responsibility for efficient management was handed over to local managers.
- Some private enterprise was allowed in areas such as catering, retailing and housebuilding. Overall, however, private enterprise remained very small.
- In agriculture peasants farmed private plots of land. In addition, compulsory deliveries of produce to the state were reduced.
- State control of trading was relaxed and enterprises were allowed to expand their trading market abroad.

RETAINING COMMUNISM

While these reforms showed a shift towards more competitive economics, Communist economies remained state controlled.

> ## QUESTIONS
>
> 1. How did the structure of the Communist economies differ from that of the capitalist ones?
> 2. What does nationalisation mean?
> 3. List three reasons for economic inefficiency in the Communist economies.
> 4. The role of the Central Planning Commissions was relaxed. In your own words, explain what this meant in terms of reform.

9.2   COMMUNIST ECONOMIES, 1970–1990

INTRODUCTION

The well-being of the previous two decades continued up to the mid-1970s in the Communist economies, after which they went into steady decline. The reforms of the 1960s were unable to arrest that trend. The economies ran up huge debts because of heavy borrowing from the West. They also failed to raise living standards sufficiently, which gave rise to mass discontent and political instability. Eventually this led to the traumatic events of the years 1989–1990, which saw the collapse of the Communist system.

EFFECT OF THE FIRST OIL CRISIS

The Communist economies did not suffer as severely as the West from the 1973–1974 oil crisis. The Comecon states were almost self-sufficient in energy largely because of the huge deposits of oil and natural gas in the Soviet Union. In the short term, in fact, the Soviet Union, Romania and Poland benefited from the crisis. The Soviet Union, being the world's biggest oil producer, capitalised on the need for oil in the West. Romania also gained from its oil exports, but by 1980 its oil supplies were running low and eventually it had to import oil from the Soviet Union. The Polish economy also received a boost from increased sales of coal. The other Comecon states bought their energy from the USSR at prices well below those on the world market. As a result, the Communist economies were sheltered from the ravages of the first oil crisis. Despite this, however, problems were not far away.

DECLINE OF INDUSTRIAL GROWTH

Between 1970 and 1975 the Communist bloc enjoyed an average industrial growth rate of around 6.5 per cent. This was the last period of sustained growth. The figure for the period 1976–1980 went down to 4.1 per cent and fell to 2.9 per cent for the period 1981–1985.

LACK OF CONSUMER GOODS

During the 1970s consumer items such as fridges, washing machines and televisions became available in Eastern Europe. This whetted the appetites of the residents in the Communist bloc for improved standards of living. Further impetus was given to this as travel from East to West became less restricted. A greater awareness developed of the higher living standards of the Western economies.

Courtesy: Bettmann/Corbis

● Oil being struck in the late 1960s in the Tyumen region (near Siberia).

THE SECOND OIL CRISIS

The 1979 oil crisis brought serious economic recession to Western Europe. This affected the Communist economies in two ways:

1. The market for East European goods was severely curtailed in Western Europe.
2. During the 1970s the Communist economies borrowed heavily from the West to finance new industries. When interest rates went as high as 17 per cent they were unable to meet repayments.

BALANCE OF PAYMENTS DEFICIT

In 1980 the gap between imports and exports totalled $300 million for Eastern Europe. Of all the Communist states Poland had borrowed most heavily and now ran into crisis.

POLAND'S FOREIGN DEBT

In 1971 Poland owed $1.2 billion in foreign debt. As imports exceeded exports that figure worsened until, by the end of 1979, Poland owed over $20 billion. Coping with this debt left very little money available for investment and growth. Unemployment rose and the demand for consumer goods was not satisfied. As inflation rose, mass discontent hit the streets and the Solidarity Party threatened the Communist regime. However, the crisis in the Eastern economies was not confined to industry.

AGRICULTURAL SHORTFALL

Agricultural output did not meet demand. State farms and collectives were generally inefficient. Throughout the 1980s food shortages and rationing became common. In 1980 the Soviet Union imported 27.8 million tonnes of grain and this became the general pattern for all of the decade.

THE SOVIET ECONOMY IN DECLINE

By the close of the Brezhnev era the Soviet economy was in trouble. Soviet technology was backward. In 1983 the Chairman of the State Committee on Science and Technology said: "Quite a few of today's enterprises are in need of radical reconstruction. Transport and communications are lagging behind the growing demands of the economy." By the early 1980s about 6 per cent of Soviet families owned a car, compared with 40 per cent in East Germany. When Mikhail Gorbachev came to power in March 1985 he attempted to turn things around.

GORBACHEV'S ECONOMIC REFORMS

- Investment in technology and new machinery was increased to reduce the Soviet Union's dependence on imports.
- Gorbachev tried to replace the inefficient and corrupt officials who controlled the economic system from the government down to the factory floor.
- The problem of excessive drinking was also confronted.

None of these measures was successful. The process of manufacturing new machinery was far too slow, the task of purging the system of corruption and inefficiency proved difficult and the anti-alcohol drive was very unpopular.

● By the early 1980s many of the Soviet Union's industrial enterprises were in decline.

Courtesy: Corbis

FURTHER ECONOMIC DECLINE

By the close of the 1980s the Soviet economic crisis had worsened:

- During the period 1988–1989 wages increased by over 20 per cent to keep pace with inflation and to avoid strike action.
- 20 per cent of Soviet expenses on imports was going on food, especially grain.
- Food shortages had become serious, leading to panic-buying and long queues outside shops; food hoarding meant that shops were frequently without basic foods such as milk, tea, meat, cheese and salt.

Courtesy: Turnley/Corbis

● After the collapse of the Soviet Union, this shipyard (dry-dock) was abandoned and the boats are just left to rust.

THE SOVIET UNION, 1991

In this, the year the Soviet Union collapsed, the economy hit a new low. Overall industrial output decreased by 18 per cent and agricultural production fell by 17 per cent. Figures for oil and coal showed a decline in output of 10 per cent. Shortages of goods drove prices up, most notably food. The Soviet economy was now so weak that Gorbachev appealed to the Group of Seven, most wealthiest nations in the world for help. By then, he had lost control of the situation and by the end of that year the Soviet Union folded. The other Communist economies endured similar difficulties.

POLAND

The foreign debt continued to rise, reaching $39.2 billion in 1987. Food prices in 1988 showed a startling rise of nearly 40 per cent. By 1987 the housing waiting list was 57 years.

HUNGARY

By the beginning of the 1980s the Hungarian foreign debt was nearly $10 billion. Between 1985 and 1989 agricultural production showed an overall decline of 2.1 per cent.

EAST GERMANY

Foreign debt had risen from $12 billion in 1981 to $20.6 billion in 1989. Proximity to West Germany led East Germans to measure their standard of living by comparison with their close neighbours. It was all too clear that they lived in disadvantaged circumstances.

SUMMARY

What we have seen in the above sections and in Chapter 7 is the steady decline of the Communist economies from the mid 1970s to the mid 1980s. From then they went into free-fall. Shortages of consumer goods, massive foreign borrowing, outdated machinery, worker apathy, cumbersome and corrupt administration, and falling standards of living all contributed to the decline of the Communist economies. Reform, in the shape of *perestroika* and *glasnost*, could not avert the fall. The main reason for this was that the old guard of traditional Communists remained in place and they resented reform. It threatened their positions, their privileges and their ability to manipulate the system for their own good. Revolution, not reform, was needed and, as we have seen in Chapter 7, that was precisely the tool that brought the Communist system down.

QUESTIONS

1. Explain why the Communist economies did not suffer as much as the West from the first oil crisis.
2. List two effects of the second oil crisis on the economies of Eastern Europe.
3. Give three reasons for the decline of the Soviet Union's economy in the 1980s.
4. List three ways by which Gorbachev hoped to reform the economy and comment on their effectiveness.
5. How did the condition of the Soviet economy compare with the other Communist economies at the time? Give a few details.

Source Document

The seeds for revolution

By the late 1980s the "shortage economy" had become the norm for Eastern Europe, sowing the seeds for revolution. In 1988 the Soviet Union admitted that its internal budget had been in deficit since 1976. Gorbachev conceded: "We lost control over the financial situation … This was our most serious mistake in the years of *perestroika*."

(Derek Aldcroft, *The European Economy 1914–2000*, Routeledge, 2001)

QUESTIONS ON THE DOCUMENT

1. What do you think Derek Aldcroft means when he describes the economy of Eastern Europe as the "shortage economy"?
2. According to Gorbachev, what was the Soviet Union's "most serious mistake" during the time of *perestroika*?

GENERAL ESSAY QUESTIONS ON CHAPTER 9

1. Examine the structure, strengths and weaknesses of the Communist economies in the period from the late 1940s to 1970.
2. Discuss the factors that contributed to the decline of the Communist economies between 1970 and 1990.
3. Compare and contrast the performance of the Communist economies in the period up to 1970 with the performance from 1970 to 1990.

10

THE OIL CRISIS, 1973
– CASE STUDY

Words you need to understand

Balance of payments deficit: When a country pays more for its imports than it earns from its exports.

Barrels: The unit of measurement used to price oil; a barrel holds 42 gallons of oil.

BPD: Barrels per day. The oil industry measures its output in BPD.

Gulf states: The oil-producing states found in the region of the Arabian Gulf, including Saudi Arabia, Iraq, Iran and Kuwait.

Nationalisation: Taking the ownership of oil production away from the oil companies and giving it to the countries where the oil had been found.

OPEC: Organization of Petroleum Exporting Countries.

Petro-dollars: Oil was always priced in dollars. The huge economic gains made by the oil producers made a very large amount of petro-dollars available for investment throughout the world.

INTRODUCTION

The 1950s has been called the golden years of the oil companies, the 1960s were called the years of the oil consumers, but the 1970s became the decade of the oil producers.

In October 1973, two events combined to set off a severe economic crisis in Western Europe. The Organization of Petroleum Exporting Countries (OPEC) dramatically increased the price of oil. Second, a war between Israel and some Arab states encouraged some oil producers to withdraw supplies of oil from countries that they believed to be supporters of Israel. The use of oil as a political weapon failed, but the resulting economic turmoil persisted for many years.

The oil business changed from a buyer's market to a seller's market. The oil crisis turned black liquid into gold. The oil crisis of 1973 took the 'gold' (money) out of Europe and sent it on to the oil-producing countries, mainly in the Arabian Gulf area.

10.1 BACKGROUND TO THE OIL CRISIS

EUROPE'S DEPENDENCE ON OIL

The prosperity and industrial expansion of Europe after 1945 depended on cheap oil supplies. The economic advantage of oil was simple. Between 1950 and 1973, the average price of a barrel of oil was two dollars.

Western Europe depended more on oil than any other source of energy for its transport systems, its industries and the new suburban consumers.

By 1972, oil provided 65 per cent of Western Europe's electricity, while coal accounted for only 22 per cent.

The plentiful supply of oil before 1973 kept prices low, as new entrants into the oil-producing business charged low prices. African countries supplied 6 per cent of Europe's oil in 1960, but over 40 per cent in 1970.

The oil producers gained from the small rise in prices between 1963 and 1972. As a result, the Gulf states increased their income almost fivefold from $1,860 million in 1963 to $8,747 million in 1972.

Courtesy: Bettmann/Corbis

● The oil pipes leading to the world's largest refinery, at Abadan, Iran. The Iranian government had nationalised the Anglo-Iranian Oil Company in 1950.

THE FORMATION OF OPEC

The emergence of a radical Arab leadership during the 1950s and in the 1960s upset the traditional arrangements with the oil companies. Many Arab leaders in newly independent countries such as Kuwait understood the importance of oil to the Western countries.

In September 1960, Saudi Arabia, Iran, Iraq, Kuwait and Venezuela set up the Organization of Petroleum Exporting Countries (OPEC) in Baghdad. OPEC changed the oil business forever. OPEC's ultimate aim was to get control of the oil fields away from the oil companies in order to increase OPEC's financial return from the sale of oil.

Country	Joined OPEC	Location
Algeria	1969	Africa
Indonesia	1962	Asia
Iran	1960*	Middle East
Iraq	1960*	Middle East
Kuwait	1960*	Middle East
Libya	1962	Africa
Nigeria	1971	Africa
Qatar	1961	Middle East
Saudi Arabia	1960*	Middle East
United Arab Emirates	1967	Middle East
Venezuela	1960*	South America

Founder members

In 1965, OPEC agreed on a standard royalty payment for producers, showing that it was possible for the producers to act in a unified manner. The price of oil rose during and after the 1967–1968 Arab-Israeli war.

In 1971, OPEC negotiated an increase of 40 cents per barrel. OPEC agreed in talks at Teheran in Iran to guarantee existing prices for five years.

However, Edward Heath, British Prime Minister, and Chancellor Willy Brandt of West Germany were worried about what would happen if a major political crisis arose in the Middle East.

Willy Brandt (1913–1992): He was mayor of West Berlin (1957–1966) and became internationally famous during the Berlin Wall crisis (1961). He was awarded the Nobel Prize for Peace in 1971, but resigned as Chancellor (1969–1974) following the discovery that an employee was a Communist spy.

Courtesy: Corbis

THE OIL PRODUCERS TAKE CONTROL OF PRODUCTION

In Libya, Colonel Muammar Gaddafi showed how the market could be upset.

Oil was a symbol of national pride and autonomy. In December 1971, he nationalised BP's (British Petroleum) territories in Libya. Between 1970 and 1973 the Libyan leader managed to achieve the largest price increases given to an Arab nation.

Colonel Muammar Gaddafi (1942–   ): A Libyan soldier, he overthrew King Idris in 1969. He promoted himself to colonel, the highest rank in the Libyan army. He supported violent revolutionaries in other parts of the world, including the IRA. In 1986 the US bombed Libya in an attempt to kill him.

Courtesy: Corbis

The increasing tension in Middle Eastern politics led Sheikh Yamani, the Saudi Arabian Oil Minister, to warn the USA in 1972 that American support for Israel would push some of the radical Arab nations to use oil as a political weapon.

Sheikh Ahmed Yamani (1930–   ): Minister of Petroleum and Mineral Resources in Saudi Arabia (1962–1986), he was a moderate member of OPEC.

Courtesy: Corbis

By 1973, most of the oil-producing countries had taken control of their oil resources, either through nationalisation (as in Iran, Libya and Iraq) or through new contracts with the oil companies.

THE TRENDS IN THE OIL MARKET FAVOUR THE OIL PRODUCERS

The global use of oil rose from around 22 million barrels per day (BPD) in 1960 to 53 million in 1972. In the 1960s the gap between supply and demand stood at 15 per cent. At the start of the 1970s the gap had lessened to 5 per cent.

The oil producers could auction off a small amount of their oil production in the open market. This often sold at a higher price than the set price agreed between the producers and the oil companies. OPEC then increased the oil price by 70 per cent, linking it with the higher auction market price, and cut production by over 25 per cent. For every barrel of oil produced in January 1973 the producers had received over two dollars. By January 1974 this had risen to eight dollars. By January 1980, the price was over 30 dollars.

The oil-consuming countries had no reason to suppose that the situation would dramatically change. In 1972 the United Nations and OECD stated that the dramatic growth rates of the 1960s and the early 1970s should continue.

QUESTIONS

1. Why did Western Europe use so much oil between 1950 and 1973?
2. Why did the oil companies have so much influence?
3. Indicate two successes achieved by OPEC between 1960 and 1971.
4. What major step did Iraq take in 1972?
5. What advantage did the oil producers get from the auction of a small amount of oil?

10.2 THE OIL CRISIS OF 1973

In October 1973 OPEC decided to set and control the price of oil on its own without negotiating with the oil companies.

THE FAILURE OF THE POLITICAL WEAPON

This strategy coincided with a political crisis. On 6 October 1973 the Arab-Israeli War started when President Sadat of Egypt invaded Israeli territory. A ceasefire was agreed in November after an Israeli victory.

OPEC decided to use the oil weapon against countries that supported Israel. No OPEC country was to send oil to the USA or the Netherlands. Countries friendly to the Arab cause would receive their usual amount of oil.

The oil trade was thrown into chaos by the OPEC decision. The immediate shock to the oil market did not produce the anticipated change in the American attitude towards Israel.

Sheik Yamani of Saudi Arabia visited Europe in December 1973. He realised that Europe could do little to change the US attitude, and that the oil crisis would not change America's support for Israel. The political (anti-American) element of the price rise would not be achieved.

● An OPEC meeting in March 1974, called to discuss crude oil prices.

Courtesy: Bettmann/Corbis

• London motorists queue for petrol during the oil crisis.

The OPEC action marked the start of the world energy crisis, creating a severe economic crisis not only in the developed countries, but also in the undeveloped countries of the Third World.

The price increases went beyond the worst expectations of the consuming countries. They had to borrow money to pay for oil and cut back on domestic services. The importing countries soon had to deal with a serious balance of payments deficit. The recession of the 1970s was caused by the instability linked with the oil price hikes.

THE IMPACT IN WESTERN EUROPE

The oil-consuming countries had no unified response to the oil embargo. They wanted the oil, almost at any price.

The EEC leaders failed to agree in December 1973 on the 'pooling' of oil among countries. It was left to individual countries to decide on the measures that they should adopt to save energy.

Countries began to restrict the industrial and consumer use of oil. Individual consumers found it hard to obtain oil for home heating or for car use. Prices escalated. Oil producers saw their revenues soar. Consumers were prepared to pay any price, and the auction market saw a tripling of prices in some cases.

A mild winter and a fall in demand for oil lessened the impact of the crisis during the winter of 1973–1974. Governments gave any available oil supplies to essential services, such as electricity stations and hospitals.

Governments ran intensive publicity campaigns, showing ways in which the consumers could save energy. Belgium and the Netherlands decided to ban Sunday driving. Belgium cancelled its national car rally. Luxembourg closed petrol stations on Saturdays and Sundays. Denmark lowered speed limits, while France asked offices to lower their central heating by two degrees.

The British Chancellor of the Exchequer, Anthony Barber, said that his country faced its "gravest situation by far since the end of the war". In the United Kingdom, posters advised couples to bathe together in order to save water.

Source Document: A

Edward Heath and the British oil companies

The British Prime Minister, Edward Heath, describes his efforts to increase the supply of oil to the United Kingdom in October 1973.

The price of petrol in Britain was far lower than in other European countries ... Naturally the oil companies were anxious not to let down customers in other countries, but ... they could make higher profits elsewhere.

With further concessions for North Sea exploration about to come up, we could have bullied the companies. I preferred a more reasonable approach.

When I invited the chairman of Shell and BP to Chequers as my guests, however, I was met with a complete refusal to co-operate. I was deeply shamed by the obstinate and unyielding reluctance of these magnates to take any action whatever to help our own country in its time of danger.

(Edward Heath, *The Course of My Life*, London, 1998, pp. 502–3)

Chequers: A country house specifically used by the UK Prime Minister.

QUESTIONS ON THE DOCUMENT

1. Heath said that the oil companies preferred to sell their oil in countries outside the United Kingdom. What reason does he give for this?
2. How did Heath hope to place pressure on the oil companies so that they would make more oil available to the United Kingdom?
3. When the oil companies refused to give more oil to the United Kingdom, how did Heath feel?

OPEC STEPS BACK FROM THE BRINK

OPEC soon dismantled their extreme measures. OPEC suppliers began to produce more than their quota to take advantage of consumers that were desperate for supplies.

Oil-producing countries that were not members of OPEC increased their output to take advantage of the price revolution. Prices began to fall when high prices acted as a deterrent on demand from the consuming countries. In April 1975, OPEC lifted the ban on sending oil to the USA.

The West swiftly reduced its dependence on OPEC oil. The danger of a collapse in the price of oil convinced OPEC that it should guarantee a consistent supply of oil.

Ironically, as a result of the reduced supply, the oil companies increased their profitability for the first time in a decade – but there was a cost. Their role had changed. Previously, they acted as middlemen between the producers and the consumers. They had also argued that any government interference would damage their role. However, after the OPEC crisis they looked to governments to protect their interests.

FURTHER OIL CRISES, 1979 AND 1991

The oil crisis of 1973–1974 was the first of three major shifts in oil supply between 1973 and 1991.

A second oil crisis in 1979 was linked with a new radical government in Iran, as well as a political agreement between Egypt and Israel. After the Iranian revolution of 1979, oil prices briefly touched $80 before dropping back to the high level of $35.

Two OPEC members, Iran and Iraq, went to war against each other in 1980, further breaking OPEC's unity.

● Saudi Aramco oil refinery, 1990.

Courtesy: Getty Images

The third price crisis came after the invasion of Kuwait by Iraq in late 1990. This led to the Persian Gulf War in 1990–1991, when oil prices reached $46 a barrel.

1. Why did OPEC cut oil supplies to the USA and the Netherlands?
2. When did Sheik Yamani realise that the Americans would not end their support for Israel?
3. Indicate one effective step taken by European governments to limit the impact of the oil crisis.
4. Why did the OPEC countries lift their ban on selling oil to the USA?

10.3 THE FALL-OUT FROM THE 1973 OIL CRISIS

GENERAL ECONOMIC EFFECTS

When the flow of cheap, imported oil dried up, the swift increase in oil prices led to **stagflation** (a very sharp increase in prices) (see page 130). The industrialised economies soon learned the meaning of recession: high inflation and high unemployment. Oil companies passed the increased costs on to consumers. Countries produced less, exported less and ran up high trade deficits.

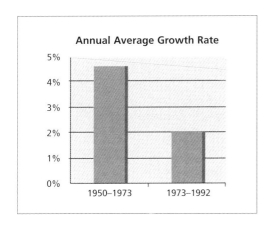

Annual Average Growth Rate

5%	
4%	
3%	
2%	
1%	
0%	
	1950–1973 1973–1992

THE LONG-TERM IMPACT ON WESTERN EUROPE

■ The oil crisis brought an end to the 'Golden Age' of economic growth in Western Europe.

■ After the 1973 oil crisis the main oil companies started to invest in new oil fields, such as the North Sea.

■ The oil-consuming countries looked elsewhere for supplies. They used non-OPEC countries, such as Mexico and the USSR, to meet their oil needs.

■ The 1973 oil crisis forced the oil-consuming countries to change their dependence on oil. Countries without oil, such as France, turned to alternatives such as nuclear power. Others, such as the UK, turned to natural gas. Iceland used its geothermal resources of energy to replace oil. High local taxes on oil in most European countries also encouraged consumers to cut down on their consumption of oil.

Courtesy: Corbis

● Western European countries looked for alternative sources of supply, and the UK started to develop its oil resources in the North Sea. This oil rig was called 'Dunlin A'.

THE LONG-TERM IMPACT ON THE OIL-PRODUCING STATES

The increase in oil prices created a bonanza for the oil-producing states – oil output in Iraq, for instance, rose from 1.5 million BPD in 1977 to 3.5 million in 1979. The income of the Gulf states increased from $7 billion in 1972 to $117 billion in 1977.

The increased revenues led to ambitious programmes of economic and social development in the oil-exporting countries. Iraq used money to develop domestic industry. Libya and Iraq invested in armament projects. Libya also invested in intensive agricultural projects.

This new prosperity led to the use of foreign labour. Many residents of Kuwait, Saudi Arabia and the UAE (United Arab Emirates) wanted high-paying desk jobs. Immigrants, such as Pakistanis, Indians and Palestinians, took lesser jobs.

The Gulf states had no banking system of their own. They loaned their new revenues, now nicknamed **petro-dollars**, to the experienced Western banking system. The bankers then loaned this money to developing countries, including countries such as Poland in the Socialist East. Arab oil money was also invested in Western Europe. Iranian money, for example, bought 5 per cent of Krupp, the German engineering company.

• The wealth and traditions of Saudi Arabia can be seen in this picture, where a mosque and modern skyscrapers stand side by side.

By 1977 the developing countries owed the commercial banks over $75 billion, most of it funded by oil money. However, the poorer countries were unable to repay this level of debt. This cycle of international debt caused a major world debt crisis in the early 1980s.

CONCLUSION

The huge rise in the price of oil caused major problems for the developed countries of Western Europe. The major price increases in 1973 helped to bring about an economic depression in Europe, the first since the second World War. The consuming countries reacted quickly to the oil crisis, lessening their dependence on oil and developing other sources of energy. By 1990 Europe imported less than 40 per cent of its oil from the Middle East.

Although the price of oil remained high, the problem of double-figure inflation in Western Europe during the 1970s softened the impact as the decade progressed. The role of the oil companies changed after they lost their monopoly over the oil fields. They no longer controlled the international flow of oil. The revenues of the oil-producing states increased substantially. The petro-dollar became a significant factor in the world economy.

QUESTIONS

1. How did countries change their dependence on oil?
2. How did the oil-producing states invest the vast increase in petro-dollars?

Source Document: B

British Petroleum (BP) took a different view to that of Edward Heath over the issue of where the available oil supply should go

It was everyone for himself in the pursuit of oil.

The chief perpetrators of the "me first" approach were Britain and France.

On 21 October, only three days after the Arabs announced their first oil export cuts, BP's chairman, Sir Eric Drake, and his Shell counterpart, Frank McFadzean, met Prime Minister Heath.

It was not a cordial party. Heath, despite being an ardent public advocate of European co-operation, kept, as Drake noted, "reverting to the problem of why British companies should look after Britain and forget about everyone else."

On 29 October, Drake met the British Defence Secretary, Lord Carrington.

Drake repeated that BP was obliged under its international contracts to treat all customers fairly and equally in the event of an oil shortage.

Any country insisting on ... normal supplies would only be worsening the situation for others.

(James Bamberg, *British Petroleum and Global Oil 1950–1975*, Cambridge 2001, pp. 481–3)

NB: Drake secretly gave extra supplies to the British government as a result of these meetings.

Embargo: Cutting back on the available supplies.

QUESTIONS ON THE DOCUMENT

1. When oil became difficult to get, how did individual countries react, according to Bamberg?
2. Bamberg, the writer, says that the meeting between Heath and Drake was "not a cordial party". What made it a difficult meeting?
3. How did British Petroleum justify its refusal to give extra oil to the United Kingdom?
4. Reread Documents A and B. What use could a historian make of the different points of view expressed in these documents?

Source Document: C

The impact of the oil crisis in the United Kingdom

Edward Heath, British Prime Minister, had to deal with the impact of the oil crisis while also dealing with a strike by coalminers that reduced the supply of coal to power stations and homes.

I announced in the House of Commons the introduction ... of a three-day working week to conserve fuel. In the meantime, industry would receive only five days' electricity every week and television would close down at 10.30 p.m. Essential services, of course, were fully protected ... With coal deliveries to the power stations down by over one-third, and the power workers now imposing an overtime ban of their own, we had to bring order to the situation ... production fell by less than 2 per cent during the three-day week.

(Edward Heath, *The Course of My Life*, London, 1998, pp. 502–3)

Source Document: D

Table 1
Oil Consumption in Europe, 1971–1992 (millions of BPD)

Year	1971	1973	1975	1977
Western Europe	13.28	15.16	13.51	14.23

Year	1979	1982	1988	1992
Western Europe	14.68	12.21	13.08	13.80

(F. Venn, *The Oil Crisis*, London 2002, pp. 135, 139, 140)

Table 2
Oil Production in Western Europe, 1973–1983 (thousand tonnes)

Year	1973	1983
Western Europe	20,420	171,050
Norway	1,600	32,040
United Kingdom	410	114,900

(F. Venn, *Oil Diplomacy in the Twentieth Century*, London 1986, p. 166)

QUESTIONS ON THE DOCUMENT

1. In Document C, what measures did Heath's government take to conserve fuel?
2. Indicate the problems that Heath had to face in bringing "order to the situation" in Document C.
3. In Document C, what success could Heath point to as a result of his actions?
4. In Document D, what statistical evidence is there to show that there was an oil crisis in 1973 and 1978?
5. Western Europe reacted to the oil crisis by looking for different sources of oil. What evidence is there in Table 2 in Document D to show that this was a successful policy?

GENERAL ESSAY QUESTIONS ON CHAPTER 10

1. Write a paragraph about each of the following.
   (a) Western Europe's need for oil.
   (b) The immediate effect of the oil price increases in 1973.
   (c) The long-term impact of the oil crisis.
2. Write a brief essay about the 1973 oil crisis. (You may include some points about the background to the crisis, why the crisis happened, its immediate impact in Western Europe and the long-term changes it brought about.)
3. "Since 1945 there has not been a really serious economic crisis" (Maurice Crouzet, 1972). Why did the oil crisis of 1973 bring an end to the period of economic growth in Western Europe?
4. "The oil crisis put an end to the Golden Age of economic growth in Western Europe." Why did Western Europe suffer so badly as a result of the oil crisis of 1973?

11

IMMIGRATION

Words you need to understand

Amnesty: To allow an unregistered immigrant to remain in a country.

Asylum seekers: People looking for permission to live in another country because of persecution in their home country.

Citizenship: Having the full rights of belonging to a country.

Commonwealth: The group of countries linked to the United Kingdom.

Emigration: Leaving one country to go to work in another.

"Illegal": A worker who does not have permission to work in a country.

Immigration: Entering a country to live and work.

Labour: A word used to describe workers.

Migrant worker: A person who moves from place to place looking for work.

Mother country: The country to which a colony was linked.

Racism: Showing hatred or disapproval of a person because of their skin colour or ethnic background.

Refugee: A person looking for protection from political, religious or racial persecution.

Repatriation: Returning an immigrant to his or her home country.

INTRODUCTION

Before the second World War, Europe sent millions of emigrants to the American and Australian continents. This pattern continued after 1945.

During the reconstruction of Western Europe in the 1950s and the 1960s, millions of workers stayed. However, millions also arrived from outside Western Europe in search of a better future.

After the 1973 oil crisis, restrictions were placed on employing workers. During the 1980s, the immigration debate was dominated by two new categories of immigrant – asylum seekers and refugees.

The scale of movement into Western Europe was so great that by 1993, the number of people living in the EU who had not been born there reached 12 million.

11.1 LARGE POPULATION MOVEMENTS, 1945–1973

REFUGEES AFTER THE WAR

Immigration into Western Europe immediately after the war mainly consisted of **displaced persons** from Central and Eastern Europe with refugees moving from East to West within Europe.

The **Potsdam Conference** in 1945 (see p. 6) agreed that German minorities could be sent from East European countries back to Germany. Twelve million people of German-origin moved to West Germany between 1945 and 1961.

TRANSFER OF WORKERS WITHIN EUROPE

The improving economy of Western Europe from 1945 to 1973 encouraged workers to move away from poorer areas in Europe (usually rural) to prosperous places (usually industrial cities).

● A transit camp for refugees after the second World War.

The less developed southern countries (such as Portugal, Spain, Italy, Greece, Turkey and Yugoslavia) sent workers to the more prosperous north (including France, the United Kingdom, West Germany, Switzerland and the Benelux countries). By 1974, about 2.7 million workers from Italy, Spain, Portugal and Greece lived in France and West Germany.

Ten million Europeans and their dependants took part in the migration movements between the 1950s and the early 1970s. Between 1960 and 1973, the number of migrant workers in Western Europe doubled, from 3 per cent to 6 per cent of the workforce.

The large-scale move from the countryside led to a decline in agriculture. In 1950, 29 per cent of the West European labour force worked in agriculture. Except in Spain, Portugal and Ireland, less than 10 per cent of people in Western Europe worked in agriculture in the early 1980s.

● An Italian immigrant working on a Volkswagen Beetle car in Wolfsburg, Germany, 1963.

THE MOVEMENT OF LABOUR FROM THE COLONIES:
UNITED KINGDOM

During the prosperous 1950s and 1960s, European countries also recruited labour from their ex-colonies. The UK had an 'open door' policy for immigrants from its former colonies. All Commonwealth residents had the right to free entry into the UK. Most UK immigrants during the 1940s and the 1950s came from the West Indies, India and Pakistan.

In 1948 the *Empire Windrush* brought 492 Jamaican emigrants to London. Attracted by the prospect of good pay, most of them had worked in England during the war.

● West Indian immigrants arrive at Southampton, England in 1956.

Courtesy: Keystone/Getty Images

• Members of the British White Defense League protest at Trafalgar Square, London against increased immigration into Britain.

By 1958 there were about 125,000 West Indians and 55,000 Asians living in the UK, working in low-paid jobs.

The **Commonwealth Immigrants Act**, passed in 1962, and the 1971 **Immigration Bill** stopped unrestricted immigration from the British Commonwealth. Immigrants needed to have a job before they arrived.

By 1967, 90 per cent of arrivals were family members joining the main wage-earner in the UK.

The last phase of colonial immigration into the UK between 1968 and 1974 saw the arrival of over 70,000 Kenyans and Ugandans, due to political problems in their own countries. By 1974 the UK had over 1 million African and Asian immigrants.

By 1992 over 2 million British residents had been born in Pakistan, India, Bangladesh or the West Indies.

Courtesy: Hulton Archive/Getty Images

• Docks, London. The immigrants are reading the local paper. What evidence is there that the people are finding it hard to adjust to the colder climate?

Source Document
The arrival of the *Empire Windrush*

The Guardian, an English newspaper, reported on the arrival of the Empire Windrush into London. This is an edited version of the original report.

What were they thinking, these 492 men from Jamaica and Trinidad, as the *Empire Windrush* slid upstream?

They had seen the advertisement of the shipping company in their local papers – a thousand berths on the troop decks vacant, £28 each – found the money, and in due time embarked with high hopes.

This morning, on the decks, one spoke with the following: a builder, a carpenter, an apprentice accountant, a farm worker, a tailor, a welder, a spray-painter, a boxer, a musician, a mechanic, a valet, a calypso singer and a law student.

And what has made them leave Jamaica? In most cases, lack of work. The cost of living is high, wages are low. Many can earn no wages. Some had been unemployed for two years. One of them said, "When the situation is desperate you take a chance – you don't wait until you die."

The Guardian, 22 June 1948

QUESTIONS ON THE DOCUMENT

1. How much had the West Indians paid for the journey to England?
2. Thirteen men described the skills they had. Which was the largest group: construction, entertainment or business?
3. Why did they leave Jamaica?

11.2   TENSIONS IN THE 1970s

The pattern of migration to the prosperous countries of the EU changed in the early 1970s.

Immigrant workers were no longer necessary in industry and other services after the oil crisis of 1973 (see Chapter 10). Governments restricted the flow of new arrivals and wanted 'guest' workers to leave. No country allowed unrestricted immigration.

In France, the first attempt to tighten the controls on legal and illegal employment of foreign labour occurred in January 1972. In Sweden, the foreign recruitment of labour was halted and immigration permits were reduced in 1972. Similarly, the Netherlands tightened its immigration controls in the late 1970s.

Southern European countries increasingly became countries of immigration (mainly from Africa), not emigration.

Source Document: A

Racial tensions in the UK

Race riots erupted as early as 1952 in Nottingham. Anti-immigrant groups such as the British Front (set up in 1967) targeted newcomers for abuse. Race riots also erupted in Brixton, London, in April 1981.

At 4.45 a young black was arrested outside a minicab office in Atlantic Road after a scuffle with a plain-clothes police officer ... the battle of Brixton had begun.

7.45: A petrol bomb sets fire to the Windsor Castle pub in Leeson Road, which is completely destroyed by 9.30 p.m. At the same time, the George public house in Railton Road is petrol bombed. An eye witness said: "There were whites as well as blacks doing it. The windows were knocked in and a long-haired white woman was doing a lot."

Mr Declan Butler, fire brigade Divisional Officer, said yesterday: "Every time we tried to attend to a fire we were attacked. We've never had this sort of disturbance before."

Edward, a black youth who did not wish to give his full name, said, … "I was expecting it. Police had been annoying us all day and everybody was getting jumpy. When it started the youths just picked up whatever they could find, bottles and bricks. We were fighting back."

Estimates spoke of 5,000 people being involved – concentrated in Railton Road with forays into Brixton Road to loot stores and the market.

(*The Guardian*, 13 April 1981)

QUESTIONS ON THE DOCUMENT

1. What incident started the "battle of Brixton"?
2. Who did the rioters attack?
3. Why did "Edward" believe that the riots started?
4. What evidence is there to suggest that it was not easy to find out what had happened during the "battle of Brixton"?

11.3   RESPONSES TO IMMIGRATION

FRANCE

In the immediate post-war years the French government needed immigrants to help France's reconstruction and to offset France's low population growth.

Before the 1960s, the majority of immigrants into France came from poorer regions of Europe and easily integrated into French society. Their children qualified for citizenship.

As a colonial power, France attracted immigrants from its colonies. Algerians were French citizens until 1962.

Courtesy: Hulton-Deutsch/Corbis

After the oil crisis of 1973, the French government suspended official immigration and even offered money to immigrants to return to their countries (voluntary repatriation). In 1976 the allowance stood at 10,000 francs. When the policy did not work, the government offered an amnesty to illegal immigrants. 130,000 availed of this opportunity.

In France, the total foreign population rose from 1.7 million in 1946 to 4.4 million in 1986. After 1974, the government allowed 'family reunification'.

● An Algerian shanty town at Nanterre, on the outskirts of Paris. Over 10,000 people lived here in 1961 when this photo was taken.

The government tightened the rules for gaining French citizenship, while eventually giving legal immigrants the same social welfare rights enjoyed by the French. In 1992 Prime Minister Édouard Balladur ended the automatic right to nationality by birth.

WEST GERMANY

With the construction of the Berlin Wall in 1961, West Germany found its supply of labour from East Germany cut off. Before the building of the Wall, some 14 million migrants from Eastern Europe had swelled West Germany's workforce.

During the 1950s, the West German government started to recruit *Gastarbeiter* (guest workers – primarily single young men) from Southern Europe to stay in West Germany on a temporary basis. Many stayed on, but the German government rarely gave citizenship rights to these guest workers.

Between 1955 and 1968, West Germany signed agreements with Italy, Spain, Greece, Turkey, Yugoslavia and Morocco to recruit workers for German businesses. By 1965 there were 133,000 Turkish workers in West Germany. By 1993, it was 2 million.

By the 1990s, it was more difficult for an immigrant from outside the EU to secure residency rights in West Germany. The foreign population in West Germany in 1993 was nearly 7 million.

Courtesy: Corbis

• The funeral of five Turkish workers in Cologne, Germany 1993. The five young men were killed in a racist attack.

RACISM

Opposition to the arrival of large numbers of immigrants increased in the late 1960s. The scale of immigration placed a large burden on the national budgets for housing, education, health, social services and social welfare. Immigration from colonial countries and other countries outside Europe led to a sharp rise in racism.

John Richards, who arrived on the *Empire Windrush* in 1948 from the West Indies, described the difficulty of being coloured in Britain: "They tell you it is the 'mother country', you're all welcome, you're all British. When you come here you realise you're a foreigner and that's all there is to it ... they say I just came off the banana boat and things like that."

In 1968 the English Conservative MP Enoch Powell wanted to halt immigration. He attacked immigration into Britain: "like the Roman, I seem to see the 'River Tiber foaming with much blood'.".

The **1968 Race Relations Act** legally banned racial discrimination in Britain, although stopping it in reality proved to be a tougher proposition.

Once seen as a 'solution' to labour shortages, immigrants were increasingly portrayed as a problem after the 1970s.

In the late 1980s, with rising unemployment, racist hostility worsened in France. In 1985 an Algerian youth was shot and killed by a café owner, who said, "I didn't want Arabs in my place, so I fired at him."

Courtesy: Getty Images

• In 1968, London dockers show their support for the racist view of Conservative politician Enoch Powell.

In a poll in West Germany in 1982, 62 per cent of West Germans thought that there were "too many foreigners" in the country, with 50 per cent backing the idea of sending immigrants "home".

In 1992, five nights of rioting at a centre for asylum seekers in Rostock, East Germany caused concern in Germany about the level of violence against immigrants.

Courtesy: Corbis Sygma

• Rostock, August 1992 – citizens demonstrate against the unequal treatment of immigrants.

11.4   ILLEGAL IMMIGRATION, 1973–1992

Governments introduced restrictive entry policies after the oil crisis, leading to the idea of **'Fortress Europe'**. However, the economic attraction of working in Europe prompted many non-Europeans to enter illegally and to work in the unofficial, or shadow, economy.

Roy Jenkins, the British Home Secretary, granted an amnesty to illegal immigrants who had arrived in the United Kingdom before 1973.

The EU Commission estimated in 1988 that Spain had 294,000 illegal residents, Portugal 60,000, Greece 70,000 and Italy 850,800. Countries offered amnesties to 'illegals'. Between 1986 and 1992, Spain, Portugal, Italy, Greece and France offered legal status to 650,000 unauthorised immigrants.

QUESTION

1. Why did Western Europe become known as 'Fortress Europe'?

11.5   ASYLUM SEEKERS AND REFUGEES IN THE 1980s AND 1990s

Courtesy: Getty Images/Time Life pictures

• Austrian soldiers search a Turkish man suspected of illegally entering into Austria, inspecting his identity papers. Why is one soldier holding a rifle?

In the 1980s the immigration debate was dominated by two new categories of immigrant – asylum seekers and refugees.

The 1951 **Geneva Convention on Refugees** asked countries to provide refuge for people with a well-founded fear of persecution in their own country.

Immigrants found it easier to travel to Western Europe. The collapse of Communist regimes in Eastern Europe also brought new immigrants from Poland, Romania, Albania and the Yugoslav region.

In 1984 there were only 104,000 asylum applications for all the EU countries. Between 1985 and 1992, applications rose from 157,000 per year to 674,000. By 1988, Germany had 800,000 refugees, France 184,000 and the UK 800,000.

Germany received over 60 per cent of all applications for asylum in Western Europe in 1992. The number of asylum applications increased in Germany from 73,832 during 1985 to 322,600 during 1993, and in the UK from 5,900 to 28,500 over the same period.

In 1992, Ireland, normally linked with emigration, received 39 asylum applications.

QUESTION

1. Explain why there was an increase in the number of asylum seekers during the 1980s.

Source Document: B

Buchi Emecheta came to England from Nigeria in 1962 when she was 18.
She arrived in Liverpool with her husband and two young children.

England gave me a cold welcome ... It felt like walking into the inside of a grave. I could see nothing but masses of grey, filth, and more grey ... It was too late now, I had sold all I had to go this far ... I was not going to allow myself to perish because if I did, who was going to look after the babies I'd brought this far.

No respectable family wanted a black family. We realised that however well educated we were, our colour which we ... regarded as natural was repulsive to others and posed a great problem. Our hosts in our new country simply refused to see beyond the colour of our skin.

(Buchi Emecheta, *Head Above Water*, London: Fontana, 1986, pp. 29, 30)

QUESTIONS ON THE DOCUMENT

1. How did the writer react to the "cold welcome" that she received in England?
2. "No respectable family wanted a black family." Why did Buchi have difficulty in finding accommodation for her family?
3. What evidence is there in Documents A and B that immigrants were determined to be successful in their new country?

GENERAL ESSAY QUESTIONS ON CHAPTER 11

1. Describe how the United Kingdom dealt with the problems of immigration between 1948 and 1992. You may use the following headings:
   (a) Where the immigrants came from.
   (b) The numbers of immigrants in the United Kingdom.
   (c) Steps taken to cut down on the number of immigrants.
   (d) Opposition to the immigrants.
2. Write about the response of the French or the West German governments to the challenge posed by immigration.
3. 'Large numbers of immigrants came to Western Europe between 1945 and 1992.' What were the main trends of immigration during this period?

12

THE WELFARE STATE

Words you need to understand

Christian Democracy: A political belief that seeks to achieve moderate reforms while maintaining institutions like the family and private property.

Nationalisation: When the state takes over property, means of production or services and uses the resources from them to benefit the nation.

Public ownership: State ownership.

Resistance movements: Organised underground movements, e.g. set up to resist Nazi occupation during the second World War.

Social democracy: A political belief that seeks to achieve gradual reforms by working through parliament rather than by revolution.

Social security: Financial assistance for unemployment, disability, pensions, etc.

INTRODUCTION

The defeat of the Fascist dictatorships and military regimes in the second World War increased popular support for the ideals of democracy. After the war, elections were held throughout Western Europe. This was a triumph for democracy.

In Western Europe, parties which stood for reform won a large share of votes. The post-war generation wanted change.

After 1945, people expected democratic governments to take responsibility for providing for the well-being of all citizens by introducing social reforms and restoring economic prosperity. The extension of democracy to include 'freedom from want' as a **duty of government** was the basis of the welfare state.

12.1 POST-WAR ELECTIONS

Political stability and economic prosperity in Western Europe after the war allowed democratic governments to implement elaborate programmes of social welfare policies. Welfare states were set up to meet the demands of the post-war electorate.

After 1945, wide-ranging social reforms were introduced by governments in Britain, Norway, Sweden, France, Italy, West Germany, Belgium, the Netherlands and Denmark.

The people who voted for Christian Democrat, Social Democrat and Labour parties expected the new democratic governments to take an active part in managing their country's economic life. They wanted their governments to protect citizens from poverty and unemployment. They believed that national wealth should be redistributed by giving state support of services for the benefit of all citizens. These ideas form the basis of the welfare state.

QUESTION

1. What reforms did the electorate expect from post war governments?

● A Labour Party election poster for the 1951 General Election in the UK.

12.2 BACKGROUND TO THE WELFARE STATE

The experience of mass unemployment during the Great Depression that followed the Wall Street crash in 1929 brought new challenges for democratic governments. While democratic capitalist countries in the West were faced with economic collapse, the USSR at the time experienced rapid economic growth. Western observers attributed the Soviet success to its Five-Year Plans. Democratic governments took on the responsibility of protecting citizens from unemployment through policies of state planning and organisation of national economies. The idea of full employment took root.

● Social Welfare payments in the US dramatically increased after the Wall Street Crash of 1929.

During the second World War, millions of ordinary Europeans faced economic hardship. Government management of the economy was necessary to ensure supplies of basic food and clothing needs. The economies of Western Europe were more mobilised during the second World War than they had ever been before.

In Britain, the wartime government appointed Sir William Beveridge to produce a report, called the 'Report on Social Insurance and Allied Services', which he published in December 1942. It became the blueprint of the post-war British welfare state and would strike a chord with post-war governments all over Western Europe.

The report was a charter for abolishing poverty. Even while fighting the war, the British government now committed itself to a welfare state and full employment. The report identified five main causes of poverty: **want**, **disease**, **ignorance**, **squalor** and **idleness**.

The hopes and expectations for a better society after the war were also evident in the resistance movements that had stood

William H. Beveridge (1879–1951): In 1942 he published the famous 'Report on Social Insurance and Allied Services', often referred to as the Beveridge Report. This report called for "full social security for all from the cradle to the grave". The Beveridge Report was the basis for setting up the welfare state in Britain.

up to the Nazis during the war. In March 1944, the French 'Resistance Charter' called for a "more just social order". It put forward an extensive package of reforms, including:

- The right to leisure and work.
- Security for workers and their families.
- Social security for all employees.
- Increased trade union involvement in economic and social life.

QUESTION

1. What were the main points of the Beveridge Report?

Source Document

The Beveridge Report

1. **Scope of Social Security:** The term 'social security' is used here to denote the securing of an income to take the place of earnings when they are interrupted by unemployment, sickness or accident, to provide for retirement through age, to provide against loss of support by the health of another person, and to meet exceptional expenditures, such as those connected with birth, death and marriage. Primarily social security means security of income up to a minimum, but the provision of an income should be associated with treatment designed to bring the interruption of earnings to an end as soon as possible.

2. **Three Assumptions:** No satisfactory scheme of social security can be devised except on the following assumptions.

   (A) Children's allowances for children up to the age of 15 or if in full-time education up to the age of 16;

   (B) Comprehensive health and rehabilitation services for prevention and cure of disease and restoration of capacity for work, available to all members of the community;

   (C) Maintenance of employment, that is to say avoidance of mass unemployment.

   (Sir William Beveridge, 'Report on Social Insurance and Allied Services', 1942, fordham.edu/halsall/mod/1942beveridge.html)

QUESTIONS ON THE DOCUMENT

1. According to the document, what is meant by 'social security'?
2. The Beveridge Report aimed to "establish full social security for all from the cradle to the grave". List some of the benefits referred to in the document.
3. What "exceptional expenditures" are mentioned in the document?

12.3 WELFARE STATES

Before 1945 most Western European states had developed basic state welfare programmes. However, it was only in the post-war period that such programmes were given stable funding and became legal entitlements for all citizens.

The various Western European states set up their own local form of welfare state depending on their different historical experiences, social conditions and government attitudes.

The welfare states in Europe fall into three types:
- Liberal Democrat.
- Social Democrat.
- Conservative/corporate.

• Social housing in blocks such as these proliferated all through Europe in the 1960s.

The following are four broad characteristics that all the welfare states share.

- **Government management of the economy:** Welfare states gave governments an increased involvement in planning and managing national economies. Goals and targets were set to improve production.
- **Public ownership of important sectors of the national economy:** Welfare states nationalised key industries and natural resources, bringing them under state or public ownership.
- **The use of taxation and social insurance contributions from those in employment to fund welfare services:** Welfare states provided social security (pensions, unemployment benefits, medical services) for all citizens. These benefits were funded by tax revenues and social insurance payments paid by all workers.
- **Broad-based co-operation between capital and labour:** Co-operation between employers (capital) and workers (labour) was a feature of welfare states. The role of trade unions in economic decision making was established.

QUESTIONS

1. List the three types of welfare state in post-war Europe.
2. Briefly explain four common features of the welfare states.

12.4 LIBERAL DEMOCRATIC WELFARE STATE: BRITAIN

In July 1945 the Labour Party came to power in Britain, promising to implement the proposals put forward in the Beveridge Report. The Labour Party's election manifesto, "Let's Face the Future", was a commitment to a programme of full employment, social security and nationalisation of key industries and resources.

There was less emphasis on state planning in Britain than in the French and Dutch welfare states. Later, under Harold Macmillan's Conservative Government (1957–1963), long-term economic planning was more in evidence in the British welfare system.

Courtesy: Getty images

● English co-ed school, 10 October 1952.

The Labour Government brought a range of industries, services and resources under public or state ownership. The following were nationalised:

■ The Bank of England.

■ Air, road, rail and water transport.

■ The production and distribution of electricity and gas.

By 1950, 20 per cent of all British industry had been placed under public ownership.

> **Means test**
>
> This was a test used to find the real income of families applying for social welfare. It was introduced in Britain in 1931 as an attempt to reduce government welfare spending and operated until 1939. Applicants for unemployment benefit had to have all forms of family income assessed, as well as the value of their furniture and other household possessions. This test was widely resented and seen as humiliating by poor families.

Courtesy: Hulton-Deutsch/Corbis

Aneurin Bevan (1897–1960): A Labour MP from 1929 to 1960. As Minister for Health in the first Labour Government, 1945–1951, he introduced the National Health Service.

The **National Insurance Act** (1946) provided unemployment and sickness benefits and old-age pensions. There was no **means test**. Everyone paid the same contributions and was entitled to the same benefits. The contributions from the National Insurance Scheme and revenue from income tax funded a range of services in the British welfare state.

HEALTH

Minister for Health, Aneurin Bevan, introduced the **National Health Service Act** (1946). The National Health Service (NHS) came into effect in July 1948. Under the Act free medical, dental and optical treatment was made available to everyone. Hospitals were placed under public control.

HOUSING

The Labour Government was committed to providing public housing. This task was the responsibility of the Department of Health, under Bevan. He also began a massive programme of state-funded house building. Between 1947 and 1950 an average of 170,000 new houses were built by the state each year. Complete new towns were also built to help deal with the housing problem.

EDUCATION

The Labour Government implemented the **Butler Education Act** (1944). Free primary and secondary education was provided for all school children. The school leaving age was raised to 15. A new exam, the eleven-plus, was introduced at the end of the primary cycle. This graded pupils on ability and aptitude for secondary education. Between 1944 and 1976 there were 15 education acts, improving access to education in Britain.

In the British welfare state trade unions became more actively involved in national decision making. Trade unions co-operated with governments and employers in promoting economic growth. Harold Wilson called this new partnership idea a '**social contract**'. Short-term labour demands were considered less urgent than long-term goals that would guarantee economic

Harold Wilson (1916–1995): In 1945 he was elected Labour MP. While he was Prime Minister a Race Relations Act was introduced in 1965 to deal with racial discrimination and limit the number of immigrants coming into Britain. As Prime Minister (1964–1970, 1974–1976), Wilson's Government introduced a number of reforms in education.

Courtesy: Bettmann/Corbis

growth and better living standards for all. Agreements between the state, employers and workers on pay and benefits were made legally binding. In 1971 the **Industrial Relations Court** was set up to intervene in industrial disputes. However, this era of co-operation between government, employers and workers came to an end in the 1970s in Britain, when a series of strikes occurred.

QUESTIONS

1. What industries and resources were put into public ownership in post-war Britain?
2. What is the NHS and how did it expand the welfare state in Britain?

12.5 SOCIAL DEMOCRATIC WELFARE STATE: SWEDEN

Sweden offers a model of the most extensive commitment by the state to provide welfare services to all its citizens. The spirit of co-operation, rather than confrontation, between social classes is central to the Swedish (and Scandinavian) model of the welfare state.

Sweden was neutral during the second World War. The Social Democratic Party came to power in 1932 and governed the country until 1976. In 1946, Prime Minister Tage Erlander's Government introduced a range of social reforms. The focus was on women and children, with generous children's allowances and state support for students to attend university. Women were encouraged into education and the workplace though state-funded child care facilities. Gender equality has always been an essential idea in the Swedish welfare state. Parental and child benefits do not depend on marital status.

● A woman training to use new computer technology, Sweden 1971.

Courtesy: Bettmann/Corbis

Old-age pension schemes and unemployment benefits were extended. Welfare benefits were universally provided for all citizens. The commitment to social equality went further than the British model and is a core feature of the welfare state in Sweden.

High taxation and compulsory contributions from employers and workers were used to fund welfare programmes. Employment in the public sector increased dramatically.

Sweden had a high level of trade union membership (over 80 per cent of the workforce). The trade unions became recognised, formal participants in regular tripartite negotiations with employers and the state. Strikes disappeared during the 1950s and 1960s. Between 1950 and 1973, Sweden had an average unemployment rate of 1.8 per cent, the second lowest in Western Europe (after Finland).

QUESTIONS

1. The Scandinavian model of the welfare state focused on women and children. Give examples of this.
2. What was the Swedish policy on nationalisation?

12.6 CONSERVATIVE/CORPORATE WELFARE STATE: FRANCE

Post-war French governments were committed to extending the welfare state. France had a stronger tradition of state involvement in social and economic affairs than most other countries in Western Europe.

In December 1945 the government appointed Jean Monnet (see p. 91) as head of a new central planning commission, the **Commissariat Général au Plan**.

In January 1947 Monnet published his first plan (see pp. 91–92). The plans brought economic success. Between 1949 and 1959 the French economy grew at an annual rate of 4.5 per cent.

The post-war government increased public control of key industries and services. The following were nationalised:

- Air France and 60 per cent of the French aircraft and automobile industries.
- About 40 per cent of the banking sector.
- Coal, electricity and gas production and distribution.
- Renault car manufacturer.

However, after this initial post-war 'clean-up', there was not much nationalisation in France until the 1980s, when the Socialists came to power.

The French social security system was linked to earnings and levels of insurance contributions. Pension and unemployment benefits were less generous than in Sweden or Britain.

Concerns about population decline made the French welfare state concentrate on the male breadwinner. Family allowances and subsidies for childbearing encouraged women to stay at home. Wives' and widows' benefits were based on their husband's social security contributions.

State spending on health between 1950 and 1984 rose from 3 per cent to 9.7 per cent of GDP, but the service was inadequate. Under the French system patients paid for doctor's visits and then applied to the local social security office for a refund.

● A poster for Air France after the company was nationalised, 1949.

Courtesy: Corbis

Government spending on education doubled between 1956 and 1965. In 1959 the school leaving age was raised from 14 to 16. The state ran 80 per cent of French schools. Attempts were made to make university education more accessible to working-class children by providing scholarships.

After the war France faced a housing crisis. The state initially focused more on rebuilding roads and railways than on providing homes. In 1948 the government began a programme of house building, but by 1953 only 45,000 houses had been built. This was not enough to resolve the housing problem. In that year the government began building high-rise housing complexes. They also built nine new towns, five of them around Paris.

As in other welfare states, French governments operated a partnership with labour and capital. In 1950 a minimum wage was introduced. Trade unions moderated their demands and co-operated in promoting industrial growth. Between 1950 and 1973 the average unemployment rate was 2 per cent.

QUESTIONS

1. How did Jean Monnet contribute to the post-war welfare state in France?
2. The French welfare state favoured the male breadwinner. Explain.

CONCLUSION

After the second World War, welfare states evolved in Western Europe. State spending on a range of services increased from 20–25 per cent of GDP before the war to 45–50 per cent by 1990, with health, education and welfare absorbing the greatest share of expenditure.

GENERAL ESSAY QUESTIONS ON CHAPTER 12

1. Write a paragraph on two of the following:
   (a) The Beveridge Report.
   (b) The Monnet plan.
   (c) The Resistance Charter.
2. Outline the reasons why the welfare state expanded in Western Europe after the second World War.
3. Discuss the origins and development of welfare states after the second World War.
4. Compare and contrast the welfare state in Britain, France and Sweden.

13

DEMOGRAPHIC AND LIFESTYLE CHANGES – EUROPE 1945–1992

Words you need to understand

Affluence: Wealth, abundant supply of riches.

Bureaucracy: A system of organisation or administration, which is usually inflexible.

Birth rate: Number of births per thousand of the population per year. Also known as the **fertility rate**.

Bourgeois: Middle class.

Death rate: Number of deaths per thousand of the population per year. Also know as the **mortality rate**.

Demography: The study of population trends.

Extramarital: Outside of marriage.

Feminism: A movement seeking political, social and economic equality of the sexes.

Gender: Classifying by sex.

Hedonism: A belief that personal pleasure and fulfilment is important.

Nuclear family: Father, mother and their children.

Patriarchy: Systems dominated by men.

Patriarchal family: Families dominated by men (father).

Stereotype: Labelling people as types based on generalised views/attitudes.

INTRODUCTION

The mood in Europe in 1945 was optimistic. Europeans faced the daunting task of rebuilding the physical environment, but having survived the horrors and uncertainties of the second World War seemed confident about rebuilding their personal lives and relationships. This confidence was reflected in the increase in marriage and birth rates in the immediate aftermath of the war.

During the war women carried out many of the jobs traditionally done by men, working in a range of industries and services supporting the war effort. In Britain, unmarried women under 30 were liable for military service after December 1941. Women played active roles in the Resistance movements across Europe. But after the war, women lost these jobs to men returning from service. They retreated to the home to devote their attention to husbands, children and housework, and they were encouraged to do so. In the immediate post-war years the emphasis in government economic and social policy was on women's role as mothers and homemakers. This emphasis was picked up by advertisers also.

The years of economic hardship caused by the war made the post-war generation eager to set up a comfortable home life.

• Women played a vital part in the British war-time effort. Here the workers are operating lathes, producing parts for the British navy, 1943.

Economic expansion after the war led to spectacular changes in lifestyles. Europeans began to enjoy some of the highest standards of living in the world. As affluence spread, so too did demands for leisure activities and consumer goods and services.

13.1 MARRIAGE AND BABY BOOM

Marriage rates increased dramatically in post-war Europe. Couples married at a younger age. Teenage marriage became more common after 1945. In 1931 in Britain, 17.1 per cent of all girls were married by the age of 19. By 1968 the figure had risen to 67 per cent.

Post-war housing shortages often meant that extended families (relatives) lived together in one household. It was not uncommon for three generations of families to share the same home.

To solve the housing shortages, welfare state governments built new towns and large suburban estates on the outskirts of big cities. Public housing projects like Sarcelles, outside Paris, or Loughborough, outside London, were built. These homes usually were one and two bedrooms, with kitchens, bathrooms, electricity and gas heating. The new towns and housing estates were designed for the single nuclear family. Sarcelles was a typical council estate built to house over 40,000 inhabitants. For many young couples, getting married was the only practical way to leave home.

• Builders at work on a new street of pre-fabricated houses. More than 20,000 such houses were constructed in 1947.

Birth rates, already rising in Britain and France during the second World War, showed a significant increase after 1945. In the last quarter of 1947 alone in Britain 193,865 babies were born. France,

Courtesy: Bridgeman Art Library

● Mother's Day, 30 May 1943, propaganda poster of the Vichy Government, 1943

a country that had experienced a declining birth rate since 1918, saw a sudden increase in birth rates from 1943. In 1938 the annual birth rate in France stood at 1.46 per cent; in 1946 it jumped to 2.14 per cent. By 1964 the baby boom had slowed down, but the birth rate, at 1.81 per cent, remained higher than in pre-war years.

The average family size changed. Households consisting of at least three people were the norm in most Western European countries. Welfare states encouraged young couples to have children by providing family allowances and tax relief. In Britain child benefit was paid directly to the mother. In 1952 it was eight shillings (40p) for the first child and increased for subsequent children.

In a speech in 1945 de Gaulle called for "12 million bouncing babies for France" within ten years. In 1935 the average number of children per family in France was two. By 1964 this rose to three children per family.

The West German Constitution (The Basic Law), introduced in 1949, placed marriage and the family "under the special protection of the state order". The government paid subsidies to non-working wives, encouraging them to stay at home and devote themselves to having and bringing up children.

13.2   THE NUCLEAR FAMILY

The nuclear family is based on the institution of marriage. It consists of husband/father, wife/mother and their children (by definition you cannot be legally called a 'husband' or a 'wife' unless you have signed the civil contract of marriage). This family type was already well established before the second World War, but it became more isolated and self-contained after the war. Sociologists refer to the trend of 'privatisation' in the post-war nuclear family. By this they mean the family unit withdrawing into itself – in the new towns and estates nuclear families were cut off from their extended families (grandparents, aunts, uncles, cousins). Often there was little or no sense of community or neighbourhood. The home became a haven of privacy and intimacy – a place of refuge in a world of strangers.

Within the home the nuclear family continued pre-war traditional values. These were patriarchal, that is, the husband/father acted as head of the household and his authority was absolute. The father was the wage earner and was legally recognised as the authority in the household. The wife/mother stayed at home to bring up the children and work in the home as a full-time housewife. The children were expected to always obey their parents.

QUESTIONS

1. How did welfare states promote marriage and birth rates after the war?
2. How did governments deal with the housing crisis after the war?
3. What were the traditional values of the nuclear family?

13.3 WOMEN IN WESTERN EUROPE

On 6 December 1944 the Queen of England thanked the women of Britain for their "magnificent efforts during the war". She praised all the women who had worked for the fire, ambulance and police services.

During the war women all over Europe had worked long hours in factories. Family life had been disrupted and homes destroyed. Women were often forced to move in with their parents or their in-laws, or live in temporary accommodation with their children. The post-war generation of women were, initially at least, glad to return to the home. Fashion, advertising and the mass media all contributed to the 'feminisation' of women during this period, consistently portraying women as house-bound.

Wartime population losses and low fertility rates reinforced women's roles as mothers. Society needed them to have children and many women recognised that. After the war there was a huge population imbalance between men and women. The high death rates of predominantly male soldiers left women outnumbering men in most European countries. In 1945 in Britain there were 1,700 women for every 1,000 men.

'War widows' were often left with families to support. Many of them had no choice but to take up employment outside the home, usually in low-paying jobs. Studies found that the women who did take up paid employment outside the home saw their jobs as a means to pay bills and provide an income. They worked because they had to.

The 1951 census in Britain showed that women made up 31 per cent of the total workforce. In France, 35 per cent of the working population were women in 1954. There was discrimination in pay in all European countries – women doing the same job as men were paid less. In 1955 Britain introduced equal pay for men and women in the civil service, teaching and local government jobs. However, in general employment women's wages remained low. In the mid-1970s women were paid 34 per cent less (on average) than men for doing the same job.

The war strengthened women's position politically. In France (1944), Belgium (1948), Italy (1946) and Greece (1952), they finally got the right to vote on the same terms as men. Before the 1960s the participation of women in politics was low. Issues that concerned women were not given priority by governments or male-dominated political parties. De Gaulle was asked if he would consider establishing a Minister for Women's Affairs. His answer was, "A ministry? Why not an Under-Secretaryship of State [junior minister] for Knitting?" Though women did become more involved in politics after 1945, they still remained under-represented in leadership (decision-making) positions until the 1980s. The issue of **gender balance** in public representation was first addressed in the European Union under the Maastricht Treaty (1992). Such emphasis requires Member States to be aware of the male/female ratios they put forward to the institutions of the EU.

Courtesy: Bettmann/Corbis

• A typical nuclear family of the 1950s. Notice the roles: mother serves dinner to father (who is in his office clothes) and son.

Courtesy: Corbis

• A room full of female typists at a nuclear development site in Britain in the 1950s. Secretarial jobs were mostly done by women.

QUESTIONS

1. How did the second World War affect women (a) in the workplace (b) in politics?

2. How would you describe General de Gaulle's attitude to women? Give reasons for your answer.

13.4   WOMEN IN EASTERN EUROPE

Courtesy: Bridgeman Art Library

• Under the red flag of Communism men and women are equal.

Equality between men and women was one of the revolutionary ideals of the Bolsheviks. In theory women had equal rights with men. However, in reality their position was not very different to that of women in the West. Many Soviet women worked long hours outside the home. Women were not free to choose their roles. Economic demands required them to work outside the home and to have children.

Equal opportunities in education gave Soviet women access to professional training and jobs. The medical profession became dominated by women, but lost financial and social status as a result.

After the second World War, when Eastern Europe became a Soviet sphere of influence, Communist ideas were imposed. Many Eastern European countries had traditional views about women and their status. These traditional views did not accept the Communist idea of equality between the sexes. They placed a strong emphasis on the family and the role of women as wife and mother. Communism, however, saw the nuclear family as a capitalist institution (bourgeois), and therefore destructive to society. In the Communist model, women were emancipated (free) workers, working outside the home for a wage.

In Poland traditional Catholic values remained strong even under Soviet rule. Both men and women supported the idea of a wife who devoted herself to the children and the home.

In Eastern Europe women had equality in the workplace, but carried the responsibility for the child care and running the home in their spare time – equality with men ceased at 6 p.m. Unlike women in the West they had few consumer luxuries or labour-saving devices in the home. Shopping often took many hours because of long queues and frequent food shortages. Many women in the Soviet bloc dreamed of staying at home and doing one job, like the housewives in the West. Access to work opportunities outside the home under Communism did not mean a better quality of life for women in Eastern Europe.

The participation of women in politics was relatively higher in the Soviet bloc than in Western democracies. Statistics show that the number of women serving in local government and in national parliaments was high in all the Eastern European countries. Communist leaders used these figures to indicate that women enjoyed greater equality under their system. However, the number of women holding positions at senior government level or in the Communist Party where real power resided, was low. In no Communist party in any Eastern bloc country did female representation ever reflect the proportion of women in the total population.

QUESTION

1. Give one example of how the roles of women in Eastern Europe were (a) different from and (b) the same as that of women in the West.

13.5   THE CULT OF DOMESTICITY

The majority of married women did not work outside the home in Western Europe during the 1950s. The general assumption, shared by many women, was that men should have priority in the job market. Women left the labour force when they got married. In 1951, 26 per cent of married women were in paid employment in Britain. In the Netherlands, France, Italy, Spain and West Germany, the numbers were significantly less.

Within the family, husbands had authority over their wives and children. In France a wife had to have her husband's permission to open a bank account or get a passport before the law was changed in 1964. Parents, and particularly fathers, controlled the lives of their children. Parental decisions carried weight even when their children became young adults.

The post-war commitment to family life, the home and traditional gender roles helped to sustain a 'cult of domesticity' in the 1950s. Women's magazines, such as *Woman's Own* in Britain and *Elle* in France, promoted the virtues of motherhood and home management. They encouraged women to be "feminine", offering them hints on how to seduce and keep their men. They promoted beauty products and the latest designs in clothing and home furnishings.

• 'Exciting stockings' from *Femina* magazine, 1950.

The new image of women portrayed in the media was the well-dressed wife and mother who reared well-turned-out children and kept a sparkling clean house full of consumer durables.

In this atmosphere of domesticity, Simone de Beauvoir's *Second Sex* received little attention when it was published in 1949. De Beauvoir argued that though women had won civil and political rights since the war, they were still economically dependent on men. There was inequality within marriage

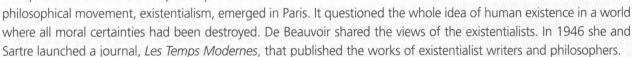

Simone de Beauvoir (1908–1986): Born in Paris in 1908 into a respected bourgeois family. While still an adolescent she gave up the strict Catholic religion of her parents and became an atheist.

In 1929 she graduated from the Sorbonne University, Paris with a degree in philosophy. She went on to study at the prestigious École Normale Supérieure in Paris. She was of the first women allowed to complete a degree there. While at the Sorbonne she met Jean Paul Sartre, who became her life-long friend, lover and intellectual companion.

Between 1941 and 1943 she taught philosophy at the Sorbonne. During this time she also published a number of philosophical works and a novel. After the war a new philosophical movement, existentialism, emerged in Paris. It questioned the whole idea of human existence in a world where all moral certainties had been destroyed. De Beauvoir shared the views of the existentialists. In 1946 she and Sartre launched a journal, *Les Temps Modernes*, that published the works of existentialist writers and philosophers.

In 1949 de Beauvoir published *The Second Sex*. The book was well received by her fellow intellectuals but did not gain any widespread appeal until the revival of feminism in the 1960s. In the book de Beauvoir gives a detailed history of women's oppression and exposes the inequalities society imposes on women.

In the 1960s de Beauvoir supported the feminist campaign to legalise abortion in France. She also spoke out against the French government's lack of financial support to unmarried mothers. In 1970 she was involved in founding the French Women's Liberation Movement. She died in 1986 and will be remembered as one of the leading feminists of the 20th century.

• Winter fashions from *Elle* magazine. These types of adverts have remained popular since the 1950s and are a typical example of what feminists object to.

because the husband was still legally the head of the household. Women, de Beauvoir claimed, were inferior in Western culture. They must challenge the values of society that kept them in an inferior role. "One is not born, but rather becomes a woman," she argued in *The Second Sex* (see page 193). Culture and society, not biology, were responsible for shaping women's opportunities and experiences. Though well received by intellectuals, de Beauvoir's comments were ignored and unseen by the majority of women at the time when they were published.

However, a number of social and economic changes were already taking place before the end of the 1950s. These changes would eventually shatter the conservative mood of the immediate post-war years and transform the view of marriage, family and the role of women.

Source Document

But is it enough to change laws, institutions, customs, public opinion, and the whole social context, for men and women to become truly equal? "Women will always be women" say the sceptics. Other seers prophesy that in casting off their femininity they will not succeed in changing themselves into men and they will become monsters. This would be to admit that the woman of today is a creation of nature; it must be repeated once more that in human society nothing is natural and that woman, like much else, is a product elaborated by civilization … Woman is determined not by her hormones or by mysterious instincts, but by the manner in which her body and her relation to the world are modified through the actions of others than herself … If we appreciate its influence, we see clearly that her destiny is not predetermined for all eternity.

(*The Second Sex*, Picador edition, 1988, p. 734)

QUESTIONS ON THE DOCUMENT

1. What must be changed for men and women to become equal?
2. What does de Beauvoir mean when she says "nothing is natural"?
3. Do you think de Beauvoir is optimistic about the possibility of changing the status of women? Give reasons, based on the document, for your answer.

13.6   DISENCHANTMENT WITH MARRIAGE

Early marriages plus a decline in mortality rates after 1945 led to longer marriages. In the late 20th century it was not unusual for a couple to expect to spend 50 years together. Previously, marriage for life was a relatively short commitment because couples married later and the levels of maternal mortality were high. Longer marriages were a factor in the growing disenchantment with the institution of marriage from the mid-1960s onwards.

After the initial post-war boom in marriages, marriage rates in Western Europe began to drop by 1960. This decline was first noticeable in the Scandinavian countries, but within a few years Britain, France, West Germany and Austria showed similar trends. In Italy and Spain, where traditional Catholic values were strong, marriage rates did not begin to decline until the 1970s.

In addition to the fall in marriage rates, divorce rates increased in most Western European countries where it was legal. In 1960 the annual divorce rate per 1,000 marriages was around two in the Netherlands, Britain and West Germany. By 1980 it had risen to 13. The rates in France jumped from 12 per cent of all marriages in 1970 to 22 per cent in 1980 and 32 per cent in 1990. The rates in Scandinavian countries were even higher than this. By 1990 Sweden had the highest divorce rate in Europe, with 50 per cent of marriages ending in divorce. Divorce was legalised in Italy following a referendum in 1974.

In Belgium, France and the Netherlands divorce rates trebled between 1970 and 1985. In countries where rates were already high, like Denmark, Norway and Sweden, they continued to increase during these years. At the same time, the percentage of unmarried couples began to rise. This trend was particularly noticeable among young couples. In France the numbers of couples co-habitating before marriage rose from 4 per cent in 1975 to 7 per cent in 1985. In Britain, 21 per cent of couples lived together before marriage in the 1980s. In 1985 there were more unmarried than married couples under the age of 30 in Sweden.

Falling marriage rates, increased divorce rates and the growing numbers of couples living together showed that Western Europeans were becoming disillusioned with the traditional institution of marriage in the last decades of the 20th century.

Legislation making divorce easier was introduced in many countries, but financial considerations often made women reluctant to seek separation or divorce. Changes in laws governing women's property rights gave them a degree of financial security. In 1970 the British **Matrimonial Proceedings and Property Act** enshrined in law the concept of **shared property rights** in marriage. A woman could now get a divorce and not expect to face economic hardship as a result. Benefits and services provided by welfare states also gave women better opportunities to leave a marriage and not have to run the risks of a life of poverty.

Divorce rates in Eastern Europe were lower than in the West. However, figures show a similar trend, with the number of divorces increasing between 1960 and 1980. In Czechoslovakia in 1960 there were 1.12 divorces per 1,000 marriages. By 1980 this figure had risen to 2.67. In the USSR the divorce rate for 1960 was 1.3 per 1,000 and in 1980 the number of divorces stood at 3.5 per 1,000 marriages. However, between 1980 and 1989 the divorce rate in the USSR increased sharply, matching rates in Western democratic countries like Britain, France and West Germany.

The number of marriages ending in divorce in Poland was relatively low compared to other Eastern bloc countries, but there too the trend showed an increase, from 0.5 per 1,000 in 1960 to 1.15 in 1980. However, marriage continued to be considered a commitment for life by the majority of Polish couples.

QUESTIONS

1. What country in Western Europe showed the highest increase in divorce rates?
2. What made it easier for women to get divorced in Britain after 1970?
3. Explain why divorce rates remained lower in Poland than in other Eastern European countries.

13.7 CRISIS IN THE NUCLEAR FAMILY

By 1980 more than half of all households in Scandinavia, Austria, Belgium, France, West Germany, Britain and the Netherlands consisted of just one or two people. The number of single-person households, or people living alone, showed a marked increase in the late 20th century. In most Western European cities, people living alone made up nearly half of all households. In 1989 one French household in four was composed of a single, widowed, divorced or unmarried person. Paris became the capital of aloneness, where one in two households had individuals living alone.

Another change in family structure is evident in the increase in the number of single-parent households. Before the dramatic rise in divorce rates, the average single-parent family was made up of widows or widowers and their children. By the 1970s, divorce and voluntary separation were the main reasons for children living in families with one parent. Nearly 20 per cent of households in Denmark consisted of children living with one parent in the 1980s, 70 per cent of them divorced. In West Germany, France and Britain, 10 per cent of households with children were single-parent families, 40 per cent of them divorced. In Sweden the majority of divorced couples remarried and stepfamilies were common. On average, 20 per cent of children lived with only one biological parent in Sweden by the 1990s.

The number of children born to unmarried couples also increased from the mid-1960s onwards. Again the Scandinavian countries show the highest figures for extramarital births: in 1990, 48 per cent of children in Sweden were born to parents who were not married. In Denmark the figure was also 48 per cent and in Norway 41 per cent. In France in 1975, 8.5 per cent of children were born to unmarried couples. The percentage rose to 18 per cent in 1984. The figures were about the same in Britain.

Courtesy: Corbis

Many conservative commentators argue that changes in family structure have resulted in the breakdown of society in Western Europe. They point to the rising divorce rates, lawlessness and crime, particularly among the young. In Britain in 1945 the total number of criminal offences was **478**; by 1994 the figure had risen to 4,598.

Family size has changed dramatically since the 1960s. All over Western Europe the number of children being born began to drop after 1965. In France the birth rate fell from 18.1 per cent in 1964 to 13.4 per cent in 1990. The figures are particularly dramatic in Italy, where traditionally the birth rate was above the European average. Between 1970 and 1990 it dropped to being the lowest, not just in Europe, but also in the world. The average number of children per woman in Italy was 2.42 in 1970; by 1990 it had dropped to 1.3.

● There was a huge rise in single parent families throughout the 1980s, where one parent carries the sole responsibility for the welfare of their children.

Even where the nuclear type of family continued to be the norm, structures within the family changed after the 1960s. Parental control, particularly the father's authority, declined. Young people enjoyed greater freedom within the family. Even in Italy, where the patriarchal family structure was strong, there is evidence of a growing decline in paternal control. A study of families in Rho, near Milan, records the story of a 21-year-old female clerk living at home in the 1960s. She tells how she dared to suggest to her father that instead of giving him all her wages (45,000 lire a month) and receiving 1,000 lire back for pocket money, she might keep her earnings and pay only her share for the upkeep of the family home. This scenario would not have happened in Italy before the 1960s. In France in the 1950s, if a father disapproved of his daughter's boyfriend she would break off the relationship. In the 1980s she would simply leave home.

Relationships between men and women, and between parents and children changed dramatically. Women and children have become more independent of the husband/father. With the changes in the nuclear family, children have become more assertive and less controlled by their parents.

Results of the crisis in the nuclear family:

- The role of the family as primary educator and social and cultural influence on children's lives has declined. With the growth in separation and divorce and single-parent families, many children attend day-care and pre-school centres to facilitate working arrangements of parent(s). This, together with universal education, has reduced the influence of the family and exposed children to outside influences, e.g. media and education system.

- Socially, the decline of the nuclear family has resulted in a growth of individualism, whereby more emphasis is placed on personal and individual achievement at the expense of community values. The traditional family fostered values of compromise and self-denial in the interest of the family unit.

- Economically, the break-up of families often brought financial hardship as both parents took on the responsibility of running separate homes. Single-parent families frequently faced financial difficulties.

QUESTIONS

1. What changes were happening in the nuclear family in the late 20th century?
2. How did relations between parents and children change after the 1960s?

13.8　THE SECOND WAVE OF FEMINISM

In 1963 an American feminist, **Betty Friedan**, wrote *The Feminine Mystique* which exposed the degree of sexual discrimination that existed in America in the 1950s. It showed how women, who made up half the population, had a disproportionate share of professional jobs, and they earned less than men for doing the same jobs.

The Feminine Mystique attacked the 'cult of domesticity', and Friedan showed that far from being content with their role as wife and mother, the majority of American women were deeply dissatisfied. When one doctor investigated the problem he found that women were suffering from "housewife's fatigue", caused not by housework but boredom.

The importance of Friedan's book was that it popularised many of the ideas Simone de Beauvoir had put forward in *The Second Sex*. *The Feminine Mystique* became a best-seller. Its message spread to Europe and inspired the feminist movement, which developed there in the late 1960s.

● Betty Friedan at a National Organisation for Women (NOW) march in New York, August 1970, marking the 50th anniversary of full suffrage for women in the USA.

Courtesy: Corbis Sygma

Germaine Greer coined the term the "second wave of feminism" in the book *The Female Eunuch*, published in 1970. The earlier feminists (first wave), Greer pointed out, were "genteel middle-class ladies (who) clamoured for reform". They focused on women's right to vote and to have access to higher education. Many of the more obvious legal discriminations against women had been

● Germaine Greer, author of *The Female Eunuch* and *Sex and the Politics of Human Fertility*, photographed in 1975.

removed as a result of their campaign. However, Greer argued, women remained second-class citizens in Western society. It was now time to launch a new campaign because:

- Since 1945 the gains made by the first wave of feminism had been eroded by the return to a male-dominated society after the war.
- Changes in the laws alone did not end sexual discrimination against women. Attitudes and behaviours would have to be transformed, as **sexism** was part of everyday life. Women themselves, often unconsciously, had come to accept society's stereotype of women as inferior to men.

Drawing on history, literature and popular culture, *The Female Eunuch* offered a powerful critique of Western society. It exposed how women were still denied real equality with men in the late 20th century. The way forward for women was not just to fight for equal treatment with men: "Womanpower means the self-determination of women, and that means that all the baggage of paternalistic society will have to be thrown overboard." (*The Female Eunuch*, Paladin 1971, p. 114).

The modern women's movement, according to Greer, needed to change the whole basis of society's values. Freedom and equality for women would require a complete revolution in attitudes between the sexes, and among women themselves.

QUESTIONS

1. What was the main message in Betty Friedan's *The Feminine Mystique*?
2. What was the "second wave of feminism"?

13.9 CHANGING PATTERNS IN EDUCATION AND THE WORLD OF WORK

The ideas of Friedan and Greer struck a chord with many women in Western Europe. The vast majority of these women were well educated and middle-class. In the immediate post-war years, 15–30 per cent of all students in most Western European countries were women. By 1980 their numbers had risen to 50 per cent or more.

More women attended university in Eastern bloc countries than in the West. By 1960 the number of female university students in Bulgaria stood at almost 50 per cent of the entire student population.

In the immediate post-war years the majority of women in paid employment were single. From the 1960s onwards there was a dramatic increase in the number of married women working outside the home. The average woman worker was older, married and a mother. Paid employment was no longer considered something single women did to make up the time between finishing school and getting married.

The availability of good child care facilities in Scandinavian countries gave married women employment opportunities, as did tax incentives that encouraged women to return to work after having children.

A study of married women working outside the home in Britain in the early 1960s showed that most of them saw their work as an extension of family duties. They worked to supplement family income. From the mid-1960s on, many families came to increasingly rely on the extra income from wives to pay for a range of consumer goods and contribute to the more affluent lifestyle that most Europeans were now enjoying.

However, in the world of paid employment women's traditional roles were often reinforced. The majority of women were employed in the service sector (catering, cleaning, retail, tourism, etc.), caring occupations (teaching, nursing, social work, etc.) or office work (banking, civil services, etc.). In Germany 77 per cent of low-grade civil service jobs were done by women. In France in 1973, 96 per cent of typists, 88 per cent of receptionists and 78 per cent of cashiers were women. In Britain in the 1970s, 74 per cent of service workers and 67 per cent of office workers were women. Throughout Europe women increasingly dominated primary and secondary teaching.

• Norah O'Neill was the first female commercial pilot, photographed here just before her first flight in 1977.

Courtesy: Corbis

By 1991 female workers were becoming more visible in greater numbers than ever before, making up 70.1 per cent of the total workforce in Denmark and 61.1 per cent in Britain. The figures for Southern Europe were lower, with 37.2 per cent in Italy, but here as elsewhere the number of women in paid employment showed an increase between 1960 and 1990.

QUESTIONS

1. What dramatic change in education took place for women after 1945?
2. What kind of work were women mainly employed in?

13.10 SEXUAL REVOLUTION

Simone de Beauvoir argued that society, not biology, determined women's roles. Once pregnant, the vast majority of women had no choice but to give birth and raise their children.

The birth control pill was invented in 1952. By the 1960s it was widely available in most Western European countries. From 1974 women in Britain were able to get contraceptives under the National Health Service. In Scandinavia family planning services were provided by the state.

In France the laws on contraception were slower to change, partly because of traditional Catholic views, but also because of French paranoia about falling birth rates. In 1920 the French government had passed a law forbidding the sale of contraceptives and banning the distribution of birth control information. The law was not based on religious objections but on demographic (population) needs. France had suffered huge population losses and the government wanted to encourage couples to have more children. This law was reformed in 1967, and since the mid-1970s contraceptives have been available from the national health service in France.

• The contraceptive pill, simply known as 'the pill' became widely available through the 1960s and 1970s.

Courtesy: Bettmann/Corbis

In 1968 Pope Paul VI issued *Humanae Vitae*, an encyclical that firmly denounces contraception. Catholics in Europe were deeply divided on the issue, but the numbers of women using the pill

increased in Catholic as well as Protestant countries. "In the Pope's own Italy … The sale of contraceptives and birth control information was legalised in 1971". (Hobsbawn p. 323)

When contraception was legalised in most Western European countries, feminists and their supporters turned their attention to campaigning for the right to have legal abortions. In the 1960s in France it was estimated that there were between 700,000 and 800,000 illegal abortions performed annually. Often women faced huge health risks, even death, when having these "back-street" abortions.

• 'Pregnant' men at a demonstration in London, 1972. These men did this to show that men are affected by the debates and political decisions around birth control.

In April 1971, French feminists published a manifesto demanding free and legal abortion. Three hundred and forty-three leading French women, including Simone de Beauvoir, announced that they had had illegal abortions. They challenged the authorities to prosecute them. In November that year women took to the streets singing "*Travail, Famille, Patrie, y en a marre*" (work, family, fatherland, we've had enough of them). A pro-abortion organisation, Choisir (Choice), was set up. As a result of its campaign the French parliament passed laws legalising abortion in 1974.

In 1983 the Socialist government in France made legal abortion available on social security, with 70 per cent of the cost refunded. In the 1980s it was estimated that there were 180,000 legal abortions in France.

In 1971 *Stern* magazine published an article declaring that 375 well-known West German women had had abortions. A petition with 86,500 names was presented to the Minister for Justice calling for the liberalisation of the existing abortion laws in West Germany (GFR). Eventually the laws were reformed to allow for abortion in certain circumstances. The interpretation of the law was left to the courts in the different states. Conservative states like Bavaria often took a narrow interpretation of the law and tried to restrict abortions.

• A pro-abortion rally in France, 1979. The banner says 'It is not up to the government, it is a woman's choice'.

Abortion was legalised in Britain, Sweden, the Netherlands and Germany in the 1960s and 1970s.

Laws on abortion and contraception were more liberal in the Eastern bloc countries. Abortion was frequently used as a method of birth control in the Soviet bloc.

The 1960s and 1970s was a time of great change in sexual attitudes and behaviours. Sex was no longer exclusively linked to marriage and procreation. Developments in medicine seemed to remove the major risks that went with sexual promiscuity. Venereal diseases were now treatable with antibiotics and pregnancy was avoidable by the use of the pill. The shift in attitudes and behaviours was so dramatic that it has been described as a **sexual revolution**.

• An anti-abortion demonstration from the 1980s. The banner here reads 'The embryo is a person'.

13.11 REVIVAL OF FEMINISM

Feminism in the 1960s was concerned with social and economic equality between men and women. At first, middle-class, educated women dominated the movement. By the 1970s and 1980s it spread to all women (through TV, film and books) and took on a political focus. Women took up leadership roles in politics in many countries.

Women became a pressure group in politics. They were prominent campaigners on green issues and environmentalist concerns, and pushed for political recognition for consumer rights and proper advertising standards. Female activists concerned with the deployment of US nuclear weapons in Britain set up the Women's Peace Camp at Greenham Common in 1981. They continued their protests there until the American missiles were finally removed in March 1991.

Women in politics campaigned on a range of social issues. They fought for maternity leave for working mothers, forcing governments to introduce legislation on this issue. They demanded the setting up of women's aid refuges and rape crisis centres. They brought the issue of violence against women in the home and in society to the forefront of politics.

By 1990 most of these issues were taken on board by political parties in many Western European states. Women had finally succeeded in having a real and lasting influence on the male-dominated world of politics.

The revival of feminism in the 1960s also had an impact on women's 'consciousness' or way of thinking. Women became more assertive about their rights. The feminists preferred to use the word gender rather than sex, e.g. gender inequalities, gender issues, etc. 'Consciousness-raising' sessions had begun in the US in the 1960s. During the 1970s they became common in the UK, France and Germany. These sessions encouraged discussion and debate on sexism. They also promoted self-esteem among women. Their slogan became **"the personal is political"**. This emphasised that sexism was present in personal relationships between men and women, even within marriage. In 1970 a group of feminists laid a wreath at the Tomb of the Unknown Warrior at the L'Arc de Triomphe in Paris. The inscription read: "There is someone more unknown than the Unknown Warrior: his wife".

Courtesy: Bettmann

● Anti-nuclear protestors at Greenham Common, England in 1983. They are blocking the entrance to the air base, so that goods and personnel cannot get through. Theirs is a passive protest (no violence).

A whole new academic study emerged. In universities around Europe, courses in Women's Studies were offered. Academic research challenged many cultural assumptions that implied that the masculine experience is the central form of human experience. In the study of history the focus moved away from the "great men", military campaigns and political developments, which had dominated the history books. The new focus turned to social history and the lives of ordinary men and women who up to now had largely been omitted from the history books. Women who generally went unnoticed in the study of history before the 1960s were now given recognition for the parts they played in the past.

QUESTIONS

1. Explain why the laws on contraception were slow to change in France.
2. What was *Humanae Vitae*?
3. List some of the political issues that concerned women in the 1970s and 1980s.

13.12   AFFLUENCE

By the 1960s jobs were plentiful, wages were good and standards of living improved dramatically. Families no longer worked to make ends meet or to provide for the necessities of life. Most Europeans could buy goods previously considered luxuries. The working classes were now able to afford goods and lifestyles that before now were only available to the middle classes and the rich. As poverty and unemployment seemed to disappear during the golden years, the traditional working class was no longer recognisable. These were the years of the "affluent worker", and by the 1960s millions of ordinary Europeans began to share the benefits of economic prosperity. Secure jobs, paid holidays and a range of welfare services meant the working class became more socially mobile. The working classes were buying cars, domestic appliances, home entertainment products and investing in private property. Labour politicians worried that they were losing the powerful working-class vote. Prosperity seemed to weaken political support for reform. Contented workers were not prepared to threaten the social and economic system that had brought such improvement to their lives.

One clear indicator of the new affluence was the growth in ownership of private cars. Between 1950 and 1964 the number of private cars in Italy increased from 342,000 to 4.67 million. By 1970 there were nearly 14 million private cars in Germany, 13 million in France and 11.5 million in Britain.

During the 1959 British general election campaign, Conservative Home Secretary R.A. Butler said, "We have developed … an affluent, open and democratic society in which the class escalators are continually moving and in which the people are divided not so much between the 'haves' and the 'have nots' as between 'haves' and 'have mores'.

QUESTION

1.   Give examples of affluence in post-war Europe.

13.13   LEISURE

In the post-war years full employment, increased wages and more paid holiday time created new patterns of consumption and leisure activities. Work, once necessary to earn a living and survive, now also became the means to pay for a range of free-time activities. Before the war the average French family spent 50 per cent of its income on food and drink. By the 1980s this had dropped to 21 per cent. This pattern of increased **disposable income** was similar in most Western countries.

The post-war revolution in transport and communications resulted in great changes in leisure habits, the greatest of which were found in the expansion of travel opportunities and in the emergence of new forms of entertainment.

Courtesy: Bettmann/Corbis

● Packing a picnic basket. An early 1960s family at a free-time weekend activity.

The motorcar brought increased mobility and a new focus for leisure-time activities. The mass production of cars and the availability of cheap petrol made car ownership a reality for millions of families. Cars like the German Volkswagen Beetle, the French Citroén DS and Renault 4 CV, the British Mini and the Italian Fiat 500 were symbols of both affluence and a new form of leisure activity. Sunday trips into the countryside by car became a popular activity for many families.

After the war, civilian use of air transport also increased dramatically. Foreign package tours, with an 'all in' price for air travel and accommodation, provided relatively cheap holidays. 'Sun holidays' became popular. Before the 1950s Spain had few foreign tourists. However, by the late 1980s over 54 million foreigners a year took holidays there. New holiday complexes were built to cater for the mass market.

Courtesy: Corbis

● Marbella beach – the Costa del Sol attracts millions of holiday-makers each summer.

In 1950 a small informal holiday camp for adults was set up on Majorca. The idea took off and was developed into Club Méditerranée (Club Med). By 1985 Club Med's annual turnover was worth 6 billion francs (€914 million) and had become the largest holiday organisation in the world.

In 1992, the giant American theme park, Euro Disney, opened in France. Situated 16 miles east of Paris, it offered a new tourist attraction modelled on the Florida and California Disney theme parks. It created 30,000 new permanent jobs and was estimated to attract 5 million foreign tourists a year. Theme parks like Gardaland on the shores of Lake Garda in Italy and at Alton Towers in Britain also became popular family holiday destinations.

The expansion of the tourist industry from the 1950s to the 1980s led to what has been called the 'grand depart'. Every July and August European motorways, railways and airports were choked by millions of holiday tourists.

The post-war communications revolution also had a profound effect on leisure activity. The most spectacular change in communications came with the arrival of television. The world's first regular television broadcasting began in 1936 with the BBC. The station had closed down during the war, but reopened in 1949. At this stage, though, TV was a luxury item and was not available to the general public. By the 1960s things had changed. In 1963 France had 3.5 million TV sets, West Germany 7.9 million and Britain 12.5 million, and by 1965 49 per cent of Italian families owned a TV set. By the mid-1980s over 90 per cent of all homes across Western Europe were equipped with TV sets.

In the 1950s TV viewing was usually a collective form of entertainment. In West Germany, TV clubs were established. People who did not have TV at home went to watch programmes in neighbour's houses. An Italian journalist wrote about the experience of one small village north of Florence. Here there were only 11 TV sets in the whole village, yet 91 per cent of the villagers watched TV. In the evenings peasants carrying chairs often came down from the mountains to watch a TV programme.

As the cost of television sets fell, more families were able to buy their own sets. In the home the family gathered around the TV set to spend their leisure time watching favourite TV shows. In 1962 the Telstar satellite transmitted the first live broadcast from the USA. On 20 July 1969, 600 million TV viewers around the world watched the first moon landing live. Cable and satellite broadcasting began in 1989. Available on subscription, viewers were given a greater choice of programmes to watch.

By the 1980s, television viewing was the most popular form of entertainment in Western Europe. A 1986 Italian survey found that 86.3 per cent watched TV every day, compared to only 46.4 per cent who listened to radio and 41.4 per cent who read a newspaper. A French survey in 1982, showed that people over 60 and those with only elementary education watched TV most frequently.

• Watching TV everyday became more and more common throughout the 1980s, attracting all generations.

Courtesy: Corbis

The high cost of producing home-based TV shows resulted in widespread importation of American programmes. By 1988, 22 per cent of French programmes, 13 per cent of British and 6 per cent of Italian were imported from America. Many saw this development as a threat to their own culture.

Telephones, computers, VCRs (video recording) and stereo music systems all transformed leisure time in the late 20th century. The boom in pop music made radio popular with music fans. However, the print media, particularly newspapers, failed to compete with TV and radio. During the 1960s the best-selling newspapers in Britain, the *Sun* and the *Star*, primarily catered for entertainment. These featured information about the lives of pop stars, the royal family, sport and soap operas.

QUESTIONS

1. How did changes in transport affect leisure-time behaviour after the war?
2. What new leisure activities were made available by the revolution in communications?

13.14   THE CONSUMER SOCIETY

The golden years of prosperity marked the rise of the modern consumer society in Western Europe. Consumption went beyond the fulfilment of basic economic needs (food, clothing and shelter) to satisfying personal desires for comfort and better standards of living.

Courtesy: Bettmann/Corbis

• A 1950 image of a 'perfect' kitchen full of appliances – a dream sold to millions of consumers.

Two distinct phases of consumption are evident between 1945 and 1992. In the earlier phase, 1945 to the late 1970s, the focus was the home and the family. Between 1958 and 1965 spending on consumer durables such as fridges, washing machines, TVs and cars doubled in Western Europe.

The advertising business played a crucial role in the expansion of consumer demands. Newspapers, magazines and TV advertising promoted the ever-growing range of labour-saving devices for the home. Advertising and marketing companies targeted women in particular. Many domestic appliances and gadgets were now considered necessities, useful and standard items for the average home.

The consumer society led to a spectacular expansion of the retail trade in general. Large supermarkets replaced small grocery shops. American-style department stores, selling everything from clothes and footwear to home and beauty products, caused a decline in the number of small individual retail businesses. The development of shopping centres from the 1960s onwards offered even greater scope for mass consumer retail spending.

Courtesy: Corbis Sygma

From the end of the 1970s on, a new phase in consumer spending took place. In the 1980s and 1990s consumption swung more towards fulfilment of personal satisfaction. Technological change revolutionised everyday life, particularly in the field of entertainment. Video recorders (VCRs), CD players and PCs became the new domestic necessities. The emphasis on the personal is evident in the increasing trend towards portability and miniaturisation. Sales of digital watches, pocket calculators, video cameras, mini discs and the ever-present Walkman rocketed. Hedonism, instant gratification and the pursuit of individual pleasure became the hallmark of the late 20th-century consumer society.

● Frantic shopping at Christmas-time, 1990s.

Another aspect of the growth of a more personal kind of consumption during this period is the remarkable expansion of consumer demand for beauty and personal hygiene products. Cosmetic sales boomed. Perfumes, deodorants and haircare products all became consumer necessities. The market in these products was not confined to women, as an Italian study found: two out of three people (men and women) in the 1990s were regularly using face creams.

Designer clothes and branded products came to symbolise good taste and superior lifestyles. Mass marketing in the late 20th century turned shopping into a performance, the consumer society's ultimate source of satisfaction.

QUESTIONS

1. What consumer products were in most demand during the 1950s and 1960s?
2. How did consumer behaviour change from the late 1970s on?

GENERAL ESSAY QUESTIONS ON CHAPTER 13

1. Outline some of the changing trends in the role of women 1945–1992.
2. Compare the situation for women in Western and in Eastern Europe 1945–1992.
3. List some of the changes in leisure activity in Europe 1945–1992.
4. Explain why the role of women in the immediate post-war years became largely confined to the home.
5. "The rights of women are the most profound of all the human rights claimed in the second half of the 20th century." To what extent do you agree with this statement?
6. What were the factors that contributed to changes in family life from the 1960s onwards?
7. Outline the arguments put forward by one of the feminist writers referred to in this chapter.
8. What were the main developments in popular entertainment in post-war Europe?
9. Describe the changing trends in consumer behaviour and attitudes in Western Europe 1945–1992.
10. "Rising affluence was the unique feature of the golden age of prosperity." Discuss.

14

LITERATURE AND SOCIAL CRITICISM: EAST AND WEST

Words you need to understand

Socialist Realism: The policy of the Communist governments that all art, including literature, must serve the state.

Dissident writing: The work of writers who disagreed with the structure of government and society in Eastern Europe.

Gulag: A labour camp for prisoners in the Soviet Union.

Zek: An inmate of the prison system in the Soviet Union.

Existentialism: The belief that man must create his own values through action and live every moment of his existence to the full without reliance on a god or a church.

14.1   EASTERN EUROPE

In the second half of the 20ᵗʰ century, writers in Eastern and Western Europe expressed their criticism of society. In the East writers were censured and pressured to shape the content of their work in a particular way. Writers in the West enjoyed a far greater degree of freedom.

Socialist realism was the first official cultural policy adopted during the long period of Stalin's reign of the Soviet Union. In 1934 the **Union of Soviet Writers** adopted **Socialist realism** as "the basic method of Soviet artistic literature and literary criticism". Basically, it said that all Soviet culture must reflect life in the Soviet Union. However, that portrayal of Soviet life would always be positive, heroic and never critical of the system.

SIMPLICITY AND LOYALTY

Under Socialist realism, literature had to be written in simple, understandable language. All literature had to support the policies of the Communist Party. Soviet workers had to be portrayed as heroic figures. Writers were expected to base their work on the advances in industry, agriculture and Soviet military strength. Until Stalin's death in 1953, Socialist realism was rigidly enforced on Soviet writers and artists. Stalin's departure gave rise to a slightly more tolerant and lenient approach to writers and artists.

THE THAW

Hundreds of writers who had opposed the policy of Socialist realism were freed from prisons and gulags after March 1953. Under Khrushchev there was a thaw in that writers were allowed greater freedom than under Stalin, but they still had to toe the Party line. The softer approach encouraged some writers to express their opposition to the restrictions placed on them.

DISSIDENT WRITING

By 1954 a small number of writers began to defy the limits set by Socialist realism. A notable outlet for these writers was the literary journal, *Novyi Mir* (**New World**), which was published monthly. One of the first dissident writers to challenge and embarrass the authorities was Boris Pasternak.

BORIS PASTERNAK

Boris Pasternak was a novelist and poet whose work was condemned by the Union of Soviet Writers in 1947 on the grounds that it did not comply with the principles of Socialist realism. In 1955 Pasternak completed his novel, *Doctor Zhivago*, which tells the story of Yurii Zhivago, a doctor and poet who at first supports the Bolshevik Revolution, but then disagrees with it because it threatens his freedom of expression as a poet.

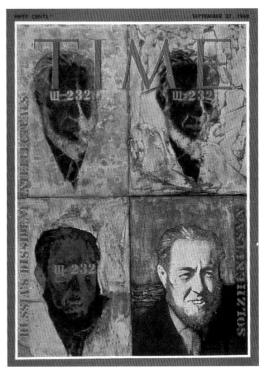

● Solzhenitsyn emerges from the shadows during the thaw of the 1960s.

Having failed to get the book published in the Soviet Union, Pasternak succeeded in having it published abroad in 1958. The following year he was awarded the Nobel Prize for Literature.

At home Pasternak's work was attacked because it concentrated on the personal experiences and feelings of the characters and paid little attention to revolutionary Socialism in the Soviet Union.

He was expelled from the Writers' Union and was forced to reject the Nobel Prize. The alternative was to be sent into foreign exile. Khrushchev later admitted that he had not read *Doctor Zhivago* before the public humiliation of Pasternak took place. Pasternak died in 1960, but by then an even more formidable dissident writer had emerged in the Soviet Union by the name of Alexander Solzhenitsyn.

ALEXANDER SOLZHENITSYN

Of all the dissident writers, Solzhenitsyn was the one who achieved the greatest fame and caused the most acute embarrassment to the authorities. In 1945 he was arrested for making "disrespectful remarks about Stalin" in a letter to a friend. He was sentenced to eight years in detention camps. On completion of this sentence he spent a further three years (1953–1956) in exile in Kazakhstan. This camp housed political prisoners. Solzhenitsyn worked in this camp as a miner and a bricklayer. His experiences in this camp provided the material for his first great novel, *One Day in the Life of Ivan Denisovich.*

● A scene from the film *Dr Zhivago*, released in 1965, shows Yuri Zhivago (Omar Sharif) and Lara (Julie Christie) kneeling over a wounded soldier.

Alexander Solzhenitsyn (1918–   ): Solzhenitsyn served in the Red Army during the second World War, rising to the rank of captain.

In February 1945 he was arrested because he made critical remarks about Stalin in a letter to a friend. He was sentenced to eight years' imprisonment. His experiences provided the basis for his novel, *One Day in the Life of Ivan Denisovich*. In 1953 he was exiled for life to southern Kazakhstan. He was freed from his exile in 1956.

In 1970 he was awarded the Nobel Prize for Literature and published the first section of *The Gulag Archipelago* in 1973. The following year he was charged with treason and deported from the Soviet Union. When the Soviet Union collapsed he returned to Russia in 1994.

Courtesy: Getty Images

ONE DAY IN THE LIFE OF IVAN DENISOVICH

The novel tells the story of how one prisoner, Ivan Denisovich Shukhov, survives a typical day in a Soviet Gulag, or labour camp. The conditions in which the prisoners (*zeks*) live and work are graphically described. The setting is mid-winter and the outside temperature is –27°C. Shukhov and his fellow prisoners spend their day in construction work in these freezing conditions. Their clothing and footwear are inadequate to counter the fierce cold. The most severe physical deprivation experienced by the *zeks* is the deliberate rationing of food by the camp's authorities. Shukhov's own observation conveys his sense of grievance at the handing out of bread rations: "He, like every other prisoner, had discovered long ago that honest weight was never to be found in the bread-cutting. There was short weight in every ration".

The novel simply describes the awful conditions, without comment. That clinical description, however, serves as a scathing criticism of the Gulag system in the Soviet Union.

GETTING PUBLISHED

Solzhenitsyn completed *Ivan Denisovich* in 1959, but kept the manuscript a secret for a couple of years. When Khrushchev openly denounced Stalin at the 22nd Party Congress in October 1961, Solzhenitsyn decided to take the huge risk of trying to get the novel published. He submitted it to Alexander Tvardovsky, the editor of *Novyi Mir*. Tvardovsky appealed to Khrushchev personally. The Soviet leader saw in the novel an opportunity to condemn Stalin's Gulag system, while at the same time strengthening his own position. The novel was published in November 1962.

PUBLIC REACTION

The public response within the Soviet Union and internationally was startling. For the first time the harshness of Stalin's prison camps was laid bare. It soon became clear to the Communist Party that the publication of *Ivan Denisovich* was a mistake and a backlash followed. When Khrushchev fell from power in 1964, criticism of Solzhenitsyn increased.

SOLZHENITSYN'S FALL FROM FAVOUR

Although he was the outstanding favourite to lift the Lenin Prize for Literature in 1964, he was overlooked. Solzhenitsyn's next novel, *The First Circle*, which is based on his time in a prison research institute, was denied publication in 1964. The novel focuses on scientists who serve their prison time doing research for the secret police. Throughout the course of their sentences they debate whether they should co-operate with the secret police. If they refuse they will be banished to the harsh world of the labour camps. In 1966 *Cancer Ward* was rejected by the authorities. The novel is based on Solzhenitsyn's personal experience of being treated for cancer in 1954. The book is implicitly critical of Stalinism.

LETTER TO THE USW

In May 1967 Solzhenitsyn responded to the banning of his books by writing a highly critical letter to the Union of Soviet Writers' Congress. The letter was a direct challenge to state censorship. In it he argued that censorship was illegal. He claimed that suppression of good literature was nothing but a disservice to the Soviet Union. He demanded that censorship be abolished. The Writers' Union, most of whom complied with the principles of Socialist realism, chose to ignore his demand. Two years later Solzhenitsyn was expelled from the Writers' Union on the grounds that he was a dangerously subversive influence.

THE NOBEL PRIZE FOR LITERATURE

In 1968 *The First Circle* and *Cancer Ward* were published in Europe. In October 1970 Solzhenitsyn won the Nobel Prize. The Communist Party condemned the award, seeing it as a hostile act by the West against the Soviet Union. Solzhenitsyn did not attend the prize ceremony because he feared not being allowed back into the country.

• Alexander Solzhenitsyn flanked by two fellow Nobel Prize winners, Harry Martinson (left) and Eyrind Johnson (right), 1973.

THE GULAG ARCHIPELAGO AND EXPULSION

The Gulag Archipelago is Solzhenitsyn's three-volume detailed account of the vast network of prisons and labour camps, most of which were set up during Stalin's regime. The work describes the process of interrogation, conviction and imprisonment of victims of the Gulag. The author supports his description with his own experiences and the testimony of other prisoners who endured the brutality of the labour camps. The first volume was published in Paris in December 1973. On 12 February 1974 Solzhenitsyn was arrested and charged with treason. The following day he was banished from the Soviet Union and deported to West Germany.

GLASNOST AND ACCEPTANCE

Gorbachev's policy of *Glasnost* eased censorship restrictions. As a result, *Novyi Mir* published extracts from *The Gulag Archipelago* in 1989. The following year saw Solzhenitsyn's Soviet citizenship restored to him and he returned to live in Russia in 1994.

Source Document

Extract from a statement by Solzhenitsyn on the tasks of a writer

It is not the task of the writer … to defend one … from a government … The task of the writer is to select more universal, eternal questions [such as] the secrets of the human heart, the triumph over spiritual sorrow …

(Francis Barker, *Solzhenitsyn: Politics and Form*, London: The Macmillan Press, 1977)

QUESTION ON THE DOCUMENT

1. In your opinion, does Solzhenitsyn's statement agree or disagree with the policy of Socialist realism?

THE INFLUENCE OF SOLZHENITSYN

The publication of *Ivan Denisovich* marked a turning point for Soviet writers who were disillusioned by the restraints of Socialist realism. As one Soviet writer put it, "After Solzhenitsyn we cannot write as before".

After *Ivan Denisovich* many Soviet writers sought to expose the harshness of Stalinism. With the departure of Khrushchev, however, censorship became more strict. The Brezhnev era clamped down on dissident writing.

Courtesy: Corbis Sygma

• Nicolas Bakov, a worker in Samizdat, was arrested in 1975. He chose exile in France over prison in the Soviet Union.

SAMIZDAT

The new wave of censorship gave rise to the emergence of *Samizdat* around 1965. This movement of underground publishing encouraged dissident writers to express themselves through novels, poems, political manifestos and petitions. Of course it was an extremely risky exercise because of the vigilance of the KGB.

CHRONICLE OF CURRENT EVENTS

Chronicle of Current Events was a notable *Samizdat* publication which first saw the light of day in April 1968. Its function was to champion the causes of freedom of information and basic human rights. The cover of each issue carried Article 19 of the Universal Declaration of Human Rights. This article upheld the right of everyone to hold and express their opinion and to acquire information from any source regardless of its origin. One of its famous contributors was Andrei Sakharov, the eminent Soviet physicist and human rights activist who caused a great deal of embarrassment for the Brezhnev regime (see p. 62).

QUESTIONS

1. What did the policy of Socialist realism demand of writers in the Soviet Union?
2. In your opinion, why did the Soviet authorities ban the publication of *Doctor Zhivago*?
3. In what sense could *One Day in the Life of Ivan Denisovich* be seen as an attack on the Soviet system?
4. Why did Khrushchev agree to the publication of *Ivan Denisovich*?
5. What was *Samizdat*?
6. How did Article 19 of the Universal Declaration of Human Rights clash with the Soviet system?

14.2   WESTERN EUROPE

The greater freedom granted to writers in the West was reflected in the wide range of issues addressed. They criticised discrimination against women, poverty, lack of opportunity and the brutality of war. Simone de Beauvoir in France, John Osborne (see p. 194) in England and Heinrich Böll (see p. 195) in Germany were three prominent critical voices during the period.

THE STATUS OF WOMEN

One of the significant changes that took place in post-second World War Europe was the greater role of women in society. During the period 1945–1990 the numbers of women entering third-level education in Europe went from around 25 per cent to almost 50 per cent. From this emerged an increased awareness of existing discrimination against women.

It also gave rise to a significant shift in women's career expectations. Increasingly, women played a more prominent role in business, the professions and politics. Two notable developments in this latter area were the accession of Margaret Thatcher to the position of Prime Minister of Britain in 1980 and that of Mary Robinson to the presidency of the Republic of Ireland in 1990. The improvement in the status of women was accompanied in the 1970s by a new wave of **feminism**, which demanded that women must be seen as individuals in their own right and not as second-class citizens. It is generally accepted that one of the

• Women in New York protest against pornography.

biggest influences on this new wave of feminism came from the pen of the French writer, Simone de Beauvoir (see page 175 for full biographical details).

THE SECOND SEX

The Second Sex is the title of Simone de Beauvoir's major work, published in 1949, which challenged the inferior status of generations of women in Western society. Using existentialist philosophy and tracing the treatment of women in history, de Beauvoir attempts to explain why women found themselves relegated to inferior social status. The central idea of the book is that women are in this situation because men see women as objects, not as equals. "One is not born, but rather becomes, a woman." De Beauvoir rejects the idea that woman is born to be feminine, but becomes so because society shapes her into a feminine figure. Her role becomes increasingly passive in contrast to the active role of man. This is demonstrated in practical, everyday life.

MARRIAGE

Essentially de Beauvoir sees marriage as an unequal arrangement where the woman is confined to the home as housekeeper, mother, cook and lover. For the woman the family home is the world and that world is dominated by the drudgery of housework. Furthermore, not being a wage-earner means she is economically dependent on her spouse.

MOTHERHOOD

On this subject de Beauvoir argues that caring for a child should be the collective responsibility of the couple. If women can take on the important task of bringing another human being into the world then she ought to play an active role in public life.

INDEPENDENT WOMAN

De Beauvoir argues that women should be independent. They should be free to earn their own living and to reject or enter into marriage and motherhood. For a woman, being unmarried should not be seen as some

• Comedienne Joan Rivers ridicules *Playboy* magazine by using it to 'spice up' the cooking.

kind of failure. If a woman is to be free then she must become economically independent. She must also have the same educational opportunities as a man and have access to facilities such as contraception and legal abortion. According to de Beauvoir, "Woman prides herself on thinking, taking action, working, creating, on the same terms as men; instead of seeking to disparage them, she declares herself their equal".

TREATMENT OF THE ELDERLY

De Beauvoir did not confine her social criticism to the rights of women – she also supported the rights of workers. She campaigned for Algerian independence from France and in 1970 she published a book called *The Coming of Age*, in which she condemns the treatment of the elderly by society in general. She attacks the notion that a person is valuable only if he or she is doing something profitable. She asserts that the real value of any person is to be found in his or her humanity, which has nothing to do with age. The elderly must not be seen as a burden on society. She also calls on the elderly to play an active role in life and to guard against drifting into boredom and inertia.

THE IMPORTANCE OF *THE SECOND SEX*

When published, *The Second Sex* was a radical book. The emphasis on individual freedom of choice challenged the long history of the suppression of women. Many who read the book saw something of their own lives in it. In time this contributed to the collective voice of feminism that emerged in the late 1960s and 1970s.

The Second Sex cannot be dismissed as simply a period piece because the issues raised are still relevant. That relevance lies in the questions de Beauvoir asks in her introduction: "How can a human being in woman's situation attain fulfilment? What roads are open to her? Which are blocked? … What circumstances limit woman's liberty and how can they be overcome?"

John Osborne (1929–1994): The emergence of the English playwright John Osborne changed the direction of the British theatre in the 1950s. His play *Look Back in Anger* shocked audiences when it was produced in 1956. It marks the point where British theatre moved out of the comfortable drawing rooms of middle-class England into the terraced houses and flats of the poorer classes. The play focuses on the lives of ordinary, lower-middle-class people and their struggle for existence. The play is a criticism of a system that limits opportunity and confines people to living in deprived and bleak circumstances. It is also a criticism of people themselves who are prepared to endure underprivileged lives in silence. It is an angry, rebellious piece of social criticism conveyed in language that audiences of the time found disturbing. In 1957 Osborne completed the play *The Entertainer*, in which he continued to level criticism at the structure of British society.

Courtesy: Corbis

Heinrich Boll (1917–1985): Boll has frequently been described as the conscience of post-second World War West Germany. He served in the German army in the second World War and his early writings such as *The Train Was on Time*, published in 1947, focuses on the futility of war. They convey the sense of hopelessness felt by the ordinary soldier and express revulsion at the brutality of armed conflict.

Courtesy: Corbis

Living in Germany in the 1930s and his experiences in the second World War gave rise to a deep hatred of Nazism. That hatred was clearly expressed in *What's to Become of the Boy*, published just before his death, where he says: "The Nazis repelled me on every level of my existence: conscious and instinctive, aesthetic and political." Boll's later social criticism is demonstrated in the sympathy he shows for the victims of society – the poor, the political refugees, the dissidents – all those who are adrift in the world. He demands that human dignity be recognised and nurtured, not violated and sacrificed. In one of his later works, *The Lost Honour of Katharina Blum*, published in 1974, he condemns the aggressive and sometimes ruthless nature of some sections of the press. The heroine of the novel, Katharina Blum, is endlessly pursued by an unscrupulous journalist. In the end, exasperated and humiliated, she is driven to taking his life. Two lives have been destroyed.

Throughout his life he campaigned for freedom of expression and he gave particular support to writers who were denied that freedom under Communism. When Solzhenitsyn was exiled from the Soviet Union in 1974 he first found refuge in the home of Heinrich Boll.

QUESTIONS

1. Explain what you think de Beauvoir means when she says: "One is not born, but rather becomes, a woman."
2. List two ways in which de Beauvoir sees marriage as an unequal arrangement.
3. Does de Beauvoir place all the blame on man for woman's inferior status? Explain.
4. Briefly summarise de Beauvoir's criticism of the treatment of the elderly.
5. What aspects of society are criticised by (a) John Osborne and (b) Heinrich Boll?

GENERAL ESSAY QUESTIONS ON CHAPTER 14

1. Show how the work of Alexander Solzhenitsyn undermined the policy of Socialist realism in the Soviet Union.
2. "Solzhenitsyn, in his writing and in his personal experience, exposed the harshness of the Soviet regime." Discuss.
3. Describe Simone de Beauvoir's view of the treatment of women in *The Second Sex* and assess the importance of the book.
4. Show how literature was employed to criticise political and social structures across all of Europe in the period 1945–1990.

15

CHANGING PATTERNS IN RELIGIOUS OBSERVANCE, 1945–1992

Words you need to understand

Celibacy: Remaining unmarried and abstaining from sexual relations.

Ecumenism: The desire for the various Christian Churches to act together on areas of common belief.

Hierarchy: A term used to describe the organisation of the Catholic Church, with the Pope at the top and cardinals, bishops and priests beneath him.

Institutional Church: A Church with established rules and regulations.

Pluralist society: A society in which the customs of different groups are treated equally.

Religious observance: Following the regulations set by a religious group, such as the Catholic Church.

Rite: The type of liturgy or religious observance chosen by a religious group.

Secular society: A society in which the major areas of society are not controlled by religious institutions.

INTRODUCTION

The religious landscape of Europe changed between 1945 and 1992. Religion became less important. The main Christian religions showed signs of decline. Fewer people attended church services on a regular basis.

Empty churches showed that society had become more secular, but a large majority of Europeans still had strong Christian beliefs as a result of an historic Christian heritage. A trend towards **ecumenism** in some religions emerged during the period, as well as a new acceptance of the voluntary character of religion. A majority of the members of Christian Churches used the Church buildings for the main turning points of life – baptism, marriage and burial (often referred to as hatching, matching and dispatching).

THE REASON FOR CHANGES IN THE EAST

The changes were brought about in Eastern Europe by political factors. Communist governments discouraged the public practice of religion in general.

THE REASONS FOR CHANGES IN THE WEST

In Western Europe, different factors came into play. The new consumer society, the rise in individualism, the popularity of feminist thought, the communication revolution, the increasing influence of the media, the rise in immigration into Western Europe as well as an increase in international travel all contributed to the decline.

The decline in religious observance was also due to the popularity of new philosophical ideas. The ideas of **existentialism** were linked with the French writers Jean Paul Sartre and Simone de Beauvoir (see p. 175). Existentialists argued that there was no such thing as eternal truths, such as the Christian God.

● Attendance at Churches fell during the period, although the fall was not equal in all countries.

EUROPE'S NEW 'CONFESSIONAL MAP'

The 'confessional map' of Western Europe can be divided into a Catholic south, a Protestant north and a number of mixed countries, such as England, Wales, Northern Ireland, the Netherlands and Germany. The decline in religious observance changed the role of the traditional family unit. The Christian Churches lost support because they usually opposed changes in moral and sexual behaviour, such as divorce, contraception and abortion. These changes were last accepted in Catholic countries such as Italy, Spain, Poland and Ireland. The Christian heritage of Western Europe co-existed after the war with an increasingly **secular** and **pluralist** society (see page 158).

A FALL IN JEWISH NUMBERS, A RISE IN ISLAMIC NUMBERS

The Jewish religion was decimated by the death of 6 million of its believers during the Nazi Holocaust. The Zionist movement, supporting a Jewish homeland in Israel, turned its energies away from Europe in the post-war period.

The trends of immigration led to large Muslim minorities in Britain, France and Germany. At the start of the 1990s, Muslims made up 3 per cent of the Western European population. Islam (with over 7 million adherents) was close to replacing Judaism as the second-largest European religion.

● The arrival of large numbers of immigrants with different religions led to the building of new facilities. In London, this 1984 photo shows the new mosque in Regent's Park.

QUESTIONS

1. Mention two changes showing how the level of religious observance changed during this period.
2. Changes in religious practice happened in Western Europe and Eastern Europe, but had different causes. How did they differ?
3. Why did Europe have a Muslim population of 7 million at the start of the 1990s?

15.1 RELIGION IN THE USSR: THE CRISIS OF THE ORTHODOX CHURCHES

THE RUSSIAN ORTHODOX CHURCH

In the Communist countries, the public practice of religion was discouraged. Before the second World War, all the activities (except public worship) of the Russian Orthodox Church were banned. After its important role in the Great Patriotic War, Stalin allowed the Church more freedom in return for state approval of many appointments in the hierarchy.

Orthodox believers who disapproved of this co-operation joined 'underground' Churches, such as the True Orthodox Church, to separate themselves from the Moscow Orthodox authorities.

The collapse of Communism and the fall of the USSR allowed the Russian Orthodox Church to practise freely. In 1989, a survey revealed that 40 per cent of Soviet citizens believed in God.

QUESTION

1. Why was the Russian Orthodox Church allowed more freedom after the second World War?

15.2 THE PRACTICE OF RELIGION IN THE SATELLITE STATES

CONTROL OF RELIGIOUS PRACTICE

In the satellite states, Communist governments restricted the practice of religion. The governments took over the running of all schools and other organisations that could challenge the social control of the state.

As a result, the main Christian Churches played an unusual opposition role to the Socialist governments. Non-believers frequently used Mass attendance to show their disapproval of the state.

Courtesy: Corbis Sygma

● In Romania, during elections held in 1980 after the overthrow of the Communist dictator, an Orthodox priest meets with protesters who did not want Communist Party officials to take part in the elections.

THE CASE OF THE ROMANIAN ORTHODOX CHURCH

In the satellite states of Eastern Europe, the orthodox religious organisations had to accept the authority of the Socialist state.

In Romania, the members of the Eastern Rite Church were forced to accept the different traditions of the Russian Orthodox Church. Thousands of clerics and ordinary followers were jailed for refusing to accept the change. Six bishops died in prison. By 1975 an estimated 900,000 Romanians worshipped in secret. Their private devotion was assisted by many underground priests. When President Ceausescu was overthrown in 1989, the followers began to worship publicly.

THE CATHOLIC CHURCH IN THE EAST

Catholic leaders in Hungary (Cardinal Mindszenty – see p. 76) and in Poland (Cardinal Wyszynski in 1953 – see p. 43) were imprisoned for long periods of time.

■ **Czechoslovakia**: Atheism was the official state philosophy. At the start of the 1950s, over 8,000 Catholic monks and nuns were imprisoned in Czechoslovakia. During the liberal period after 1968 in Czechoslovakia (see pp. 111–13), the Catholic Church was permitted to take charge of religious education. A 1988 petition demanded religious freedom and less state interference in Church affairs. After restoration of religious freedom in 1989, the Catholics welcomed Pope John Paul II in 1990.

- **Poland**: The Catholic Church operated as the main opposition to the Communist regime. During the period of Communist rule, Poles adopted a strong Catholic identity not only for religious purposes, but also for nationalist and anti-Soviet identity. The Polish Church was identified with modern themes such as freedom, human rights and democracy.

- **Hungary**: The Catholic Church operated as a 'Church within Socialism'. Three priests were elected to the parliament in 1985. After the dissolution of Communism, religious freedom was allowed, but people did not go back to the Hungarian Catholic Church in large numbers.

• In January 1981, Pope John Paul II meets with Lech Walesa, leader of the Polish independent unions, in Rome. Pope John Paul II supported human rights in the socialist satellite states.

- **The Catholic Church after the fall of Communism:** The Catholic Church emerged as a major public influence in Poland, Hungary, Slovenia, Croatia and the Czech and Slovak republics. After an initial celebration, the drift away from institutionalised religion could also be seen in Eastern Europe.

- **Religious tensions**: One unwelcome trend in post-war Europe concerned the identification of religion with politics in certain areas. During the Bosnian War of the early 1990s, religion played a key role in distinguishing between opposing groups – the Catholic Croats, the Orthodox Serbs and the Muslim groups in Bosnia and other new territories.

- **Current situation**: The issue of the return of property to the Churches in the former Communist states caused problems. Conflicts with the present users led to a crisis of confidence where it seemed that the Churches could benefit from the new acquisitions. Decades of Communist controls and the influence of the welfare state had limited the acceptable areas where the Churches could operate.

QUESTIONS

1. How did the Orthodox Church in Romania respond to the order to transfer its allegiance to the Russian Orthodox system?
2. Why did the Communist governments restrict the practice of religion?
3. What special role did the Catholic Church have in Poland?
4. How important was religion during the Bosnian War?

15.3 CHANGES IN RELIGIOUS OBSERVANCE IN WESTERN EUROPE

According to the historian Eric Hobsbawn, during the period 1945 to 1992 the modern generation moved away from the "old moral vocabulary of rights and duties, mutual obligations, sin and virtue, sacrifice, conscience, rewards and penalties" (Hobsbawn, *Age of Extremes: The Short Twentieth Century, 1914–1991*, London 1994, p. 338).

The churchgoing population of Western Europe increased in age, decreased in size and became overwhelmingly female. In the West, churchgoing attracted higher numbers of the well-educated

• Pope John Paul II promoted meetings of young people, to take place on 'World Youth Days'. This meeting took place in Paris in 1997.

and professional classes. In central Europe, in contrast, the less-educated rural population attended church in higher numbers.

The number of infants who were baptised fell over the period. In the UK, for instance, the numbers of infant baptisms in the Church of England fell from 50 per cent of births in 1945 to 25 per cent in 1990. In France, Catholic baptisms fell from 92 per cent of births in 1958 to 58 per cent in 1993.

The change from the traditional to the new pattern of observance was also clearly seen in the Netherlands. The numbers attending Church fell quickly as a result of the liberal social movements of the 1960s.

THE DECLINE OF OFFICIAL RELIGION IN THE TWO GERMANYS, 1945–1992

The experience of the Holocaust had a traumatic effect on the German Churches. In 1945, the German Protestant Churches publicly accepted that they had been guilty of many failures during the Nazi era. The population movements after the war brought many Protestants to West Germany, creating an almost equal balance of Catholics and Protestants.

In East Germany, for every seven Protestants there was one Catholic. While people were guaranteed religious freedom, membership of a Church was discouraged. Church membership barred people from state employment, state organisations and higher education.

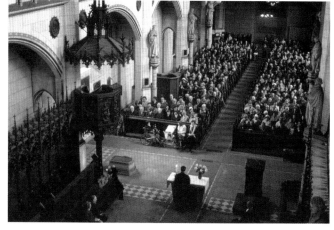

• A Protestant congregation in an East German church, in Wittenberg. The Socialist government allowed freedom of assembly in churches.

West Germans could pay a part of their income tax to their Churches, and this income reached 17 million Deutschmarks in 1992. At the start of the 1990s, 300,000 people a year were withdrawing from this scheme. The Lutheran and Catholic Churches used this money to build community centres, hospitals and other social facilities in both Germanys. This tax practice was also followed in the Nordic countries.

In the GDR the local Church was the only area where freedom of assembly was allowed. The Churches provided a venue for protest during the 1980s. By 1989 the ministers joined the new peaceful civil protest movements. After the freer elections of March 1990, the first freely elected GDR government contained two Protestant ministers in its cabinet.

After the fall of Communism, the Church in the GDR lost the importance it had gained during the protests of the 1980s.

Living under a highly secular regime for over 40 years had diluted religious beliefs. In the 1990s, less than one-quarter of Germans in the former East Germany belonged to either the Catholic or Protestant Churches, while in the former West Germany the total was one-third.

THE MOVE TOWARDS INDIVIDUAL CHOICE IN WESTERN EUROPE

Individuals began to choose the level of religious practice they wanted rather than following a standard pattern set by a Church. Other voluntary organisations also experienced a fall in active numbers, such as political parties, trade unions and local community groups that relied on unpaid workers. A new trend of 'believing without belonging' had emerged in European societies, with Europeans less inclined to 'belong' to anything (G. Davies, *Religion in Britain since 1945: Believing without Belonging*, London: Blackwell 1994).

More people chose to co-habit rather than marry, either in a Church or a civil ceremony (see pp. 177–178). A majority of European couples still went through a religious marriage ceremony, although the levels of marriage were much lower in 1992 than 30 years previously.

In countries where the main Christian Church was weak, large numbers of people still stated that they had a religious faith based on belief in a God, in the existence of a soul and in life after death.

While Europeans stopped attending church, they still expected it to be there when they wanted it (for baptism, marriage and burial).

Courtesy: Hulton-Deutsch/Corbis

● Many couples decided not to marry in a church, and the proportion marrying in a registry office rose.

OBSERVANCE IN THE NORDIC STATES

The move towards voluntary observance after the war was most obvious in the Protestant states of Northern Europe.

In the Nordic countries, the registered membership of Churches was high, but the numbers attending Church remained much lower. About 90 per cent of the Swedish population were members of the Swedish state Church, the Evangelical Lutheran Church. Every newborn child was registered as a member of the Church once one of the parents was a member. This regulation remained until 1996. In Iceland, the state Lutheran Church received financial assistance from the state. As in Sweden, a small number of people attended Church services, while most citizens were registered as Church members.

QUESTIONS

1. What was the main difference between churchgoers in Western and Central Europe?
2. How did the Lutheran Church and the Catholic Church benefit from the special tax arrangement in Germany?
3. What does Grace Davies mean by 'believing without belonging'?
4. Why did the Lutheran Churches in Sweden and Iceland have a high membership?

15.4 JOHN PAUL II

Pope John Paul's reaction to the changes in religious observance can be viewed in two parts. The first concerns his experiences in Poland until he was elected as Pope in 1978. The second deals with his conservative reaction to the decline in European religious observance.

JOHN PAUL II'S CHALLENGE TO COMMUNISM AS A YOUNG MAN

Karol Wojtyla (pronounced *voy-tea-wah*) lived under the rule of Nazis in Poland during the second World War. As a priest, a bishop and finally a cardinal in Communist Poland, he challenged the Communist restriction on the public practice of religion. He criticised

Courtesy: Corbis

● Pope John Paul II travelled more than any other pope. Here, he waves to crowds in Mexico in 1978.

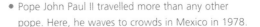

Communism because it "violated the dignity of the person", not for its economic short-comings. He said of the government: "I am not afraid of them, they're afraid of me."

The Polish government refused to build a Church for the workers of the new city of Nova Huta, having first granted a permit in 1958. Crosses appeared in the Church site, but were removed by the authorities. Due to Wojtyla's persistence, a church was built in 1977. A sculpture in the new church was made of shrapnel (bomb pieces) taken from the bodies of Polish soldiers.

JOHN PAUL II'S CHALLENGE TO COMMUNISM AS POPE

John Paul II was the first non-Italian Pope for 455 years. When he was elected, Yuri Andropov (see p. 65), future leader of the Soviet Union, warned the Soviet Politburo that there could be trouble ahead.

Courtesy: Bettmann/Corbis

● Pope John Paul II as a priest in 1945. He was an active person. "I also was once 20 years old. I loved sports, skiing, reciting poetry, I studied and worked. I had hopes and worries … when the land of my birth was wounded by war, and then by a totalitarian regime."

Within a week of his election John Paul II met Cardinal Wyszynski (who had been imprisoned, see p. 43), highlighting the suffering of the Church in Communist Europe. John Paul II helped to undermine the Communist system, telling the Polish people, "Do not be afraid." His support for the banned Solidarity trade union movement also encouraged a wave of revolt that rippled through the Soviet bloc.

Even former Soviet Premier Mikhail Gorbachev agreed that John Paul II was very important: "Everything that happened in Eastern Europe in these last few years would have been impossible without this Pope."

JOHN PAUL II'S RESPONSE TO THE CRISIS OF RELIGION IN EUROPE

John Paul II spoke out regularly and powerfully on modern issues, such as divorce and abortion. The Pope, as head of a Church with a standard moral view, was a critic of the modern trend towards the 'privatisation' of morality.

In the early years of his papacy he encouraged the Vatican to use satellite transmissions and to produce video recordings. A media-pope, he was the only pope to appear in an American comic book, produced by Marvel comics in 1983. He became the most-travelled pope in history, going on 56 apostolic visits between 1979 and 1992.

QUESTIONS

1. What was Wojtyla's attitude towards the Communist government in Poland?
2. How important was John Paul II's role in bringing about the fall of Communism?
3. How did John Paul II succeed in spreading his views?

15.5 THE EXPERIENCE OF THE CATHOLIC COUNTRIES

Throughout Europe the authority of the Catholic Church seemed to erode very quickly, as those attending for Mass every Sunday declined. Many Catholics began to lead lives that did not always follow the rules of their Church. Even in Spain, the generation born after the early 1950s mainly looked to the Church as a venue for baptism, marriage and burial service.

Catholic Europe held on to the churchgoing habit for longer than the Protestant north. By 1990, outside France a quarter of Catholics attended Church on a weekly basis. With the exception of the

Calvinists in Holland and Switzerland, less than 10 per cent of Protestants attended Church services.

The numbers choosing to train as priests, nuns or brothers fell sharply while the average age of priests kept rising. This concern became so great in the 1990s that people began to talk about 'Europe without priests'. France had 41,000 priests in 1965, 29,000 in 1985 and 20,000 in 1995. In 1989, the average age of a French priest was 66.

The Catholic Church witnessed the growth of new religious communities, made up mainly of laypeople. The Spanish organisation Opus Dei (The Work of God) had 75,000 lay members in more than 80 countries at the start of the 1990s. Emphasising membership in a community, it was the Catholic Church's fastest-growing, and wealthiest, society.

Courtesy: Corbis Sygma

● Pope John Paul II created more saints than any previous pope. In 1992, he began the process of beatification of the founder of Opus Dei, Josemaría Escrivá.

CONCLUSION

By 1992 it was clear that the major challenge facing the large Christian Churches was how to minister to a multicultural, secularised Europe while showing respect for others' opinions. If the Churches tried to impose their views, the new trend of individualism meant that many people would no longer accept being told what to do. The changing pattern of religious observance had weakened the influences of the main Churches.

QUESTION

1. Give one example that shows how the Catholic Church lost its control over many Catholics.

Source Document: A

Historians often have to make judgments based on statistical information. The following tables give a flavour of the changing times for religion in Europe since 1945. The changes in religious belief and religious practice have been recorded by pollsters, i.e. groups of professional people who regularly ask a different group of people the same group of questions over a number of years. The European Values Survey has been the most valuable indicator of change.

Belief in life after death in Western Europe, 1947–1990

Read the table and answer the questions that follow. The table records the percentage of people surveyed who said they believed in 'life after death'.

	1947	1968	1981	1990
Norway	71	54	41	36
Finland	69	55	n/a	44
Netherlands	68	50	41	39
France	58	35	35	38
Britain	49	38	46	44
West Germany	n/a	41	36	38

QUESTIONS ON THE DOCUMENT

1. What is one difference between the figures for 1947 and 1990?
2. What is one difference between the figures for 1968 and 1990?
3. Select one piece of statistical information from the table above that helped you to understand the changes in religious belief.
4. Find a statement in the chapter that is similar to the trend identified in the table. Then write a new sentence combining the two pieces of information.

Source Document: B

A disagreement among historians

Jonathan Kwitny wrote a biography about John Paul II, called Man of the Century.

He posited the following about Karol Wojtyla during his time as Bishop of Krakow: "He forged the Solidarity revolution – in his philosophy classes, his secret ordination of priests, his clandestine communications seminars, the smuggling network he oversaw throughout the Eastern bloc."

(Jonathan Kwitny, *Man of the Century: The Life and Times of Pope John Paul II,*
London: Henry Holt & Company, 1998)

Posited: Suggested.
Clandestine: Secret.

Source Document: C

Two American researchers, Jean Barnes and Helen Whitney, found some errors in Kwitny's evidence

Barnes and Whitney spoke to some of the people interviewed by Kwitny and found serious errors of fact.

■ Kwitny stated that Joanna Szczesna, a veteran of the Polish resistance, was Jewish: "In truth, she's Catholic. She laughed when we showed her the reference."

■ Karol Wojtyla had not directed a workers' strike in Warsaw, as he was in Krakow at the time. "He was not one of the political priests," according to Szczesna.

■ Had Wojtyla ever sent Father Bardeicki to the Ukraine to gather intelligence on the Church there? "No. I was only in the Ukraine before the war when it was part of Poland. After the lines were redrawn, we were not allowed to go."

■ Did Wojtyla oversee a vast smuggling operation throughout Eastern Europe? "Smuggling Bibles and literature happened," Father Bardeicki assured us. "But it was [Cardinal] Wyszynski's operation, Wojtyla was just a parish priest."

Unfortunately, before they could raise their questions with Jonathan Kwitny, he died of a brain tumour. Because of his sudden, untimely death, he never had the chance to defend the book he'd spent a decade writing.

(Jane Barnes and Helen Whitney, *John Paul II and the Fall of Communism*, www.pbs.org/wgbh/pages/frontline/shows/pope/communism/)

QUESTIONS ON THE DOCUMENTS

1. Name two successes that Kwitny associated with Bishop Wojtyla in Document B.
2. Give two examples of errors found by Barnes and Whitney.
3. Why was it not possible for the Americans to interview Jonathan Kwitny to ask him about Father Bardeicki's criticisms?
4. Do Jean Barnes and Helen Whitney succeed in showing that Kwitny's biography was unreliable? Explain your answer.

GENERAL ESSAY QUESTIONS ON CHAPTER 15

1. Write about changes in religious observance under the following headings:
   (a) The reasons for change.
   (b) The role of the Catholic Church in Eastern Europe.
   (c) The decline in church attendance.
   (d) The response of Pope John Paul II to the 'crisis' in religion.
2. "The pattern of religious observance changed radically between 1945 and 1992 in Europe." What were the principal trends of this change?

16

THE SECOND VATICAN COUNCIL – CASE STUDY

Words you need to understand

Aggiornamento: Updating or modernising the Church's views.

Anti-Semitism: Anti-Jewish actions or feelings.

Atheists: People who do not believe in a God.

Collegiality: Working together.

Council: A meeting of all the bishops, archbishops and cardinals of the Church.

CPC: Central Preparatory Commission, which prepared the documents for the Council.

Curia: The civil service within the Vatican City, run by a number of cardinals.

Dogma: A belief within the Catholic Church.

Ecumenism: Promoting dialogue with other religions.

Encyclical: A statement issued by the Pope.

Heresy: A belief that is contrary to and not acceptable to the authorised teachings of the Catholic Church.

Liturgy: The format the Catholic Mass follows.

Mixed marriage: Marriage between people of two different religions.

Papal infallibility: The view that the Pope is right when he speaks about matters of belief and faith for Catholics.

Rite: The type of liturgy or religious observance chosen by a religious group.

Roman numerals: VI, six; XII, twelve; XXIII, twenty-three.

Theologians: People who study religions.

INTRODUCTION

The Vatican Council 1962–1965 was the most significant event in the life of the Catholic Church in the 20th century. It changed many of the practices and attitudes of a very conservative institution and updated many of the practices and rites in the modern world.

The impact of the changes was difficult to assess because of the movement away from organised religion in continental Europe during the second half of the century.

16.1   BACKGROUND TO THE SECOND VATICAN COUNCIL

THE ELECTION OF POPE JOHN XXIII

On 25 October 1958, at the age of 77, Angelo Roncalli, the son of a poor peasant family from the north of Italy, was elected as Pope John XXIII. He asked Catholics not to look on him as a prince of the Church, but as a priest, a father and a shepherd.

During the second World War, Roncalli saved the lives of thousands of Jews from Romania and Bulgaria, especially children, by issuing blank baptismal certificates.

Roncalli's experience of the world encouraged him to reach out to the members of other religious denominations. During his short time as Pope (less than five years) he brought about a revolution in the life of the Catholic Church.

Source Document

The character of Pope John XXIII

Pope John XXIII took English lessons when he was elected as Pope.

Under Monsignor (Desmond) Ryan, who then headed the English-language section of the Secretariat of State, John took up his study of English. It was not a marked success.

A huge and hearty man, Monsignor Ryan said, "I believe Pope John felt a bit less of a father to the English-speaking people he met because he could not say anything to them in their own tongue. So he tried to learn, not to make speeches, but just to say a few words of greeting. But of course he was past 77 and when we got together he was much happier telling stories about the olden days."

Even more characteristic, says Ryan, were the heavily accented words he did manage for a group of Americans during an audience in 1960. "I do not speak English well," he said, "but my heart speaks to you."

(L. Elliott, *I Will Be Called John: A Biography of Pope John XXIII*, London 1974, pp. 278–9)

• Angelo Roncalli, Pope John XXIII, in 1958.

Courtesy: Bettmann/Corbis

QUESTIONS ON THE DOCUMENT

1. Who tried to teach English to Pope John XXIII?
2. Why did Pope John XXIII fail to make much progress in learning English?
3. John XXIII spoke to American pilgrims at a papal audience in Rome. What can we learn about his character from the words he used?

• Pope Pius XII speaking at a press conference, 1 June 1944.

Pope John XXIII was a major contrast to Pope Pius XII (1939–1958). While Pius XII insisted that the Vatican gardeners should leave the Vatican gardens when he walked there, John XXIII welcomed their presence. John XXIII visited the sick in Roman hospitals, the elderly in care homes as well as prisoners in jail.

One of John XXIII's first acts was to eliminate the term 'treacherous Jews' from a prayer used on Good Friday. His attitude to Judaism contrasted with that of Pius XII, who has been criticised for not speaking out on the Nazi holocaust.

QUESTIONS

1. What was Pope John XXIII's name before he became Pope?
2. What indications were there that Pope John XXIII had a 'common touch'?
3. John XXIII was willing to introduce change into the Catholic Church. What evidence is there that he wanted to bring about change very quickly?

• Pope John XXIII at his first consistory in the Vatican, Rome, 1958.

JOHN XXIII ANNOUNCES THE VATICAN COUNCIL

In 1959, after 90 days in office, John XXIII called all Catholic bishops to a Council in Rome. Cardinal Montini, who would succeed him as Pope Paul VI, told a friend, "This holy old boy doesn't realise what a hornet's nest he's stirring up."

Vatican II, as the meeting was called, opened the Roman Catholic Church to the modern world. Pope John XXIII used the term *aggiornamento* (updating) to describe his new perspective on the world.

QUESTION

1. Why was Cardinal Montini concerned that a Council had been called?

THE PREPARATIONS FOR THE COUNCIL

The preparations for Vatican II took almost four years. The Central Preparatory Commission (CPC), set up to organise the Council and employing 1,000 officials, was split between conservatives and progressives.

The progressives wanted to reform and modernise the Church, while conservatives wanted to stick to traditional practices and attitudes. The Curia representatives, who lived in Rome and ran the Pope's civil service, were the strongest conservative group.

Over 9,000 reports were sent to the CPC. Ten groups prepared 13 discussion documents for the bishops.

QUESTIONS

1. What was the difference between the progressives and the conservatives in the Central Preparatory Council?
2. Why did the CPC send documents to the bishops?

16.2 THE SECOND VATICAN COUNCIL IN SESSION

THE SCALE OF THE VATICAN COUNCIL

More than 2,500 delegates attended than had attended the previous 20 Councils held by the Church. The largest group of bishops (over 1,000) came from Europe, while 489 came from South America, 404 from North America, 374 from Asia, 296 from Africa, 84 from Central America and 75 from Oceania.

The assembly was organised in terms of rank. The most senior of the cardinals sat nearest the altar, while junior bishops sat further away. The future Pope John Paul II sat near to the door of St Peter's Basilica, about 500 feet from the cardinals.

The Pope had appointed all bishops. No woman, ordinary priest or layperson attended the Council. Vatican II was not a parliament of the Church. Any reforms that it suggested could only be introduced with the Pope's consent.

- A photograph of the Vatican Council in session, September 1962. This area of St Peter's Basilica was sectioned off for one session. The meeting area was known as the 'Great Hall'.

JOHN XXIII OPENS THE COUNCIL

The opening of Vatican II on 11 October 1962 brought the largest-ever gathering of bishops in the history of the Catholic Church. The Council took place in a huge meeting space in St Peter's Basilica, the Aula Maxima (Great Hall).

In his opening address to the Council, Pope John XXIII said that he wanted to promote peace and the unity of all humankind. He set an optimistic tone for the work of the Vatican Council. Above all, he wanted a Council that was predominantly pastoral (guiding) in character.

Previous Councils had been called to face up to attacks on the Roman Catholic Church. Pope John XXIII resisted pressure from some bishops to include a condemnation of Communism in his opening address. He spoke of the '**Church of Silence**', a reference to areas of the world where Catholics could not practise their religion in public.

- This painting by Franklin McMahon shows the opening processions of Vatican Council II. Vatican City is a country with its own diplomatic service.

ORGANISING THE WORK OF THE COUNCIL

The Council was the first to take advantage of modern communications. Newspapers, magazines, radio and television reported the Council's work and progress.

Pope John XXIII did not attend the Council sessions; instead, he had a live radio link in his own library to listen to the debates.

All the official business of Vatican II took place in Latin – Pope John XXIII's opening speech was given in Latin, the speeches were in Latin and all the original documents were issued in Latin.

Bishops were given timetabled slots in the debates. Cardinal Cushing of New York was not a Latin expert. After one session he famously said, "It is all Greek to me." Cushing suggested that a simultaneous translation system be used, like the United Nations, but his suggestion was rejected.

• The *observatores* watch from the balcony, in a very good position to see what is happening in the Great Hall. This painting looks down from the Pope's perspective.

The prospect of listening to so many speeches in Latin convinced some bishops to hand in the written copy of their speeches and not to present them in the Aula Maxima. Many of them passed the time at the two coffee bars that came to be known as Bar Abbas and Bar Jonah.

The Council was attended by 93 non-Catholic observers (called *observatores*). They were often consulted, formally and informally, about the drafts of the Council's business.

Some bishops complained that the *observatores* were given better facilities than the bishops themselves. They were given special access to the Council Hall and sat just to the left of the high altar of St Peter's Basilica. A special languages group translated the Latin speeches into modern languages – a facility not available for the bishops.

Source Document

The dialogue between the Catholic Church and the Jewish faith

In October 1965, Pope Paul VI issued an encyclical, Nostra Aetate *(In Our Time). It dealt with the difficult relationships between Jews and Christians. As a result of* Nostra Aetate, *Rabbi A. James Rudin said that more positive encounters between Catholics and Jews took place during the years after the Vatican Council than had taken place during the previous 2,000 years of the Church. Rabbi Rubin wrote about the impact the ecumenical effort had on his family:*

But in 1965 the declaration drew sharp criticism. For many Jews, it was a clear case of much too little far too late. Catholic critics of *Nostra Aetate* could see no reason to build "mutual respect and knowledge" between what they saw as the one true faith and a spiritually exhausted one.

Although my wife, Marcia, strongly supported my efforts to build the "mutual respect and understanding" described in *Nostra Aetate*, others in my family, clearly reflecting long centuries of painful Jewish history, did not understand or fully believe what I was doing.

[It] is clear the Second Vatican Council marked the beginning ... of a long effort to eradicate ... anti-Semitism within the Catholic Church.

(*National Catholic Reporter*, 4 October 2002)

QUESTIONS ON THE DOCUMENT

1. Not all Catholics or Jews welcomed the Vatican declaration *Nostra Aetate*. What evidence is there in the first paragraph to support this statement?

2. Why didn't Rabbi Rubin's family share his optimism about this new dialogue between Jews and the Catholic Church?

3. What process was begun by the Vatican declaration?

THE COUNCIL GETS DOWN TO WORK

Vatican II was a turning point in the modern history of the Catholic Church. The Council held four sessions:

- Session 1: October to December 1962.
- Session 2: September to December 1963.
- Session 3: September to November 1964.
- Session 4: September to December 1965.

The first working day lasted only 50 minutes. The bishops received voting papers to elect people to the various committees. However, the bishops demanded, and were given, three days to make their choices.

The first important debate on liturgy, between 22 October and 13 November 1962, heard 38 Latin speeches, each an average of ten minutes long. The liturgy debate showed that a majority of the bishops favoured the Pope's call for renewal.

JOHN XXIII IS REPLACED BY PAUL VI

After the first session, Pope John XXIII issued the encyclical *Pacem in Terris* (Peace on Earth) in April 1963, emphasising the importance of human rights. He started writing the encyclical during the Cuban Missile Crisis (see pp. 37–8).

It was addressed not only to the Catholic bishops, clergy and faithful, but also "to all men of good will". Pope John XXIII viewed his role as not only confined to the Catholic Church, and he wanted to promote a dialogue with non-Catholic groups.

The following is a quotation from the *Pacem in Terris* encyclical, published in 1963: "Every human being has the right to life, to bodily integrity, and to the means that are necessary and suitable for the proper development of life: food, clothing, shelter, rest, medical care and the necessary social services."

Pope John XXIII died in June 1963, before the second session of the Council. Cardinal Giovanni Montini was elected as his successor. As Pope Paul VI, he presided over the last three sessions of the Council. He announced that the Council would follow the directions outlined by Pope John XXIII.

Unlike previous popes, Pope Paul VI started to travel overseas, visiting the Holy Land in 1964 and the United Nations in New York in 1965. The future pope, Pope John Paul II (from Poland), took Paul VI's advice to visit the Holy Land.

THE COUNCIL CONTINUES ITS WORK

In total the Council produced 16 major documents, divided into three groups – constitutions, declarations and decrees. The major **constitutions** dealt with liturgy, divine revelation and the role of the 'Pilgrim' Church in the modern world.

● Pope Paul VI visited Jordan (part of the Holy Land) in 1964 and encouraged his bishops to go there as well.

The **declarations** dealt with religious liberty, education and non-Christian religions. **Decrees** were issued on ecumenism, relations with Catholic Eastern Churches, missionary activity and the role of the bishops, priests and laypeople.

Courtesy: Corbis

An American Jesuit, Thomas Reese, described the scale of changes made by the Council: "We must remember that with Vatican II, we made a quantum jump from the 16th century."

The Church's sacraments and practices were simplified so that all Catholics could participate more fully in the life of the Church, if they wished.

The Church before Vatican II

The universal language of the Catholic Church was Latin.

The priest said Mass with his back to the people.

The Catholic Church was seen as the Church of God.

The Catholic Church was identified as the one true Church.

The Catholic Church was engaged in a monologue, teaching its views to ordinary Catholics.

The Catholic Church was traditionally hostile to and suspicious of other religions.

The ordinary Catholic was expected to pray and obey, to accept the views of the Church.

The Church after Vatican II

Mass is to be celebrated in the vernacular (or local) language.

The priest says Mass facing the people.

The Catholic Church is viewed as the people of God, as an ecumenical community.

Salvation is not seen as the sole possession of the Catholic Church.

The rites and sacraments of the Church have been simplified to encourage its members' fuller
    participation.

The Catholic Church started to formally talk to other Churches.

The ordinary Catholic is encouraged to have a role as an educator and Eucharistic minister.

PROMOTING ECUMENISM

Ecumenism, or taking part in conversations with other religions, was a major theme of Vatican II. The Catholic Church recognised the spiritual values in many of the world's major non-Christian religions.

● Pope Paul VI, as part of his encouragement of ecumenism during Vatican II, met the leader of the Eastern Orthodox Church in Jerusalem in January 1964. It was the first meeting in over 500 years between the two Churches.

Courtesy: Bettmann/Corbis

Vatican II documents stated that the Church should enter into dialogue with a wide range of groups to show "its solidarity and respectful attention for the whole human family to which it belongs."

The council promoted reconciliation towards the Jewish faith. The papal encyclical *Nostra Aetate* rejected the idea that Jewish people had a "collective guilt" for the death of Jesus. The declaration condemned "all outbreaks of hatred, persecutions and manifestations of anti-Semitism that have been directed against the Jews at any time by anyone."

After the 1964 ***Decree on Ecumenism***, a series of conversations with other Churches took place. The Church spoke to Lutherans, Orthodox Christians, Anglicans and Methodists, among others. They talked about the differences in sacraments (such as baptism) and the difficulties of mixed marriages.

Two events in 1965 showed the good will that had developed between the main Christian Churches since the opening of the Council in 1962. Firstly, before the Council closed, Pope Paul VI led a special prayer service with the non-Catholic *observatores* who had attended Vatican II.

Secondly, the Roman Catholic Church and the Orthodox Church had split nine centuries earlier. Pope Paul VI in Rome and Patriarch Athenagoras in Istanbul each expressed regret for past mistakes just before the closure of the Council.

PAUL VI AS A CAUTIOUS POPE

The council closed on 8 December 1965. Pope Paul VI had to change almost every part of Church life. He was slow to initiate change, as he needed to bring conservatives along with him.

Source Document

A nun responds to the changes of Vatican II

What I experienced personally was the transition from our lifestyle of the 16th century to the 20th century. We were 'allowed' to read the newspapers and watch TV news every day. We could look at ourselves in a mirror. In the 1970s, there were still some of us who felt uncomfortable when our new constitutions identified us as 'women'. For me, the whole change was a process to be a normal human being with common sense.

(Mercedarian Sister Filo Hirota, a member of the Oratory of St Francis Xavier, an order of nuns based in Rome)

(*National Catholic Reporter*, 4 October 2002)

QUESTIONS ON THE DOCUMENT

1. What is the major change identified by Sister Filo?
2. Name two changes that took place in her daily life.
3. Did Sister Filo support the changes? Give a reason for your answer.

QUESTIONS

1. How many bishops attended the first meeting of the Second Vatican Council?
2. Would the Council be able to implement its own policy?
3. What did John XXIII hope to achieve at the Council?
4. What problems were caused by holding the Council's proceedings in Latin?
5. What special privileges were given to the non-Catholic observers?
6. How did the bishops show their independence at the Council?
7. What new audience did John XXIII address in *Pacem in Terris*?
8. Give one example of how the Catholic Church tried to improve its relations with the other Churches.
9. Why was Pope Paul VI slow to introduce changes?

Source Document

Pope Paul VI presided over the Second Vatican Council after the death of Pope John XXIII. Before he was chosen as Pope and before the Council began, Cardinal Montini spoke about what the Council might achieve.

The Council is not like a parliament elected by the people. It is an organism composed of ecclesiastics and … of pastors and doctors of Christ's Church.

The Council, I think, will thunder no curses on the world.

First will be the Council's call to separated Christians to enter Christ's one true Church. This, as we know, is intended to be one of the ecumenical Council's main aims, together with the Church's inner reform and a firm affirmation of the true Christian religion.

If the Council does not succeed in celebrating the return of the separated brethren it will at least succeed in opening the doors of the family home to them.

(Paul VI, *The Mind of Paul VI*, London 1964, pp. 230, 231, 265)

Ecclesiastics: Bishops of the Catholic Church.

QUESTIONS ON THE DOCUMENT

1. Name the three groups that would take part in the Council.
2. What do you think the statement that the council "will thunder no curses on the world" means?
3. What phrase did Cardinal Montini use to describe Christians who were not members of the Catholic Church?
4. According to Montini, what were the three main aims of the Council?

16.3   THE IMPACT OF THE COUNCIL

CHANGING THE FACE OF THE CATHOLIC CHURCH

The Council changed Catholicism, the world's largest religious faith, more than any other event since the Protestant reformations of the 16th century. According to the banned theologian Hans Küng, Vatican II was a major turning point. He called Pope John XXIII the 'most significant pope of the 20th century" for opening up the Church to renewal "in keeping with the time."

The popes and cardinals of the Vatican since 1965 saw themselves as sensitive and truthful interpreters of the Council. However, their critics suggest that they have avoided genuine and radical change, shutting the windows to the modern world that had been opened by John XXIII.

IMPACT AT LOCAL LEVEL

The Council relaxed many restrictive rules surrounding the daily life of religious clergy. It allowed greater collegiality (co-operation), gave bishops more responsibility in the life of the Church, promoted social justice and gave a greater role to the laity.

The most visible change at local level came with the introduction of a new Mass. The priest used the local language (the vernacular) instead of Latin. Male clergy and nuns were allowed to dress in a more casual manner.

Bishops were encouraged to implement the Council's changes in their dioceses. Bishop Karol Wojtyla, the future Pope John Paul II, attended every session of the Council and indicated that he owed a great debt to Vatican II.

In his Polish diocese he introduced the many changes decreed by the Council. As Pope, he insisted that Vatican II was primarily a religious event, not a political contest.

Courtesy: Corbis

● This unusual church design in Helsinki, Finland in 1988 was carved from solid rock.
What features can be seen here that shows this is a post-Vatican II church?

Source Document

The impact of the Council

George Weigel, an American biographer of Pope John Paul II, describes how the lessons of Vatican II reached him in America.

The Council then meant glossy photo essays in *Life* magazine and the occasional lecture at my parish ... I vividly remember Pope Paul VI coming to the United Nations during the fourth session and the Council fathers passing the 'Declaration of Religious Freedom', but I did not 'meet' the Council in its texts until years later. Truth to tell, I never seriously read the texts of Vatican II until the mid-1970s, despite eight years in high school and college seminary and two years of graduate studies in theology. I don't think I was alone in this ... The actual texts of the council got short shrift, as battalions of theologians and 'consultants' and facilitators and what-not worked overtime to implement a council whose documents were not widely read, and were even less carefully studied.

(*National Catholic Reporter*, 4 October 2002)

QUESTIONS ON THE DOCUMENT

1. What was Weigel's clearest memory of the Council as a teenager?
2. When Weigel says that he "was not alone in this", what is he referring to?
3. What final comment does Weigel make about the Council's documents?

IMPACT ON THE JESUITS

The major Catholic orders changed their roles. In 1965, Pope Paul VI encouraged 36,000 Jesuits to battle against atheism. Fr Pedro Arrupe, the 'general' of the Jesuits, insisted that this 'battle' should be identical with a battle against poverty.

In 1983, Fr Peter-Hans Kolvenbach committed the Jesuits to identifying with the "poorest of the poor", insisting that this principle had to be included in the work of their 2,000 universities, schools and colleges throughout the world.

DISAGREEMENTS WITHIN THE CHURCH

The changes linked with Vatican II led to conflict and controversy. Prior to the Council, the Catholic Church saw itself as unchanging. Vatican II accepted the need for *semper reformanda* (constant reform) in the life of the Church, up to a point decided by the Pope.

Disagreements between theologians and the Pope after Vatican II challenged the Pope's authority. The books of banned theologians, such as Hans Küng, became instant best-sellers. In 1979, the Vatican banned Küng from teaching as a Catholic theologian.

Conflict between bishops and priests became more public. The idea of clerical celibacy was challenged. Pope Paul VI issued the encyclical *Humanae Vitae* (Of Human Life) in 1968, stating that Catholics should not use artificial contraception. It highlighted a major difference between the official views of the Church and the private lives of Catholics.

Archbishop Lefebvre, from France, rejected the new vernacular form of the Mass and other various changes. He formed his own Church in 1988, training and ordaining priests. At the start of the 1990s he had over 250,000 followers. Lefebvre died in 1992.

Courtesy: Bettmann/Corbis

● In 1979, Pope John Paul II visited the Nazi concentration camp at Auschwitz. He visited the cell of Father Kolbe. Kolbe had given his life in exchange for one of the other prisoners. The sign over the gate reads 'Work makes free'.
What other evidence is there in the photo that this was a Nazi camp?

POPE JOHN PAUL II AND ECUMENISM

Vatican II had started an important debate between Christians and Jews. John Paul II continued that dialogue. He was the first pope to visit the Jewish synagogue in Rome. In April 1986 he condemned anti-Semitism "by anyone – I repeat, by anyone." At the end of the meeting, he recited a Hebrew version of Psalm 118. He was also the first pope to visit the Holocaust memorial at the Auschwitz concentration camp. He established diplomatic relations between Vatican City and Israel in 1993. He called Jews "our elder brothers".

THE CATHOLIC CHURCH, THE ANGLICAN CHURCH AND WOMEN PRIESTS

The Catholic Church and the Anglican Church in the UK disagreed on the issue of women priests. The Anglicans first discussed the ordination of women in 1988. Some Anglican ministers who opposed the ordination of women joined the Catholic Church, as it also opposed the ordination of women as priests. The first ordination of women ministers within the Anglican religion took place in March 1994. Pope John Paul II stated that the ordination of women was a clear "obstacle to unity" between the two Churches.

CONCLUSION

In October 1992, the Vatican apologised for its treatment of the scientist Galileo, who in 1633 had been forced by the Catholic Church to deny his view that the Earth orbited around the Sun. Such an apology by the Church, even after almost four centuries, would not have been possible in the years before Vatican II.

For this small change and the many major changes that took place since the Council, Vatican II turned out to be one of the most influential of Catholic Councils.

In 1995, an estimated 1 billion Catholics lived under the influence of the changes brought about by Vatican II, even though the impact may have fallen short of its ideals and there is still no agreement about what its legacy has been.

QUESTIONS

1. Although Küng was a critic of the Church, why did he praise John XXIII?
2. What was the most visible change at local level?
3. What new role did the Jesuits take?
4. How did Archbishop Lefebvre react to the reforms of Vatican II?

GENERAL ESSAY QUESTIONS ON CHAPTER 16

1. Write a paragraph on each of the following:
   (a) Pope John XXIII and the calling of the Second Vatican Council.
   (b) The changes in the Catholic Church brought about by the Second Vatican Council.
2. Write a brief essay on the Second Vatican Council. You may include some points about the reason it was called, the organisation of the Council, the changes it brought about and the impact it had within the Catholic Church.
3. According to the theologian Hans Küng, Vatican II was a major turning point for the Catholic Church. Assess the impact that the Second Vatican Council had within the Catholic Church.

17

YOUTH CULTURE

Words you need to understand

Avant garde: A group expressing modern ideas in society.

Autonomy: Freedom or independence.

Elite: Superior, higher.

Haute Couture: High fashion.

Mass media: Various means of communicating to a large number of people.

Media barons: Powerful and influential people in control of the media.

Sit-in: Peaceful occupation of an area as a way of protest without violence.

Taboo: Forbidden.

Vanguard: Leaders of a movement.

17.1 YOUTH CULTURE

The idea of young people having their own distinctive and unique culture is a relatively new one that emerged in Europe after the second World War.

Educational reforms allowed them spend a longer time in full-time education. Young people also had spending power and free time. These new freedoms gave youth a sense of identity. Caught between childhood and adulthood, they saw themselves as being different. For the first time in history young people became mass consumers of products designed specifically to cater for them as a distinct group in society. This group spent their money on trendy clothes, cosmetics and music.

● A young person using their clothes to carry a message – this one showing Bill Gates (see p. 254) as the devil.

Courtesy: Corbis

Source Document

Leisure and pop music, 'Summer Holiday'

Cliff Richard made a film, Summer Holiday *(1963), and the title song showed how consumerism and the media had combined in Britain during the early 1960s.*

> We're all going on a summer holiday
> No more working for a week or two.
> Fun and laughter on our summer holiday,
> No more worries for me or you,
> For a week or two.
> We're going where the sun shines brightly
> We're going where the sea is blue.
> We've all seen it on the movies,
> Now let's see if it's true.

(written by Bruce Welch and Ray Bennett, 1972)

QUESTIONS ON THE DOCUMENT

1. How long did the holiday last?
2. What was the holiday destination?
3. Where had the holiday-makers learned about the destination?
4. What influence of American popular culture can be seen in this British song?

TEENAGERS

Teenagers belong to the age group that ranges from 13 to 19. The term was first used in America in the 1940s and was imported to Britain in the 1950s. By the end of that decade it was used all over Europe.

AMERICAN INFLUENCE

The British 'teenage boom' began in the 1950s. It regarded Hollywood movie stars like James Dean and Marlon Brando as heroes and role models. Elvis Presley sold millions of records in Europe. American rock and roll became the anthem of the post-war generation of teenagers in Europe.

Courtesy: Corbis

Courtesy: Corbis

● 1980s teenagers cheering at a concert.

● All over Europe and America, pop culture dominated this period. This photo was taken at a concert after John Lennon's death (see p. 221).

In Eastern Europe young people came together to listen to rock music and paid small fortunes on the black market for American records and blue jeans. To teenagers in Soviet-controlled Eastern Europe, American culture, particularly rock and roll, represented a way of rebelling against political authority.

In France authorities also regarded American influences as subversive. The French government introduced a law restricting the amount of time given over to playing foreign music on the radio.

WORKING-CLASS VALUES

Young men found new ways to express themselves by copying the clothes, music and even the language of the urban working classes. In Britain, the Teddy boy was a symptom of proletarian rebellion. They got their name from the style of clothes they wore, which was an exaggerated version of the clothes worn by upper-class men in Edwardian England (1902–1910) – hence the name Teddy. The Teddy boy cult was eventually replaced by other fashion trends: in the 1960s the mods and rockers, and in the 1970s and 1980s the punks. Each of them had uniquely working-class roots and set the tone for male youth culture in general.

• Teds at Wembley, 1 January 1972.

• Generation gap, 1958. An elderly couple ignore the youths behind them.

QUESTIONS

1. Explain how a distinctive youth culture emerged after the second World War.
2. How and why did American trends influence European teenagers in the 1950s?

17.2 THE SWINGING SIXTIES

By the early 1960s Britain had become the centre for youth culture. The young pop group from Liverpool, the Beatles, broke into the UK Top 20 in December 1962 with their first hit single, 'Love Me Do'. Following the release of their first album, *Please, Please Me*, the band appeared on national TV and attracted an audience of 6 million viewers. The Beatles created a whole new trend in music and in fashion, particularly in hairstyles.

BEATLEMANIA

The media called the new craze started by the Beatles 'Beatlemania'. Screaming teenage girls attended Beatle concerts and formed fan clubs all over Europe. Beatles concerts became a licence for mass hysteria.

• Beatlemania transferred very early to the USA, as this 1966 concert at Shea Stadium shows.

John Lennon (1940–1980): He formed his first band, the Quarrymen, when he was 16. Lennon met Paul McCartney in 1957 and invited McCartney to join the band. George Harrison and Ringo Star joined later and the band changed its name to the Beatles. Lennon and McCartney co-wrote most of their biggest hit songs. In 1969 Lennon married Yoko Ono, a Japanese artist and writer. They received huge international media attention for their seven-day 'bed-in' at the Amsterdam Hilton Hotel, a protest against war and violence in the world, particularly against the war in Vietnam.

In 1970 the Beatles officially broke up. Lennon pursued a solo career, releasing the song 'Imagine' in 1971. In 1975 Lennon went into seclusion, living with Yoko and their son Seán in New York. In 1980 he and Yoko released *Double Fantasy*. On 8 December Lennon was shot by a deranged fan, Mark Chapman.

To adults Beatlemania was a kind of epidemic. They believed young fans to be at risk of serious corruption and moral contamination. In an interview in 1966, Beatle John Lennon caused a storm of reaction when he claimed "we're more popular than Jesus Christ now". The band gave their last live performance that year, but continued to produce hit records until they finally broke up in 1970.

LONDON FASHION

Paris remained the centre of *haute couture* fashion, but the trend-setters for youth styles were the London designers. In 'Swinging London', Mary Quant, who created the miniskirt, attacked Paris fashion for being outdated. In 1963 popular demand for her clothes was so great that she moved into mass production. The new look had no waist, no heels, and breaking completely with tradition, no hat, gloves or stockings.

Twiggy, a 17-year-old Cockney (someone from the East End of London) rose to fame in 1966 as a model. She portrayed a new image of feminine beauty and made 'skinny' fashionable.

MASS PRODUCTION

Mass production made chic clothes cheap to buy. Less expensive imitations of designers' style could be found in Carnaby Street, which until the 1960s was a run-down back alley off Regent Street. Here an entire outfit could be bought for as little as £15. Traditional standards of decency were shattered by the miniskirt and pants suits for young women, as well as bright-coloured shirts and trousers for young men. In 1965 French clothing manufacturers produced more trousers than skirts for the first time. Blue jeans, like rock music, became the badge of identity for young men and women all over Europe.

The explosion of spending on 'style' by young people led to the creation of a new kind of 'aristocracy' in Britain. Members of this exclusive club came from the world of fashion, music, media, entertainment and sport. Among them were fashion photographer David Bailey, son of an East End tailor, and his French wife, actress Catherine Deneuve. Their wedding guest list, which included Mick Jagger of the Rolling Stones as best man, was a roll call of London's 'beautiful people'.

• A fashion model stands in front of a mural displaying the clothing designs of fashion designer Mary Quant, Carnaby Street, London.

• Fashionable men on Carnaby Street in the 1960s.

The event, in July 1965, received widespread media coverage. Social magazines like *Tatler* and *Harper's & Queen* covered this new rich club of fashion and media celebrities.

In April 1966, *Time* wrote: "In this century, every decade has its city … and for the Sixties that city is London." The mood of Swinging London was captured in the popular 1966 film *Blow Up*.

Source Document

Banning the Rolling Stones

Pop music was often controversial, and the publicity usually worked to the advantage of the artist.

The Rolling Stones' latest single disc is being banned by some American radio stations. The reason given by the station executives: "It could incite further riots here." Mick Jagger said today, "I'm rather pleased to hear they have banned 'Street Fighting Man' as long as it's still available in the shops. The last time they banned one of our records in America it sold a million."

(*Evening Standard*, London, 4 September 1968)

QUESTIONS ON THE DOCUMENT

1. Why was the song 'Street Fighting Man' banned in the USA?
2. How did Mick Jagger react to this?

17.3   STUDENT REVOLT

Baby boom – a term coined in the USA to describe the increase in birth rates during the 1940s and early 1950s. By 1965 these war and post-war babies had reached their late teens or early 20s and became known as 'baby boomers'. In 1951, the under-20 group made up 8 per cent of the population in Britain; by 1966 this had increased to 10 per cent.

The remarkable expansion of education in post-war Europe produced a new generation of well-educated young people. The baby boom changed the age structure of all European countries. Demographic changes, together with welfare states' commitment to provide better educational opportunities, ensured a dramatic rise in Europe's student population.

University attendance between 1950 and 1965 more than tripled in France, tripled in West Germany and doubled in Italy. By 1975, 39 per cent of the student population in Western Europe was female, while in Eastern Europe it was 48 per cent.

The experience of mass education in post-war Europe gave students a sense of shared identity and became a powerful force in shaping the cultural values of a whole generation.

● A modern-style poster of the revolutionary cult-figure, Che Guevara.

Courtesy: Corbis

● Protestors at an anti-Vietnam War rally, 1967.

Courtesy: Corbis

Disillusioned with Soviet Marxism, and with Stalin in particular, many students looked for inspiration and heroes in the developing world. The 1960s generation of students looked to youthful Third World revolutionaries like Che Guevara, Fidel Castro and Mao Tse-tung for inspiration.

INTERNATIONAL BACKGROUND

Across Europe a generation of students found a common cause in their shared reaction to these four events: The Vietnam War, the Chinese Cultural Revolution, revolution in Latin America and the Prague Spring (see pp. 50–2).

PROTEST

In late 1967, students in Italy, France, West Germany and Britain demanded reforms in university education. They began to stage sit-ins, forcing their way into university buildings and occupying them. The police were called in to remove the protesters, and violent clashes often developed. The radical student leader Danny Cohn-Bendit led a sit-in at Paris University in March 1968. Some teachers joined the protest. Militants were arrested and the university was eventually closed on 2 May. The next day students at the Sorbonne protested. The police were sent in to arrest the leaders. Over 1,000 people were injured in rioting. The police used tear gas and baton charges against the demonstrators. Students threw bricks and Molotov cocktails (petrol bombs) at the police.

● Paris, 1968. Thousands of students demonstrated for educational reform, while carrying symbols of revolution: posters of Mao Tse-Tung, Castro, Lenin and Che Guevara.

Courtesy: Bettmann/Corbis

President de Gaulle wanted to send in the army, but other ministers cautioned against this, fearing it would provoke full-scale civil war.

By mid-May, workers had joined the protests. 10 million people were on strike in France, turning the situation into a serious threat for the government. To diffuse the situation the government made wage concessions to the workers and conceded educational reforms. The excesses of the student demonstrations, however, lost them middle-class support and they found themselves isolated. In the June elections de Gaulle won a majority.

Courtesy: Bettmann/Corbis

Unrest quickly spread to universities across Europe, where students marched to demonstrate against the war in Vietnam and the invasion of Czechoslovakia. They attacked the material comfort, affluence and conformity of middle-class culture. The Western student rebellion widened the gap between the generations.

The youth cultural movement discovered new levels of intensity in the 1970s. In that decade the 'counter-culture', or 'hippie' youth movement spread from the USA to Europe. Older critics called it the 'permissive society'.

QUESTION

1.   How did conditions in universities lead to student unrest in the late 1960s?

● An anti-Vietnam war demonstrator throws a tear-gas canister at police.

17.4   THE PERMISSIVE SOCIETY

Historian Eric Hobsbawn said, "The cultural revolution of the later 20th century can … best be understood as the triumph of the individual over society." *Age of Extremes*, Penguin, 1994.

Courtesy: Corbis

The cultural mood of Europe's younger generation after the 1960s was experimental, critical and hostile to traditional social values.

Youthful rebellion had previously been contained by the controlling influences of family and religion.

Old values that rewarded sacrifice, obedience, duty and 'good living' were abandoned in favour of endless consumption and personal gratification. Youth celebrated excess, in dress, music, drugs, sex and spontaneous living in defiance of older cultural values.

● A man paints a woman's face during the Summer of love-in at Haight Ashbury, San Francisco, California, 1967.

FORBIDDEN TO FORBID
The popular slogan of the Paris 1968 rebellion, "It is forbidden to forbid" became the motto for youth rebellion in the 1970s. It formed the basis for personal, as well as social, liberation of young people everywhere. The satisfaction of private individual desires and feelings inspired a new code of conduct in youth culture.

Courtesy: Corbis

TUNE IN, TURN ON AND DROP OUT
The hippie counter-culture originated in America during the 1960s. It represented a cultural rebellion against the materialism of American consumer society of the 1950s. The slogan "tune in, turn on and drop out" expressed their rejection of middle-class society. This cultural movement spread to Europe during the 1970s. Amsterdam and Copenhagen became hippie centres in Europe.

● Peace and love. Musicians play bongos and a sitar at a hippy festival of the early 1970s.

DRUG USE AND SEXUAL EXPRESSION

During the 1960s British rock bands openly promoted drug taking. The Beatles released their hit album *Sergeant Pepper's Lonely Hearts Club Band* in 1967. It was a departure from their earlier musical style and was clearly influenced by drugs. One song on this album, 'Lucy in the Sky with Diamonds', was said to stand for LSD, a new chemical substance believed at the time to enhance consciousness. Mick Jagger (see p. 222), the lead singer with the Rolling Stones, and other band members were arrested for possession of drugs. The most popular drug among Western young people was marijuana, but later a market for cocaine developed among the more prosperous middle-class youth. During the late 1980s ecstasy (known as E) became a popular drug among young people, associated with a new movement in music known as 'acid house'.

● Merry pranksters decorate the bus in preparation for the Acid Test Graduation celebration, San Francisco, California, October 1966.

Post-1960s youth culture also believed in freer sexual expression. In the permissive society individuals indulged in pre-marital sex. Such attitudes became more widespread with the greater availability of the contraceptive pill. During the 1980s gay pride parades became familiar demonstrations of rebellious sexuality and social difference in many European cities.

● Group of punks, February 1989.

In Eastern Europe, Western-style rock music festivals were a beacon to young people attracted to free love and drugs. Here youth culture was generally more political – drugs, sex and rock and roll were an expression of opposition to Communist repression.

QUESTIONS

1. What were the distinguishing features of the hippie counter-culture of the 1970s?
2. Show how the development of a drug culture among young people in Europe was linked to rock music.

17.5 POPULAR CULTURE

After the second World War new cultural trends emerged in Europe. This was the age of the masses – mass production, mass consumption and mass media. Traditionally culture had been divided into 'high' and 'low', or elite and popular culture.

From 1945 the situation changed dramatically. Radio, television and cinema have all made culture universal, transmitting it to all classes. No longer confined to theatres, art galleries, museums or concert halls, by 1992 culture was available daily in the home via radio, television and home entertainment systems.

Courtesy: Getty Images

● Elvis Presley in full swing, 1957.

Technology has also changed the expression of culture. The camera has turned photography into an art form. Drama and theatre have found new means of communication in film. Producers of film soundtracks and popular music records share the cultural world of classical musicians. The tastes and styles of ordinary people, i.e. popular or mass culture, were dominant in Europe between 1945 and 1992.

After the war the continued American military presence in Europe helped to spread the influence of rock music. By 1960 there were over 400,000 US military personnel in West Germany. The Marshall Plan helped to spread American cultural influences. Europe became a market for Coca-Cola, Hollywood films, rock records and the entire American way of life.

Courtesy: Corbis

Home-grown variations of rock musicians sprang up in cities all over Europe. In Britain, Tommy Steele, Lonnie Donnegan and Cliff Richard competed with American stars in the charts during the 1950s. In the 1960s the French popular rock singer Johnny Hallyday borrowed American music and dress.

In the 1970s glam rock and punk rock rebelled against the earlier music and dress styles of the 1950s and 1960s. In Britain, glam-rockers dressed up in sequins and bell-bottom trousers to attend David Bowie's concerts. Punk bands in the late 1970s transformed older rock musical forms. The British band *The Sex Pistols* first played live in November 1975. They represented youthful excess and spontaneous expression.

● David Bowie, in his persona of Ziggy Stardust, typified 1970s glam rock.

Source Document

Sex Pistol murder in New York

Sid Vicious, the punk singer from the British band The Sex Pistols, *murdered his girlfriend in New York.*

Sid Vicious, bass guitarist of Britain's spitting and stomping *Sex Pistols* punk rock band, yesterday was arrested and charged with stabbing his sultry blond girlfriend to death in their room at Manhattan's famed Chelsea Hotel.

His face pale and scratched, the dazed-looking Vicious muttered curses and "I'll smash your cameras" as he was led from the hotel, where the body of Nancy Laura Spungen, 20, was found crumpled under the bathroom sink.

Both Vicious and Miss Spungen had said they expected to die young – "I'll kill myself as soon as the first wrinkle appears," she once said.

(*New York Post*, 13 October 1978)

QUESTIONS ON THE DOCUMENT

1. What was the musical reputation of *The Sex Pistols*?
2. How did Vicious behave when he saw the cameras?
3. Spungen had stated that she expected to die young. What does this say about the extreme expectations of some punk rockers?

The 1980s saw the arrival of yet another wave of youth culture in Europe. Unlike the liberalising 1960s and 1970s, the 1980s youth culture was conservative. These were 'Thatcher's children', who had lived through less prosperous economic times than the rock fans before them. The rates of youth unemployment were high in this decade. In Britain between 1982 and 1988, 20 per cent of young people were unemployed. In Spain during this time, 40 per cent of young people were unemployed. Club culture, and its later offshoot, raves, became the shared experience of the generation. A new and distinct dress code, dance styles, music genres and rituals, which included and often centred around illicit drug taking, emerged. However, the focus was on personal liberation more than on any attempt to change the system.

• Ravers in the late 1980s.

Courtesy: Corbis

Each new movement of youth culture received widespread media attention. After initial shock reactions from the older generations and established authority, the trends were eventually absorbed into mainstream popular culture. Youth culture could be seen and heard everywhere. It was part of everyday life. Furthermore, it crossed all class and national boundaries.

QUESTIONS

1. What was the 'permissive society'?
2. How did European popular culture reflect American influences after the second World War?

17.6 SPORT

After the second World War, sport became commercial in the consumer society. It was packaged and sold as a product. Advertising sold goods and services by connecting branded products with popular sports stars; for example Sharp, an electrical company, sponsored Manchester United in the 1980s.

The growth of the mass media, television, radio, newspapers and magazines brought sports into everyday life.

Attendance at sporting events has generally declined, but television viewing of all sports grew dramatically. In 1972 the Munich Olympic Games were broadcast to an audience of 450 million. All national networks offered regular sports programmes, enjoyed by all classes. England's 1966 World Cup victory at Wembley Stadium in London turned soccer into an acceptable sport, enjoyed by all classes and generations. Until then it had been regarded as a working-class pastime.

Since 1945 many sports formerly considered elitist became more accessible to all classes. In France the number of private sailing boats and yachts rose from 20,000 in 1960 to 647,000 in 1985. Membership of tennis and golf clubs, once the preserve of the rich, became available to all classes. Horse racing, the traditional sport of aristocrats, became a popular working-class sport with the growth of betting shops across Europe. In 1960 the British government passed the **Betting and Gambling Act**. This allowed for off-course betting on horse races, turning horse racing into a popular sport.

Courtesy: Getty Images

● Cassius Clay (Muhammad Ali) at the Rome Olympics, 1960.

Since 1945 there has been a marked emphasis on winning in sports. This has often resulted in the politicisation of sports, evident in the nationalism displayed in events like the Olympics and the football World Cup. During the Cold War the Olympics were frequently reduced to another form of conflict between East and West. At the 1960 Olympic games in Rome, Soviet gymnasts won every event in the women's competitions. Four years later at the Tokyo Olympics, the Americans won 12 of the men's swimming events and broke seven world records.

Football hooliganism was first identified as a serious problem in Europe during the 1960s. Emphasis on winning often provoked violent clashes from sections of fans on the losing side. In the late 1970s and 1980s racism became a factor in football violence. In 1985 Liverpool supporters caused a riot at the Heysel Stadium in Brussels. Thirty-nine fans were killed and more than 200 injured. Following this, English clubs were banned from European competitions.

Like rock music and films, sports provided young people with heroes and icons to follow. The young footballer George Best became a role model for millions of British fans during the 1970s. Playing for Manchester United, he impressed fans as much with his lifestyle and attitude as he did with his football skills. Best was banned from playing for one month in 1970 because of 'disreputable' behaviour. However, this did not diminish his popularity.

The cult of the sports celebrity was not confined to soccer. In continental Europe cycling and motor racing attracted large support and produced a number of sporting heroes.

Courtesy: Corbis Sygma

● English football hooligans square up to police in riot gear outside a French international match, 1985.

Courtesy: Hulton-Deutsch/Corbis

● George Best at Manchester United.

Source Document

Sport: the celebrity of the individual

Peter Dobereiner, a British golf journalist, describes the importance of getting a good quote from a player.

Once upon a time it was the custom of newspapers to carry reports of sporting events. These days readers are not interested in what a player did. They are fascinated to learn what a player *said* he did. Unless a player can talk a good game he is nothing.

(In Yorkshire, Bernard Hunt was interviewed.)

"What happened at the fourteenth", we bayed. It was like drawing teeth; but we persisted and bit by bit it came out. As he was addressing the ball, Hunt's club was struck from his hands by lightning.

"What did you do when the lightning struck you?"

"I picked up the club and hit the ball. Front left about twenty feet." It was a start.

(P. Dobereiner, *The Golfers*, London 1982, pp. 50–1)

QUESTIONS ON THE DOCUMENT

1. What major change has taken place in reporting on sports?
2. What evidence is there that Hunt was not happy to discuss this incident?
3. "It was a start." What does this comment tell us about the writer's attitude towards this new demand for celebrity quotes?

Competitiveness in sports resulted in many drug-related scandals. The use of performance-enhancing drugs became an all-too-common feature of many sports. At the 1988 Seoul Olympics, Ben Johnson, the Canadian world record holder of the 100 metre title, was disqualified and had his gold medal taken from him when he failed a drugs test. At the Rome Olympics in 1960, a young Danish cyclist, Knut Jensen, collapsed and died during a race. A post-mortem found that he had taken a stimulant drug before the race.

Since the 1970s the new obsession with health and beauty, together with increased leisure time, raised participation in sports. Between 1979 and 1989 the number of sports centres in Italy grew from 45,494 to 118,712. New stadiums have been built in most European capitals. The number of tennis courts tripled in France between the 1970s and the 1980s. By the 1990s participation in sporting activities were higher than ever before in Europe.

Courtesy: Bettmann/Corbis

● Olympic sprinter Ben Johnson, disqualified for steroid use in 1988. Of the eight finalists of that race, four of them have tested positive for drug use since 1988.

QUESTIONS

1. How have sports become more popular since 1945?
2. What were the results of growing competitiveness in sports 1945–1992?

17.7 THE MASS MEDIA

Courtesy: Corbis

• A selection of 1960s paperbacks, widely available to the mass market.

The mass media includes the print media (newspapers, magazines and books) and the electronic media (radio, television, sound recordings, films and the Internet). The paperback revolution (no longer putting expensive hard boards on the front and back) has made books widely available and cheap to buy. Between the late 1960s and 1981, paperback sales in France doubled from 50 to 100 million copies a year.

Newspapers have had to compete with television and circulation figures have declined since 1945. Newspapers adapted to the mass consumer market by including popular features on sports and entertainment. Television listings became an important marketing feature for newspapers. In 1962 the London *Sunday Times* began publishing a colour supplement. Most newspaper publishers in Europe quickly followed the trend. The tabloid press reached mass audiences. Offering wide coverage of sports, entertainment and sensational gossip, they have enjoyed popular appeal.

Magazine sales also rocketed during this period. The most successful magazines were directed to specific interests. There was something to suit all age groups, all classes and all leisure interests. News magazines catered for middle-class professionals. Women's magazines, such as *Ideal Homes*, *Women's Own* and *Elle*, were big sellers. The market in sports magazines expanded dramatically, offering a huge range to suit all sporting tastes. Music fans also found magazines to cater for their interests. With the growth of youth culture since the 1950s, magazines marketed directly at young teenage girls advertised clothes, cosmetics and boys. However, the best-selling magazines were those associated with television programming and personalities.

After the war, and particularly since the 1960s, popular demand for entertainment changed much of radio's programming content. Radio received a brief setback when television first appeared, but by catering to popular demand for rock music its share of the market began to increase again in the 1960s. The development of the transistor and battery-operated radios made this medium transportable. The later 'ghetto blaster' radio was popular with Europe's urban youth.

Technological improvements in sound recording brought the long-playing record (LP) to consumers in 1948. During the 1970s individual music choices became widely available and transportable with the arrival of the cassette tape. By the early 1990s, compact discs (CDs) significantly improved the quality of sound, replacing vinyl records and cassette tapes.

By the 1960s television had become the most popular form of communication in the mass media. In Eastern Europe it remained under strict government control, but in the West it was largely in

Courtesy: Corbis

the hands of new media barons, such as Silvio Berlusconi, Robert Maxwell and Rupert Murdoch. Most Europeans were turning to television by the 1990s. Television and not parents, teachers or religious leaders influenced the values of young people from a very early age. The American pop music video television station, MTV, became popular with young people throughout Europe in the late 1980s.

• Publishing magnate Rupert Murdoch at one of his many newspaper printing presses. He also owned TV stations in every continent, and he controlled SKY television, Britain's first satellite channel.

Cinema, like radio, went into decline when television first appeared on the scene. Videocassette recorders (VCRs) made the latest films available for viewing in the home. The boom in television and VCR ownership in the 1960s and 1970s saw a decline in cinema-going. However, attendance revived during the 1980s, but the age profile of those choosing this form of entertainment changed. In France in 1989, 73 per cent of them were under 35.

By 1992, Europeans were spending nearly half their leisure time using mass media. Most of that time was spent watching television, but also listening to radio, playing CDs, watching films and playing video games.

QUESTIONS

1. List some changes which have occurred in electronic media in the 20th century.
2. How have the print media changed to meet competition from television and radio?

GENERAL ESSAY QUESTIONS ON CHAPTER 17

1. Show how America influenced European youth culture after the second World War.
2. What factors made London the centre of youth culture in Europe during the 1960s?
3. Write a short account of the student revolt in Paris in 1968.
4. How did John Lennon represent youth culture during the 1960s?
5. Explain how sports became an important part of popular culture during the period 1945–1992.
6. Outline the impact of the mass media on European popular culture 1945–1992.
7. Discuss the factors that led to the emergence of youth culture in post-war Europe.
8. Discuss the changes in popular culture in Europe 1945–1992.
9. Assess the importance of London as a trend-setting city in the 1960s.
10. "At the heart of the student movement lay an irreverent anti-authoritarianism." Discuss.
11. Discuss the importance of sports in European popular culture 1945–1992.
12. "John Lennon in particular served as inspiration to an entire generation." Discuss.
13. Assess the development of the mass media, and show how it dominated life in the period 1945–1992.

18

ADVANCES IN THE BIOLOGICAL SCIENCES, 1945–1992

Words you need to understand

Biotechnology: The use of living bacteria in the industrial production of goods.

Double helix: A helix is similar to a spiral staircase. The shape of a double helix crosses over and back like the cords in a rope.

Genetics: The study of how the characteristics of one generation are passed on to the next.

Human genome: The total number of genes in the full set of chromosomes of a person.

Patent: An exclusive right to use a new invention.

INTRODUCTION

The biological sciences deal with the study of living things: human beings, microbes, plants and animals. The developments in biological sciences since 1945 raised hopes that scientific research would provide many 'magic bullet' solutions to problems or diseases that had previously been out of reach. Advances in biological sciences were catapulted forward by the discovery of the structure of the DNA molecule in 1953. The new and exciting areas of molecular biology, genetics and DNA technology have substantially expanded our knowledge about living things.

ADVANCES IN MEDICINE

Major advances were made in the field of medicine. Public health was improved by successful research into infectious diseases. Just before the second World War, Alexander Fleming, a Scot, discovered penicillin – an effective aid in fighting bacterial infection. After the war, many vaccines emerged to fight against typhoid, tuberculosis, cholera, smallpox and malaria.

Polio, a crippling illness, was almost eliminated in Europe following a mass vaccination campaign. The United Nations declared in 1978 that smallpox had been wiped out as a serious threat, and this was one of the great achievements of medicine in the late 20th century.

The prospects for patient health improved as the safety of surgery improved, allowing doctors to extend the range of facilities. Dr Christiaan Bernard performed the first heart transplant in 1967. This technique was so successful that thousands of transplants had been performed in Europe by 1992. Permanent artificial hearts and pacemakers were developed.

These improvements allowed people in Europe to live longer. Health care for older people cost more, adding to government welfare spending. In 1992, a patient over 75 years old cost Britain's National Health Service nine times more than a patient between 15 and 64 years.

> ### What is DNA?
> DNA is the carrier of genetic information in the human body and is the key to the transmission of physical characteristics from one generation to the next. Its scientific name is *deoxyribonucleic acid*.

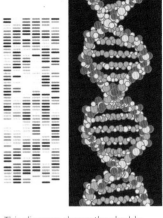

Courtesy: Corbis

● This diagram shows the double helix structure of DNA.

18.1 THE RACE TOWARDS DNA FAME

In 1866, Gregor Mandel described how **heredity** worked, or how physical characteristics were passed from one generation of a family to the next. His idea was not taken up until the 20th century.

THE DNA RESEARCHERS

Five people took part in the race to discover the structure of DNA. According to Bill Bryson, "victory fell to an unlikely quartet of scientists in England who didn't work as a team, often weren't on speaking terms and were for the most part novices in the field" (*A Short History of Nearly Everything*, London, 2003, p. 488). Dr Linus Pauling, an American scientist, was also involved. Pauling discovered, after studying X-ray patterns, that many proteins had the shape of a triple helix. Dr Francis Crick, a British biophysicist, and Dr James Watson, an American geneticist, worked on their DNA studies in Cambridge University.

Dr Maurice Wilkins and Dr Rosalind Franklin were the main DNA researchers at King's College, London.

In his book *What Mad Pursuit*, Weidenfeld 1988, Crick stated, "Jim and I hit it off immediately." They both had a "youthful arrogance, a ruthlessness and an impatience with sloppy thinking." They had chosen the "right problem". He admitted that they had luck on their side: "By blundering about we stumbled on gold, but the fact remains that we were looking for gold."

Courtesy: Time Life Picture/Getty Images

● Maurice Wilkins shown in 1962 with a model of DNA structure. He worked with Franklin during the race to discover the make-up of DNA.

Franklin and Wilkins, independently working in London, used an X-ray beam to bombard crystals of DNA. The resulting X-ray photographs helped Franklin to build up an image of the **double helix** structure of DNA. These images were not made available to other researchers. Franklin and Wilkins protected their research, even from each other.

Crick and Watson built a triple helix model of the DNA structure using wood, metal and paper. Franklin was prepared to help them. She pointed out that they had made a mistake in their mathematical equations after she saw their model.

> **James Watson (1928–2004):** Watson was an American biologist who came to work in Cambridge because of his interest in DNA. He worked with Francis Crick between 1951 and 1953 investigating the structure of DNA. He returned to America to work in Harvard University in 1955. He started the Human Genome Project in 1990.

Courtesy: Getty Images

Francis Crick (1916–2004): Crick was a British physicist who joined a molecular biology laboratory at Cambridge in 1949. Despite an age difference of 12 years, he worked with James Watson to discover the structure of DNA. He continued his genetic studies after his major DNA discovery.

Courtesy: Getty Images

WATSON AND CRICK WIN THE RACE

Watson and Crick were told by their employers to stop working on DNA and to concentrate on their other work. This did not stop them thinking about possible solutions to the DNA puzzle.

In December 1952 Crick and Watson heard that Dr Pauling was about to publish research showing that DNA had a triple helix structure. Pauling was due to travel to England to meet DNA researchers in May 1952, but the US government refused to let him leave the country because of his liberal political views.

Courtesy: Educational Co.

Rosalind Franklin (1920–1958): She took the first photographs that showed the double helix structure of DNA. She was close to discovering the secret of DNA, but Watson and Crick got there first. She made a major contribution to the discovery and properties of DNA. She died at 37 years of age because of her exposure to radiation.

At this point, Franklin made an essential contribution to the discovery of the DNA structure.

She would not publish her research until she had definite proof of the DNA structure. Her reluctance to publish straight away left an opening for Watson and Crick. Maurice Wilkins, without Franklin's permission, showed copies of her double helix photograph (called 'photograph 51') to James Watson.

It was the key event, the most important moment in the race. Watson later said, "The instant I saw the picture my mouth fell open and my pulse began to race." On his way home in the train, he sketched the double helix structure from memory in the margin of his newspaper. With the help of Wilkins and the research of Franklin, Watson and Crick had finally cracked the DNA jigsaw.

The DNA molecule is like a twisted ladder. Two interlinking lines of DNA folded around a central axis to form a curving double helix, like two spiral staircases curving around each other. When one section of a DNA string breaks away, another one forms and the new DNA string is an exact copy of the first molecule.

Source Document: A

James Watson outlines why Francis Crick and himself solved the structure of DNA before anyone else.

First, we thought it was the most important problem around. Others didn't realise that. Second, most people thought it couldn't be solved by building models – they thought you needed to get the answer primarily from X-ray crystallography of DNA. Rosalind Franklin made that mistake.

Third, we had each other. It helps to have someone else to take over the thinking when you get frustrated.

Fourth, we were willing to ask for help and talk to our competitors. Again, Rosalind was so intelligent that she rarely sought advice.

Fifth, you have to be obsessive.

Finally, both Francis and I knew that we would have careers even if we failed, so we weren't desperate.

(Time, 3 March 2003)

Source Document: B

Watson and Crick published their work in *Nature*, a scientific magazine

We wish to suggest a structure for desoxyribose nucleic acid (DNA). This structure has novel features which are of considerable biological interest.

A structure for nucleic acid has already been proposed by Pauling and Cory. They kindly made their manuscript available to us in advance of publication. Their model consists of three intertwined chains.

We have also been stimulated by a knowledge of the general nature of the unpublished experimental results and ideas of Dr. M.H.F. Wilkins, Dr. R.E. Franklin and their co-workers at King's College, London.

(Nature, 2 April 1953)

QUESTIONS ON THE DOCUMENTS

1. What comments does Watson make about Rosalind Franklin in Document B?
2. From his other comments in Document A, what do you think was the most important reason that Watson and Crick discovered the structure of DNA?
3. How do Watson and Crick define the new nature of their discovery in Document B?
4. What credit did they give to Pauling, the American chemist?
5. What tribute did they pay to Wilkins and Franklin?
6. While Watson and Crick were credited with the discovery, what evidence is there in Document B that they acted in an ethical way towards other researchers?

DNA IN THE PUBLIC DOMAIN

The British magazine *Nature* published a letter from Watson and Crick in April 1953, outlining their findings. When Franklin published her own work on DNA, she had to write that her research was in line with the "model proposed by Crick and Watson", since they had published their theory first.

Watson, writing about Franklin in his book *The Double Helix* (1978), was critical of her presentation: "her dresses showed all the imagination of English blue-stocking adolescents". He did not appreciate the difficulties that a female scientist faced. The scientific world of the 1950s often regarded women, Watson stated, as "mere diversions from serious thinking".

Franklin died in April 1958, at only 37 years of age. Her ovarian cancer was caused by exposure to the radiation emitted by X-rays. In the 1950s, she did not wear a protective lead apron and the machines themselves were not shielded, so the radiation was not adequately contained.

A NOBEL PRIZE FOR THE SURVIVING DNA PIONEERS

Courtesy: Getty Images

● In 1962, American biochemist James Watson (right) receives the Nobel Prize for Chemistry, before a standing, applauding crowd dressed in formal attire, Stockholm, Sweden.

In 1962, three people were awarded the Nobel Prize for Chemistry because of their work on the molecular structure of DNA – Maurice Wilkins, Francis Crick and James Watson. Franklin might have been included in this group, but a Nobel Prize cannot be given posthumously (after death).

HOW IMPORTANT WAS THE DISCOVERY OF DNA?

It was one of the great discoveries of the 20th century. On the day that Watson and Crick solved the puzzle of DNA, Crick told his friends at his local pub that they had discovered the secret of life.

The importance of the discovery was not clear to all observers. Their employer, Lawrence Bragg, read their report in *Nature* and said, "It's all Greek to me."

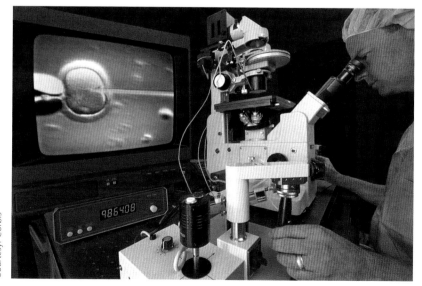

Courtesy: Corbis

● A doctor uses microscopic technology as part of a procedure using in vitro fertilisation.

The historian Eric Hobsbawn recalled that he had met Crick at that time: "Most of us were simply not aware that these extraordinary developments were being hatched in laboratories we passed regularly, and pubs where we drank" (Hobsbawn, *The Age of Extremes*, p. 527).

The significance of the discovery was noticed by others. According to the historian H.F. Judson, "Watson and Crick knew the entire [DNA] structure: it had emerged from the shadow of billions of years, absolute and simple … seen and understood for the first time."

Dr Sydney Brenner, a molecular biologist, said that Watson and Crick would be "remembered as the biologists of the 20th century … much as Darwin is remembered as the biologist of the 19th century" (Darwin is the author of *The Origin of the Species*, which puts forward the theory of evolution.)

QUESTIONS

1. What advantage did Watson and Crick have because they were working as a team?
2. Where did Watson find the inspiration for the double helix solution to the DNA mystery?
3. How important was the part played by Rosalind Franklin in the discovery of the structure of DNA?
4. How important was the discovery of the structure of DNA, as seen by contemporaries and later commentators?

18.2   THE WORLD AFTER DNA

DNA opened the door to a world of scientific discovery. Building on the 1953 discovery brought fame to many scientists.

British biologist Frederick Sanger discovered the sequence of RNA (ribonucleic acids), and was awarded his second Nobel Prize for Chemistry in 1980.

An American scientist, Kary B. Mullis, discovered how to examine tiny fragments of DNA during the 1980s. His work made it possible to detect bowel cancer by examining DNA cells, without having to do invasive surgery on the patient. He received the Nobel Prize for Chemistry in 1993.

The Human Genome Project
The Human Genome Project, involving Britain, France and Germany, as well as the USA and China (among others), set out to map the entire genetic make-up of the human body, starting in 1990. The difficulties of this investigation were immense, as the range of possible DNA base pairs is 3 billion.

Dr James Watson directed the project until 1992. The project was completed in 2003.

THE RISE OF GENETIC ENGINEERING
The revelation of the DNA structure revolutionised biological science. The major developments in genetic engineering, starting in the 1970s, produced many startling results that would have not have been possible before the discovery of the DNA structure. Genetics examines, amongst other things, how family features are passed through *genes* from parents to their children.

The commercial potential of genetic engineering meant that private companies pioneered the research because of the profits they could make. Private corporations could **patent** (own exclusive rights) over any discoveries they made once plants or bacteria were **genetically modified**.

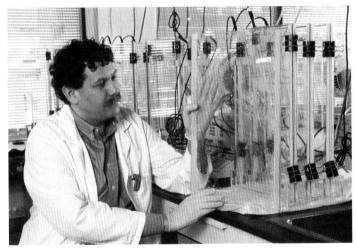

Courtesy: Corbis

● Eric Lander, a biologist, in a laboratory used to map the genes of mice.

In 1988, an American patent was issued for a mouse that had been created through genetic engineering. This set the pattern for commercial exploitation of new biotechnological discoveries.

Biotechnology, a new science
The term 'biotechnology' was first used in 1979 for technologies that develop practical (industrial and commercial) uses for new discoveries. It draws together many different disciplines, including genetic engineering, molecular biology and biochemistry.

MEDICAL BENEFITS OF BIOLOGY RESEARCH

Once the DNA structure was discovered, scientists used DNA to develop new medical techniques.

As a result of genetic engineering, scientists were able to help diabetics by producing insulin in the laboratory. The first insulin made through genetic engineering was sold in 1982.

Developments in biology allowed many infertile couples to have children. It made it possible for a woman to have a child using IVF (in vitro fertilisation). The first 'test-tube baby', Mary Louise Brown, was born in 1979 in England. The work of two surgeons, Patrick Steptoe and Robert Edwards, at the Centre for Human Reproduction led to the birth of over 1,000 children. Concerns about the use of science to develop human embryos prompted a major legal and ethical debate.

Cloning, a challenge for society

In 1973, a calf was born for the first time using a frozen embryo. Sheep embryos were cloned in 1984. In 1993, researchers cloned the first human embryos, raising the possibility that humans could be produced who would be exact copies of their parents. Such ideas had previously only been discussed in science fiction.

Other groups used birth control to limit family size or exclude the possibility of becoming pregnant. The development of the contraceptive pill lowered the possibility of unwanted pregnancy, and contributed to the sexual revolution starting in the 1960s. The Catholic Church condemned the use of 'artificial' contraception (see pp. 181–2).

Research into the human genome challenged existing views on how genetic information should be used in medicine, in food production or in society at large.

More controversially, the advances in biological sciences enabled scientists to clone animals, with the possibility that humans could be cloned. A clone is developed from only one parent and is genetically similar to it.

WHAT IMPACT DID DNA DISCOVERY HAVE IN SOCIETY?

There seems to be no end to the new worlds revealed by DNA analysis.

The use of DNA for identification has helped police forces to revisit many unsolved crimes, and to prove the innocence of others. A method of 'genetic fingerprinting' was developed in 1984, when Alec Jeffries perfected a test that could show the DNA links between members of one family.

In 1988, Colin Pitchfork received a life sentence in England for murdering a schoolgirl. He was the first murderer to be convicted when his DNA was matched to a sample left at the scene of the crime.

In the legal system, DNA tests can settle who a child's biological parents are. In ecology, DNA has been used to prove theft of eggs from the nests of protected birds..

The examination of DNA in old skeletons compared with modern samples of DNA has overturned many accepted truths. DNA analysis showed that early humans left Africa less than 100,000 years ago. Many Icelandic women are descended from Irish people rather than Norwegians.

After the fall of Communism in the USSR, DNA was taken from members of the royal family in Britain. It matched the DNA of skeletons found in Ekaterinburg, proving beyond doubt that the remains were those of the Russian royal family, executed by the Bolsheviks in 1918.

GENETICALLY MODIFIED FOOD

In agriculture, DNA has led to the development of genetically modified (GM) crops. Scientists injected genes into plants, making them stronger to fight disease, thereby increasing the production of the crop. In Europe, concern was voiced, especially by environmental groups, that the crossover into native crops as a result of even experimental GM would be irreversible, and if the GM crops proved dangerous, the results could be disastrous.

• 'Green protesters' tear up genetically modified crops in a field of experimental crops.

Courtesy: Corbis

CONCLUSION

By 1992 a United Nations report listed the benefits associated with biotechnology, showing the optimism that science could provide a wide range of benefits to society. The United Nations Conference on the Environment (UNCE) said that biotechnology would play a major role in health care, improve farming practices (thereby potentially making Third World starvation a thing of the past) and deal with pollution caused by chemical wastes.

Although there was general agreement that the first stage of the DNA revolution had brought many benefits to society, concerns were expressed about the ethical and possible military uses of genetic engineering. Great challenges remained in 1992, especially to find cures for cancer and AIDS.

In 1984, David Baltimore, a Nobel Prize winner in 1975, encouraged people to "integrate the techniques of the future into our lives" (*Nature*, November 1984, p. 151). As well as bringing about a revolution in biology, the discovery by Watson and Crick changed the way in which life itself was viewed.

QUESTIONS

1. Give one example to show how DNA research was seen as being very valuable to scientific research.
2. Why did private companies become involved in genetic research?
3. Give two examples to show the medical benefits that arose from DNA research.
4. How did the introduction of new DNA technology change people's interpretation of the past?

GENERAL ESSAY QUESTIONS ON CHAPTER 18

1. Write a brief description of the race to discover the structure of DNA under the following headings:
   (a) The friendship between Francis Crick and James Watson.
   (b) The contribution of James Wilkins and Rosalind Franklin.
   (c) The discovery of the 'secret of life' by Watson.
   (d) The publication of Watson and Crick's discoveries in *Nature* magazine.

2. The changes brought about in society by DNA research have been many. Write a brief description of changes in the following areas:
   (a) The new science of biotechnology.
   (b) Medical benefits.
   (c) Impact in society.

3. "The discovery of the structure of DNA revolutionised biological research." How true is this statement for the period 1953–1992?

19

THE IMPACT OF NUCLEAR POWER

Words you need to understand

Decommission: To take out of operation.

Nuclear fission: The splitting of an atom, resulting in the release of great amounts of energy.

Nuclear reactor: The chamber in which nuclear fission takes place.

INTRODUCTION

Nuclear technology was originally developed for the purpose of producing atomic bombs.

After the war, nuclear scientists began to look to nuclear power for its potential in producing electricity. As a result, nuclear power had an immense impact on European society. However, the use of this new technology led to many conflicts and controversies.

19.1 THE EXPANSION OF ATOMIC WEAPONS

Four countries had developed a nuclear weapon by the 1960s – the USA, the USSR, France and the United Kingdom. By 1990, the USSR had over 27,000 nuclear warheads.

The French leader General de Gaulle, who became president in 1959, favoured an independent foreign policy. In tests in the Pacific, France exploded its first nuclear bomb in 1960. De Gaulle set up France's own nuclear weapons programme.

After the collapse of the USSR, the new Russian president, Boris Yeltsin, signed a **Strategic Arms Reduction Treaty** with the USA to reduce nuclear weapons by 50 per cent in less than ten years. In June 1992, another agreement limited the number of nuclear warheads to be held by the USA and Russia to a maximum of 3,500 by 2003.

Courtesy: Corbis

● Military uses of nuclear weapons continued during this period. This picture shows the explosion after a shell was launched from an artillery gun.

QUESTION

1. Why did President de Gaulle set up a nuclear weapons programme?

19.2   THE PEACEFUL USE OF NUCLEAR POWER

After the Allied victory in 1945, the USSR used German scientists to develop a nuclear programme, both military and civilian. Once they developed their nuclear bombs, the USA and USSR used the new nuclear techniques to generate electricity.

Nuclear power appealed to governments as it allowed electricity to be produced at a lower cost than using oil or coal. Its greenhouse gas emissions were at a lower level than fossil fuels.

The first nuclear power stations began operating in the 1950s (see Chapter 10). In 1954 the USSR operated the world's first nuclear-powered electricity reactor. Nuclear reactors could be used for ships and submarines. The first nuclear-powered ships were in use in 1959.

Courtesy: Corbis

• The nuclear reactors at Three Mile Island, Pennsylvania, caused one of the most serious nuclear incidents in 1979, when one of the reactors went into melt-down.

The progress of nuclear energy was so swift that by 1957 the **Euratom Treaty** (promoting nuclear energy) was one of the three treaties that launched the European Economic Community (see pp. 89, 95).

The economic import of nuclear power was important. In Britain, 10,000 people worked in the nuclear industry in 1975. An English writer, G.R. Bainbridge, indicated the optimism linked with this new industry. He saw it as a virtue that nuclear stations were built "well in the countryside, on estuaries, on the coast," and, that they "do not pollute the atmosphere".

The fear over the potential damage of nuclear energy prompted a number of important international agreements to limit the spread of nuclear technology. In 1960, 14 countries accepted an agreement on the liability of any country that contributed to nuclear damage. Nuclear conventions signed in 1963, 1979 and 1986 also promoted nuclear safety.

FRANCE: A COUNTRY IN FAVOUR OF NUCLEAR POWER

France has historically been in favour of nuclear energy. In 1946, the **Commission for Atomic Energy** was set up. France built nuclear power stations because of its dependence on imported oil. The proportion of energy produced from oil rose from 7 per cent in 1960 to 39 per cent in 1973.

Nuclear power offered an energy alternative. A slogan outlined the choices for French people – "No oil, no gas, no coal, no choice!" The push for nuclear energy in France met with substantial local opposition, especially from communities who opposed the location of nuclear waste storage facilities in local underground depots.

The French government decided after the oil crisis of 1973 to increase the country's nuclear power generation. By 1981, France was opening five nuclear stations each year. Every two years, it built the same amount of nuclear capacity that Britain built in 30 years. France had over 60 nuclear stations by 1991.

The use of nuclear energy cut the cost of expensive fuel imports. Oil imports as a share of total French energy consumption fell from 69 per cent in 1973 to 43 per cent in 1985. By 1990 only

4 per cent of its energy was produced by oil-burning stations. As a result of its successful nuclear programme, France was the European country least polluted by energy generation.

By 1993 France had spent over 990 billion francs (in 1993 terms) on the promotion of nuclear energy.

This investment in nuclear power meant that France, having to import electricity during the 1970s, became the world's largest exporter of electricity in the 1980s. By contrast, its neighbour, Italy, did not build any nuclear reactors and became Europe's largest importer of electricity.

● One of the many nuclear stations built by the French government, Paluel Nuclear Plant is located on the Normandy coast.

THE IMPACT OF THE OIL CRISIS, 1973

After the oil crisis of 1973 (see Chapter 10), nuclear power emerged as an alternative source of energy for countries with no guaranteed access to oil supplies.

By 1996 nuclear power accounted for 12 per cent of all energy in Western Europe and 5 per cent in Eastern Europe.

QUESTIONS

1. Why did governments favour the use of nuclear energy for the production of electricity?
2. What evidence is there that France had a successful nuclear industry?

19.3 OPPOSITION TO NUCLEAR POWER

PROTEST CAMPAIGNS AGAINST NUCLEAR WEAPONS

The ever-present threat of nuclear war between the USA and the USSR led to the establishment of strong anti-nuclear campaigns. Even political leaders feared the consequences of nuclear war. According to Khrushchev, "In a nuclear war, the living will envy the dead."

Protest movements, called peace movements, complained about the spread of weapons. Critics of the peace movements accused them of supporting the USSR. The protests had very little impact on the development of nuclear weapons.

Prominent scientists supported public concern about the increase in nuclear weapons. In 1955 Albert Einstein warned that nuclear war could lead to mutual destruction.

● A huge crowd of CND (Campaign for Nuclear Disarmament) supporters in Trafalgar Square after their Easter march from Aldermaston to London.

In 1957 the United Nations set up the **International Atomic Energy Agency** (IAEA) to encourage peaceful uses of nuclear power.

TO DAY IS THE 18ᵗʰ ANNIVERSARY OF THE DROPPING OF THE ATOM BOMB ON HIROSHIMA.

"... EVERY HUMAN FAMILY CAN LIVE FROM NOW ON FREE FROM THE FEAR THAT THEIR UNBORN CHILDREN MAY BE AFFECTED BY MAN-MADE POISON IN THE AIR" -LORD HOME, ON SIGNING THE TEST BAN TREATY YESTERDAY

Courtesy: The Centre for the Study of Cartoons and Caricature

• Sir Alec Douglas-Home (the British Prime Minister) signed a treaty in 1963 banning the testing of nuclear weapons.
1. Why did he support the ban?
2. How does the cartoonist convey the horror of nuclear war?

The Nobel Prize-winning scientist, Linus Pauling, called for an end to the testing of nuclear weapons (see page 233). Nine thousand scientists supported his petition. Pauling presented the petition to the United Nations General-Secretary, Dag Hammarskjold.

For his peace campaign, Pauling received his second Nobel Prize in 1962, this time for Peace. As a result of these protests, a **Test Ban Treaty** (1963) limited the spread of nuclear weapons.

PROTEST IN THE UNITED KINGDOM

In the UK, the **Campaign for Nuclear Disarmament** (CND) was founded by Bertrand Russell and Canon John Collins. CND held an annual protest march from 1959 to 1963 between Aldermaston and London.

In 1961 over 100,000 people marched. Fears about nuclear war were so great that in 1965 the BBC decided not to show a drama called *The War Game*. It showed the impact of a 'nuclear winter', the aftermath of a nuclear explosion.

During the 1980s, the USA based more nuclear missiles in Europe. In Western Europe, the deployment of nuclear weapons led to the biggest anti-nuclear demonstrations of the Cold War period.

Courtesy: Getty Images

• Nuclear Protesters in 1960 supporting a refusal to pay tax to the UK government because of the money spent on nuclear defence.
1. Can you suggest a reason why so many women are taking part in this demonstration?
2. One woman wears a fur coat. What does this suggest about her economic status?
3. 'No Tax on War except War on Want'. What other use is the male protester suggesting for the money spent on nuclear weapons?

The British writer J.B. Priestley believed that the peaceful campaign against the nuclear menace could be won: "Alone we defied Hitler – alone we can defy this nuclear madness into which the spirit of Hitler seems to have passed, to poison the world."

PROTEST IN SPAIN

Nuclear opposition in Spain was less restrained. Spain had built the first of ten nuclear reactors in 1968. Opposition to nuclear power attracted a series of direct political actions.

The Basque area in the north of Spain opposed the building of nuclear facilities on their territory. Large demonstrations from local political parties and councils organised against the proposals.

However, the armed paramilitary group called ETA (who fought for Basque independence from Spain) bombed electrical pylons and distribution centres, and killed two managers employed by nuclear plants.

This campaign, both political and violent, succeeded in postponing the construction of a nuclear plant at Lemoniz. In

September 1982 the Spanish government then decided to completely stop work at Lemoniz and announced that it would not build any new nuclear plants.

QUESTIONS

1. Indicate three different ways that the anti-nuclear protesters tried to publicise their case.
2. How did anti-nuclear protest in Spain differ from the anti-nuclear protests in England?

19.4 NUCLEAR SAFETY PROBLEMS

Substantial concerns about the safety of nuclear production emerged after a number of nuclear incidents.

Nuclear radiation was extremely dangerous, as the fuel used remains radioactive for thousands of years. The storage of **spent fuel** posed a major problem for governments.

West Germany had 19 nuclear reactors that produced one-third of the county's power. After the reunification of Germany in 1990, Soviet-designed reactors in the old East Germany were closed, citing safety reasons. It takes at least 100 years to 'decommission', or make safe, a nuclear site.

The transportation of nuclear materials by rail or sea was also potentially hazardous.

• Nuclear power stations were often dangerous places. In this picture, can you locate two hazards (problems) linked with the production of nuclear power?

Courtesy: Corbis

In 1957, poor waste control at Russia's Mayak reprocessing plant in the Urals led to an explosion. High levels of radiation around the plant led to the evacuation of over 20,000 people over the next ten years. More than 15,000 square kilometres of land could no longer be used for agriculture. The USSR government only admitted in 1989 (32 years later) that the explosion had taken place.

Courtesy: The Centre for the Study of Cartoons and Caricature

"If that doesn't work we can always change its name again."

• In 1986, BNFL changed the name of Windscale nuclear plant to Sellafield.
1. The man on the right carries a funeral wreath. Why?
2. What does the cartoon tell us about the safety reputation of nuclear plants?

Courtesy: Hulton-Deutsch/Corbis

● Cows grazing near a nuclear power plant at Windscale, England.

Courtesy: Getty Images

● Heavy equipment surrounds the Chernobyl nuclear plant after the explosion in 1986.

More seriously, in 1957 a fire at the British Windscale site (later renamed Sellafield) sent significant amounts of radiation into the atmosphere. The accident remained secret for several decades.

THE CHERNOBYL NUCLEAR INCIDENT

The most serious nuclear accident occurred in the Ukraine, which in 1986 was still part of the USSR.

On 25 April 1986, an increase in steam pressure lifted a reactor's 1,000 tonne cover plate, releasing huge amounts of radiation into the atmosphere. The unstable Soviet reactor design, combined with the poor training of staff, contributed to the explosion.

The explosion destroyed the Chernobyl Unit Four reactor, killing 30 people. Over 5,000 tonnes of materials were dropped into the reactor's burning core.

Courtesy: Corbis

Chernobyl Unit Four was cased in a large concrete skin. The other reactors at the plant continued to produce electricity. Within a week, 160,000 residents who lived within 30 km of the reactor had to leave their homes.

The reactor fire lasted for nine days, and the radiation was carried on easterly winds over almost all of Europe.

In the UK, restrictions on the movement of sheep remained in place in some local areas for over ten years. By 1995, the Nuclear Energy Agency estimated that 140 million cures of radiation had been released, over three times the original estimate.

● The abandoned houses and farms in Chernobyl show the wasteland left after the Chernobyl nuclear explosions.

In 1995 the World Health Organization stated that the Chernobyl accident caused nearly 700 cases of thyroid cancer among children and younger people. Another Chernobyl reactor was closed in 1991 after a fire.

The nuclear disaster convinced Gorbachev that more *Glasnost* (openness) was needed. News of the problem first emerged from the West rather than from within the Soviet Union. Gorbachev declared that the "event shook us immensely".

The Chernobyl nuclear incident in 1986 graphically highlighted the potential dangers connected with the peaceful use of nuclear energy. It turned out to be the worst peacetime nuclear incident in the world.

19.5   THE GREEN MOVEMENT

The success of popular protest movements contributed towards the development of more organised structures during the 1970s and the 1980s. In West Germany an anti-nuclear campaigner, Petra Kelly, moved from nuclear protest towards the broader world of politics.

She founded the German Green Party in 1972. Elected to the **Bundestag** (West German parliament) in 1983, she campaigned on ecological issues during the 1980s.

The emergence of the Green Parties prompted substantial opposition to the use of nuclear reactors. Environmentalists promoted the idea of renewable or sustainable alternatives to nuclear energy, including solar, tidal, geothermal and wind sources of energy.

Courtesy: Corbis

● Members of the French Green Party (Les Verts) stage an anti-nuclear protest against the building of a dam. The power of public opinion succeeded in cancelling the dam project.

CONCLUSION

The fall in the price of oil after 1986 made nuclear power too expensive. In 1990, Greenpeace suggested the closure of British nuclear stations on economic grounds alone. In the UK, a Liberal Democrat MP, Chris Davies, complained, "The advocates of nuclear power have led us up a blind alley."

The post-war period saw the optimistic feeling that nuclear power would provide the answer to Europe's ever-widening energy needs, but by 1992 the balance of public and official opinion had swung against nuclear power.

After Chernobyl, with the exception of France, nuclear construction stopped in Europe. Austria and Italy closed down their reactors in the early 1990s. Sweden said it would not use nuclear power after 2010.

The legacy of environmental damage, the fear of catastrophic explosions (as in Chernobyl) and the link of the nuclear industry to the powerful war machines of the USA and the USSR led to substantial opposition and disillusionment.

Source Document

"Look, I keep telling you, this stuff is absolutely safe."

Courtesy: The Centre for the Study of Cartoons and Caricature

QUESTIONS ON THE DOCUMENT

1. What are the protesters' demands?
2. How does the dumper respond?
3. How does the cartoonist show his support for the protesters?

Source Document

Scientists campaign against the atom bomb

Bertrand Russell, the British philosopher, wrote to Albert Einstein, the scientist, on 11 February 1957, looking for his help in publicising the dangers of the nuclear arms race. Einstein agreed to help him.

I think that eminent men of science ought to do something dramatic to bring home to the public and governments the disasters that may occur. Do you think it might be possible to get say, six men of the very highest scientific repute, headed by yourself, to make a very solemn statement about the imperative necessity of avoiding war?

(R.W. Clark, *Einstein: The Life and Times*, London: Hodder and Stoughton, 1973, p. 584)

QUESTIONS ON THE DOCUMENT

1. What did Russell want scientists to do?
2. What did he ask Einstein to do?

GENERAL ESSAY QUESTIONS ON CHAPTER 19

1. Why was nuclear energy used to produce electricity after the second World War?
2. France benefited from its use of nuclear energy. Give three examples how.
3. Write a paragraph about the Chernobyl nuclear incident.
4. Why did opinion swing against the use of nuclear energy by 1992?
5. "The use of nuclear energy in Europe after the second World War played a vital part in the economy, but also held great dangers for society." Is this a fair assessment of the peaceful use of nuclear energy between 1945 and 1992?

20

THE IMPACT OF THE COMPUTER

Words you need to understand

Integrated circuit: A complete electronic circuit, placed on a very small piece of silicon, called a silicon chip.

Microprocessor: The heart of a computer, it contains the complete computer instructions on a chip.

Transistor: An electrical component that controls a current, it is the basis for the integrated circuit.

INTRODUCTION

During the second World War, electronic digital computers were used for the first time in the military environment. The emergence of the small transistor (or **microprocessor**) in 1948 made it possible to use computers outside government buildings or universities.

Between 1945 and 1992 the computer came out of the laboratory and into individual ownership, moving away from the team environment of large business and the university.

20.1 THE FIVE PERIODS OF THE COMPUTER

The development of modern computers can be divided into five phases, each one called a **generation**.

THE FIRST COMPUTER GENERATION: 1945–1956

Between 1945 and 1956, each computer had to be given special instructions on **punch cards**, before it could work.

The earliest computers were used as massive calculators. These computers were stand-alone machines. They stood in large rooms and needed a group of employees to make them work. Computer users shared the machine and rented time to use it.

Courtesy: Bettmann/Corbis

• This 1950 computer, based in New Jersey, was hailed as a new type of electronic brain that would save years of time and millions of dollars in the design and construction of guided missiles, ships, planes and submarines.

The ENIAC computer in 1946 stood on 1,000 square feet of ground. It was built in three years. The complex construction made it 1,000 times faster than any other computer. It could do 5,000 operations in a second.

In March 1949 a magazine called *Popular Mechanics* praised the ENIAC: it was "equipped with 18,000 vacuum tubes and weighs 30 tons, [but] computers in the future may have only 1,000 vacuum tubes and perhaps weigh one and a half tons."

Source Document

Dr G. Jefferson, writing in the *British Medical Journal* in 1949, set a challenge for computer scientists when he stated the limits of computers

Not until a machine can write a sonnet or compose a concerto … could we agree that machines equal brains. No mechanism could feel pleasure at its successes, grief when its valves fuse, be warmed by flattery, be made miserable by its mistakes, be charmed by sex, be angry or depressed when it cannot get what it wants.

(*British Medical Journal*, 1949)

QUESTIONS ON THE DOCUMENT

1. What would a computer have to do to equal "brains"?
2. Dr Jefferson called the computer a "mechanism". Mention two human sensations that a "mechanism" cannot feel.

By 1948 the transistor (with electronic units) began to replace the large vacuum tube in televisions, radios and computers. The first multi-frame machine (the UNIVAC machine) came at the end of the 1940s. In 1949, Thomas Watson Jr., employed by IBM, the American computer firm, said that the mechanical parts in computers would all be replaced by **electronics** within a decade.

THE SECOND COMPUTER GENERATION: 1956–1963

Transistors were installed in computers by 1956, and lasted until 1963. This type of computer was smaller, processed information faster and was more reliable than the first series. Unlike the first generation, each computer did not have to be programmed on an individual basis: the computer could **retain** instructions or data in its memory.

The 'supercomputers' had many features that can be seen in modern computers: memory banks, operating systems, storage or saving of data onto disks rather than magnetic tape. The second-generation computers created a new level of technical jobs, such as computer programmers and computer analysts. By 1965 many large corporations used the second-generation computers to process their financial information.

THE THIRD COMPUTER GENERATION: 1964–1971

While transistors brought computers to a new level, they generated so much heat that they damaged the other sensitive parts in the computer. The introduction of the **integrated circuit** in 1958 using small **silicon chips** replaced the transistor.

The third-generation computer included an operating system that let machines run different programs at the same time.

In 1964, the **mouse** was introduced so that users did not have to write instructions into the computer. By 1970 the **floppy disk** made it easier to move data from one computer to another.

The Philips electronics firm switched from radio valves to transistors during the 1960s. Its revenues increased from almost 5 billion Dutch guilders in 1961 to 18 billion guilders in 1971.

Courtesy: Hulton-Deutsch/Corbis

• IBM was one of the leading computer firms. The mainframe computer had its own permanent assistant to ensure that it was continually working. Photograph from 1954.

Courtesy: Getty Images

• The political importance of computers was shown by the visit of Soviet Premier Khrushchev to the IBM Center in California in 1959. He sampled American food in IBM's canteen.

Courtesy: The Centre for the Study of Cartoons and Caricature

"THE ERA OF TECHNOMANIA IS PASSING – AND HIGH TIME TOO." (WEDGWOOD BENN)

• An English MP, Tony Benn, praised new technology in 1967.
  1. Name the three types of technology shown in the cartoon.
  2. Why does the cartoonist show Tony Benn as a robot?

Courtesy: Corbis

• A businessman slips a diskette into his pocket. On the table, the essential components of the computer can be seen – monitor, keyboard, hard drive and a mouse. The telephone link was also used to connect to the Internet.

THE FOURTH COMPUTER GENERATION: 1971–1992

Scientists later managed to fit even more components on a single chip, called a **microprocessor**. As a result, computers became ever smaller as more components were squeezed onto semiconductors. By the 1980s, hundreds of thousands of components could fit onto one chip.

Source Document

Ted Hoff also had a problem convincing some of the Intel marketing team in 1971 of the benefits of the new microprocessors

It is now an industrial legend that Hoff went to one Intel marketing expert and was told: "Look, (computer companies) sell 20,000 microcomputers a year. And we're latecomers to this industry. If we're lucky we'll get 10 per cent. At 2,000 chips a year, it's just not worth the trouble."

(M.S. Malone, *The Microprocessor: a biography*, New York 1995, p. 15)

QUESTIONS ON THE DOCUMENT

1. How did the marketing man try to convince Hoff that the microprocessor was not such a great idea?
2. Why did the story become an "industry legend"?

By 1985 supercomputers could carry out 1 billion operations a second. Intel marketed the 4004 microprocessor in 1971. The American spacecraft Pioneer 10 in March 1972 was the first spacecraft to use a microprocessor.

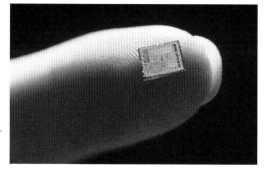

Courtesy: Corbis

• Computer chips became smaller and more powerful. This miniaturisation can be seen in this 1980s Intel microprocessor. George Moore, of Intel, coined 'Moore's Law' – that the processing power of the microchip (how fast it worked) would double every 18 months.

The importance of the computer was recognised by *Time*, the influential American magazine. Each year it named a Man of the Year. In 1982 it named the computer as its Machine of the Year: "Computers were once regarded as distant, ominous abstractions, like Big Brother. In 1982, they truly became personalised, brought down to scale, so that people could hold, prod and play with them." Ironically, the reporter wrote this article on a typewriter.

Even though the size of the computer kept reducing, manufacturers did not make computers for the individual user, either in the office or at home. Even in 1977, Ken Olson, in charge of the large computer company, Digital, stated, "There is no reason anyone would want a computer in their home".

When production costs fell at the start of the 1990s, computers became smaller, cheaper and more widely available. The average person could buy a computer.

The **miniaturisation** of the computer led to the invention of cellular phones, commonly referred to as **mobile phones**. Sales of Nokia mobile phones increased from Finnish mark (FIM) 2.3 billion in 1990 to FIM 6.3 billion in 1993.

Courtesy: Corbis

• Magnified view of IBM computer on a chip (actual size ¼ inch).

Compact disc (CD) music players were first sold in 1982. In 1984, the introduction of the CD-ROM meant that large amounts of data could be stored on a circular disc. William Gibson, a science fiction writer, coined the word **cyberspace** in 1985 to describe the silent space found inside computer networks.

In 1980 the Sony electronics company produced the Walkman, a hand-held personal tape recorder and radio. Desktop computers were supplemented by the invention of the **laptop** and the even smaller palmtop computer.

The content and purpose of the computer also changed as it found a firm niche in the entertainment industry. Steve Russell, an American university student, invented the first computer game in 1962.

In the early 1980s the development of arcade games for the small computer ignited a consumer boom for the video game industry. Games such as *Pac-Man* moved the video game industry from the large public games arcade to the intimacy of the family home.

Computer technology also revolutionised the making of major films. Animators used **computer graphics** to create the first entirely computer-generated character for the 1991 film *Terminator 2*. The special effects of realistic dinosaurs for *Jurassic Park* (released in 1994) were already being made in 1992. The Oscar-winning film *Forrest Gump* (1994) also used computer technology, with the main character being inserted into historic news footage, 'virtually' meeting President John F. Kennedy and John Lennon.

THE FIFTH COMPUTER GENERATION: THE POTENTIAL BEYOND 1992
Computer scientists continued to develop ever more compelling uses for computers. This fifth generation of computers (as yet unrealised) focuses on the development of AI (artificial intelligence), when computers do not need to be programmed by people. In 1950, Alan Turing set the challenge known as the Turing test: can a computer think?

Courtesy: Educational Co.

This speculation was developed in the science fiction film based on Arthur C. Clarke's novel, *2001: A Space Odyssey* (released in 1968). The film showed the potential problems that can be caused by a computer that could control people. The computer (called HAL) was independently intelligent and talked to the astronauts on the spaceship. HAL eventually took over the spaceship, causing chaos.

Alan Turing (1912–1954): English mathematician and logician, he was part of the team that broke the German Enigma Code during the war. In 1936, he described a "universal computing machine", known as the Turing Machine, well in advance of the digital computer.

QUESTIONS

1. Mention two elements that contributed to the success of computers in the 1940s.
2. What features of the ENIAC computer made it a first-generation computer?
3. In 1949, what prediction did the magazine *Popular Mechanics* make about computers?
4. How did the computers of the second generation differ from those of the first generation?
5. Why did *Time* magazine nominate the computer as Man of the Year in 1982?
6. Ken Olson's comment in 1977 revealed an important attitude of the people involved in selling computers. What mistake did he make?
7. Computers became very important in the entertainment industry. Give one instance that showed the impact of computers in this industry.
8. What question did Alan Turing ask about computers?

20.2 THE IMPORTANCE OF INTEL AND MICROSOFT

Courtesy: Corbis

• Andrew Grove, one of the founders of Intel, sits on top of an enlarged diagram of one of Intel's microprocessors.

Courtesy: Corbis

• Bill Gates, chairman and one of the founders of Microsoft, makes a presentation at a business conference.

In 1968 George Moore, Andy Grove and Robert Noyce founded **Intel** (the name comes from "integrated electronics"). They concentrated on increasing the numbers of transistors to be placed on a single chip. In 1993 Intel's Pentium processor held over 3 million transistors and performed 100 million instructions per second.

During the 1980s Intel silicon chips made possible the launch of three new series of computers, the 286, the 386 and the 486.

While Intel provided the 'brain' for the personal computer, Bill Gates and Microsoft provided the 'heartbeat' by producing software that made the computer do what the user wanted it to do. In November 1990 Gates stated that he wanted to make "computers more personal, making them indispensable, making them something that you reach for naturally when you need information."

Gates introduced the visual notion of **Windows**. Windows are simply display boxes. They let the user open different programs at the same time, one in each window. Although the Windows technology was introduced in 1983, the release of Windows 3 in May 1990 became the fastest-selling software product in PC history.

QUESTION

1. Intel and Microsoft aimed at two separate areas of the computer market. What were these two markets?

20.3 THE GROWTH OF THE INTERNET

At the start of the 1960s, the US Defence Department wanted a system of communication that could not be destroyed in any one enemy attack.

The **Advanced Research Projects Agency**, an American government organisation, developed the **ARPAnet**, using radio and satellite networks to spread information. It allowed each computer on the network to talk to any other computer without having to go through the same host computer. It was a **decentralised** rather than a centralised system of communication.

● People with no access to the Internet could use the facilities of internet cafés to access information. Young people, students and travellers were the most frequent users.

This new method of networking computers based in different places became known as the **Internet**.

Computer scientists and other academics in universities used the Internet to exchange information, to share ideas and to 'talk' to each other.

An Englishman, Tim Berners-Lee, wrote the rules for the infant **World Wide Web** in 1990. Berners-Lee brought order to the chaotic Internet by introducing new standards that could be understood by all users, such as WWW, URL, HTML and HTTP.

By 1991 the Internet infrastructure had grown to over 700,000 linked computers. The transmission of data over this computer network led to a new term for the Internet – the **information superhighway**.

The principal growth of the Internet came after 1992, when the cost of computing fell, allowing home users to access the Internet from their homes. The explosion in the number of individual users saw the emergence of **e-mail** as the most common use of the Internet.

QUESTIONS

1. Why did the Americans develop the ARPAnet to promote the use of communication by computer?
2. Why was the Internet used by an increasing number of Internet users by 1991?

Source Document

A virus is a computer program that tells a computer to disobey the instructions of the software and it can wipe out all the data on the computer's hard drive. A Bulgarian virus writer called the 'Dark Avenger' gave an interview in 1992 describing why he wrote viruses. The interview with Sara Gordon took place over a five-month period through computer messages and conversations.

Sara: People have wondered why you wrote your first virus.

Dark Avenger: I wrote it because I had heard about viruses and wanted to know about them. I decided to write my own one. I put some code inside it that intentionally destroys data, and I am sorry for it. I started working on it in September 1988.

Sara: Then why did you put destructive code in viruses?

Dark Avenger: As for the first virus the truth is that I didn't know what else to put into it.

At that time there were few PCs in Bulgaria, and they were only used by a bunch of hotshots (or their kids). I just hated it when some asshole has a new powerful 16 MHz, and didn't use it for anything, while I had to program on a 4.77 MHz with no hard disk (and I was lucky if I could ever get access to it at all).

First law of computer security: don't buy a computer. Second law of computer security: if you ever buy a computer, don't turn it on.

(W.M. Grossman, *Remembering the Future: Interviews from Personal Computer World*, London 1997)

QUESTIONS ON THE DOCUMENT

1. The virus writer called himself the Dark Avenger. Why did the Dark Avenger start to write virus programs?
2. The Dark Avenger envied those who owned computers. What evidence is there for this statement?
3. What was the Dark Avenger's second law of computer security?

20.4 THE IMPACT OF COMPUTERS

THE INFORMATION REVOLUTION

Bill Gates suggested that the change brought about by computers was as great as that brought about by the spread of printing in Europe during the 16th century. Others stated that the potential of information technologies was so vast that it could only be compared to the introduction of steam for the first industrial revolution and electricity for the second industrial revolution.

The advances in computer technology led to what has been called an **information revolution**. Technological improvements brought about an explosion in the sharing of knowledge. Computers made it possible to work out the genetic codes of the human genome. Computers managed and transferred huge amounts of data, thereby increasing access to information. Advances in miniaturisation led to the development of the heart pacemaker, the mobile phone and the microwave oven.

The special technical vocabulary of the computer became part of daily life. In September 1945, Grace Hopper, working for the American navy, noted the first ever computer 'bug'. A moth had become stuck on her Harvard Mark II computer.

SOCIAL ISSUES

The high cost of owning a computer made it impossible for many social groups to benefit from computer technology. This reality led to the **digital divide** between those who own or have access to computers and those who lack access.

Computers allow governments to closely monitor the activity of citizens, as they have instant access to a wide range of records, including medical, financial, educational and other data. Large

Courtesy: Corbis

- The combination of the computer and access to the Internet enables many workers to work from home. "Teleworkers" have to be very disciplined to separate their "work" life from their "personal" life.

Courtesy: Corbis

- An architectural technician uses a computer-aided design (CAD) program to prepare building plans. This computerised system replaced the traditional role of the draughtsman.

business corporations and government departments increasingly depend upon computers for their daily work.

COMPUTERS IN THE WORKPLACE

Computers completely changed traditional professions such as architecture with the introduction of computer-aided design (CAD). Architectural drawings were no longer done by a **draughtsman**, using traditional skills. Publishing was similarly affected.

New computer technology reduced employment in large industries such as coal or steel production. Jobs lost in these **smokestack** industries would not be replaced.

The early prospect of a 'work-free' society turned sour as the numbers of new jobs created by the computer revolution did not replace the large numbers who had been displaced from traditional low-skill or manual occupations.

QUESTIONS

1. Bill Gates saw the computer revolution as very historic. What comparison did he use?
2. What was the digital divide?
3. Give two instances of how computers changed the workplace.

CONCLUSION

The computer revolution between 1945 and 1992 revolutionised almost every aspect of society. Post-war prosperity provided a market for the dramatic developments in computer technology.

The inventors or owners of the new inventions tried to take advantage of their commercial potential and to make them available for customers as soon as possible.

By 1992, computers were available for home use for a wide range of purposes. Society had been changed in ways that could never have been foreseen by the computer developers.

Source Document

Ted Hoff was part of the Intel engineering team that developed the 4004 and 8008 microchips. However, having the new products was one thing, but convincing industrialists to use them in 1971 was another.

People were used to thinking of computers as these big basic pieces of equipment that had to be protected and guarded and babied and used efficiently.

I remember one meeting in which there was all this concern about repairing microprocessors and I remember saying, "A light bulb burns out, you unscrew it and throw it away and you put another in – and that's what you do with microprocessors." But they just couldn't accept doing that with a computer.

(M.S. Malone, *The Microprocessor: A Biography*, New York 1995, p. 14)

QUESTIONS ON THE DOCUMENT

1. What attitude did people have towards the "big" computers?
2. What argument did Hoff use to convince people microprocessors should not be repaired?

GENERAL ESSAY QUESTIONS ON CHAPTER 20

1. Write a paragraph on each of the following:
   (a) The five generations of the computer.
   (b) The growth of the Internet
   (c) The impact of the computer on jobs and learning.
2. "The development of computers brought about significant changes in society." How did these major changes take place?

INDEX